Culture and Consumption II

Grant McCracken

Culture and Consumption II

Markets, Meaning, and Brand Management

INDIANA
UNIVERSITY
PRESS

BLOOMINGTON AND INDIANAPOLIS

This book is a publication of

Indiana University Press
601 North Morton Street
Bloomington, IN 47404-3797 USA

http://iupress.indiana.edu

Telephone orders   800-842-6796
Fax orders   812-855-7931
Orders by e-mail   iuporder@indiana.edu

The paper used in this publication meets the minimum requirements of American National Standard for Information Sciences—Permanence of Paper for Printed Library Materials, ANSI Z39.48-1984.

Manufactured in the United States of America

Library of Congress Cataloging-in-Publication Data

McCracken, Grant David, date-
    Culture and consumption II : markets, meaning, and brand management / Grant McCracken.
        p. cm.
    Includes bibliographical references and index.
    ISBN 0-253-34566-9 (cloth : alk. paper) — ISBN 0-253-21761-X (pbk. : alk. paper)
    1. Consumption (Economics)—History. 2. Culture—History. 3. Social values—History. I. Title.
    HC79.C6M384 2005
    339.4′7—dc22
                                                                                2004028466

1 2 3 4 5   10 09 08 07 06 05

*This book is dedicated to Mish Vadasz,
with my profound thanks.*

Contents

Acknowledgments

Montrose Sommers for my introduction to marketing; Margot Acton, Michael Adams, Joan Adelman, Ken Ames, George Anastaplo, Jeanne Beker, Hargurchet Bhabra, Gloria Bishop, Suzanne Boyd, Jeff Brown, Laurie Brown, Ewen Cameron, John Clippinger, Pip Coburn, Tyler Cowen, John Cruickshank, Jim Dingwall, Amy Domini, Denise Donlon, Gwynne Dyer, Dave Dyment, Charles Paul Freund, David Frum, Nick Gillespie, Nick Harney, Adrienne Hood, Henry Jenkins, Shaista Justin, Bob Kincaide, Mark Kingwell, Joan Kron, Eugene Lee, Nadja Lesko, Simon Leung, Roger Martin, Julia Matthews, Lars Meyer, Alan Middleton, Louise Milne, Michael Valdez Moses, Sarah Mundy, Annie Pedret, Virginia Postrel, Rita Rayman, Gilbert Reid, Ellie Rubin, Charles Saumerez Smith, Lindsay Sharp, Lee Simpson, Evan Solomon, Rick Stacey, Suzanne Stein, Diana Stinson, Wodek Szemberg, Clive Thompson, William Thorsell, Liz Torlee, Rikk Villa, Danny Virtue, Wentworth Walker, Margo Welch, Lisa Werenko, Rick Wolf, Richard Worzell, Culyer Young, Nora Young, Marilyn Zavitz, Philip Zimmerman, Moses Znaimer, Andrew Zolli, and especially Leora Kornfeld for discussions on contemporary culture; Matt Ariker, Vinita Bali, Rae Burdon, Richard Burjaw, Jim Carfrae, Chris Commins, Pat Crane, Tomohiri Doai, Denise Fonseca, Pat Garner, Peter Grossman, Rob Guenette, Nick Hahn, Robert Hall, Stephanie Hancock, Reid Hankin, Rob Heyvaert, Dan Hunter, Stephen Jones, Murray Kaiserman, Jim King, Jim Koch, Holly Kretschmar, David Lamb, Judie Lannon, Shelly Lazarus, Ian Leslie, Diane Lockwood, Lowell London, Tom Long, Mike Lotti, Tom Luke, Andy Macaulay, Margaret Mark, Noel Marts, Jake McCall, Scott Miller, Mary Mills, Mark Murray, Charlotte Oades, Bill O'Connor, Scott Pederson, Tony Piggott, Abigail Posner, James Potoki, John Prevost, Claire Quinn, Tess Resman, Sheri Roder, Paula Rosch, Monica Ruffo, Matt Ryan, Barry Schwartzblatt, Nick Shore, Dave Snell, Ricardo Solera, Sir Martin Sorrell, Myra Stark, Rick Sterling, Ben Stone, Michael Stoner, Richard Stursberg, Michelle Sullivan, Bob Thompson, Michael Troutman, Charlie Veraza, Stephen Verba, Lanny Vincent, Martin Weigel, Wendy Weissman, Mike Welling, Stewart Whitney, Tim Wingrove, Mark Workman, Khalil Younes, and Sergio Zyman for the chance to see marketing from the consultant's point of view and for the resources with which I wrote this book; James Alexander, Ken Ames, Eric Arnould, Bill Baffin, Ann Bermingham, Jim Bettman, John Brewer, Kemal Büyükkurt, Bobby Calder, Karin Calvert, Colin Campbell, John Carey, Cary Carson, Fiona Caulfield, Rita Denny, John Docker, Richard Elliott, Eileen Fischer, Susan Fournier, Mark Grayson, Steve Greyser, David Halle, Ronald Paul

Hill, Elizabeth Hirschman, Morris Holbrook, Douglas Holt, Tim Jackson, Henry Jenkins, Philip Kotler, Rob Kozinets, Theodore Levitt, Sid Levy, Rich Lutz, John Lynch, Jean-Sebastien Marcoux, Ed McQuarrie, David Mick, Daniel Miller, Paul Nunes, Jerry Olson, Nelson Phillips, Richard Pollay, Jules Prown, Marsha Richins, Mark Ritson, Dennis Rook, Kirsten Sandberg, Leigh Eric Schmidt, John Schouten, Michael Schudson, Linda Scott, Simon Shama, Al Silk, Paula Silver, Penny Sparke, Warren Susman, Craig Thompson, Sarah Thorton, James Twitchell, Alice Tybout, Melanie Wallendorf, Bill Wells, Irv White, Richard Wilk, Terrence Witkowski, and especially John Sherry and Russ Belk for their work in consumer research; Kevin Clark and Mark McNeilly for the chance to participate in the IBM Marketing Advisory Council; Gil McWilliam and John Deighton for our informal seminar at Harvard in the late 1990s; David Arnold, Kent Bowen, Tiziana Casciaro, Sam Chun, Kim Clark, Brian DeLacey, Rohit Deshpandé, Bob Dolan, Jed Emerson, Marty Frobisher, John Gourville, Pryce Greenow, Steve Greyser, Charles Hale, Linda Hill, Neil Houghton, Nigel Killick, Kip King, Gabe Knapp, Nancy Koehn, Joe Lassiter, Alan MacCormack, Youngme Moon, Das Narayandas, Kash Rangan, Shaka Rasheed, Miklos Savary, Al Silk, Luc Wathieu, Susan Wolf, Gerry Zaltman, and especially John Deighton and Kay Lemon for the year I spent teaching at the Harvard Business School; Giselle Amantea, Simona Bealcovschi, Joumane Chahine, Alain D'Astous, Jim Gough, John Gundy, Johanne Lamoureux, Guy Lanoue, Alain Lapointe, Don McGregor, Dayna McLeod, Janice Merson, Karl Moore, Wade Nelson, Margaret van Nooten, Monica Ruffo, Rita Schaeffer, Will Straw, Martha Townsend, Kevin Truit, Michel Verdon, Peter White, and especially Daz for encouragement in Montreal.

The following articles are reprinted courtesy of their original publishers listed below:

"Living in the Material World." *Globe and Mail,* October 26, 1990.

"Homeyness." In *Interpretive Consumer Research,* edited by Elizabeth Hirschman, 168–183. Provo, Utah: Association for Consumer Research, 1989.

"Marilyn Monroe: Inventor of Blondness." In *Big Hair,* Grant McCracken, 78–87. Toronto: Penguin, 1995.

"Who Is the Celebrity Endorser?" *Journal of Consumer Research* 16 (1989): 310–321.

"The Strange Power of Uncle Meyer's Wallet." *Globe and Mail,* August 21, 1990.

"Culture and Culture at the Royal Ontario Museum I: An Anthropological Approach to a Marketing Problem." *Curator* 46, no. 2 (2003): 136–157.

"Advertising: Meaning or Information?" In *Advances in Consumer Research,* edited by Paul Anderson and Melanie Wallendorf, 121–124. Provo, Utah: Association for Consumer Research, 1986.

Culture and Consumption II

Part One
Introduction

Book Strategy:

The strategy of this book is to move beyond the usual platitudes about the consumer society into a more detailed, exacting anthropological treatment.

The architecture of the book uses a pairing device. In each section, a brief essay is paired with an academic article. The essay is designed to offer a quick provocative glimpse of the topic. The article gives a deeper anthropological treatment.

Section Strategy:

The essay for this section of the book begins with a broadside against the now thoroughly conventionalized attack on the consumer culture.

The article recounts my appearance on the *Oprah Winfrey Show* and draws one or two conclusions about our treatment of the consumer culture.

1 Living in the Material World

Enough! Recently, on this page, Brian Fawcett and Ron Graham did the most alarming duet. In "Fifth Column," Mr. Fawcett mocked some Soviet visitors for wanting consumer goods and called the rest of us "devouring beasts." In an adjoining essay, Mr. Graham accused consumers of having sold their souls to the devil. Ladies and gentlemen, guard your loved ones. A new species of nonsense is loose upon the land.

Materialism is fast becoming the villain of the piece. Increasingly, it's the explanation we resort to when things go wrong. Drugs on the rise, divorce rate up, kids dropping out of school? Must be our love of consumer goods. The case against the consumer society is the new orthodoxy, a staple of classroom, cocktail circuit, and media commentary. We have found a new flag in which to wrap ourselves. We have found a new incendiary for our "searing" acts of social criticism. Most of all, we've got ourselves an all-purpose explanation for the ills of contemporary life.

This argument is familiar and widespread. It says modern Western societies, driven by the engines of marketing and materialism, have developed a soul-destroying obsession with consumer goods. It says these goods have turned us away from high culture, from real spirituality, from the ideals of community, self-sacrifice, and a common good. Goods are shackles for the self. We all know the argument well enough to sing it by heart.

This argument is a dangerous misrepresentation of the facts. It is, in my opinion, alarmist, accusatory, rich in assumption, poor in research, and almost entirely wrong. It creates alienation where none is necessary, self-loathing where none is warranted, and sends our collective misgivings rabbiting off in all the wrong directions.

Consumer goods are an important medium of our culture. They are a place we keep our private and public meanings. Cars and clothing, for instance, come loaded with meanings, meanings we use to define ourselves. We are constantly drawing meanings out of our possessions and using them to construct our domestic and public worlds. Shackles of the self? In Western societies, the reverse is true. Consumer goods are one of our most important templates for the self.

Why do goods play this role? In our society, individuals are free to construct the self. We no longer presume to tell people who they must be. Increasingly, we leave them to make this choice for themselves, to choose how they will define their gender, age, class, and lifestyle.

Goods help us make this choice. They help us make our culture concrete and public (through marketing and retailing). They help us select and assume new meanings (through purchase). They help us display new meanings (through use). And they help us change meanings (through innovation). Goods help us learn, make, display, and change the choices required of us by our individualistic society. They are not shackles but instruments of the self.

This does not mean the consumer society is above criticism. Let us note, for instance, that goods do contain stereotyped meanings. They contribute to the confines we place upon the self-definition of women, immigrants, the elderly, and the young. But let's remember that this could not be otherwise. When goods reflect the meanings of our society, they must necessarily reflect the benign meanings and the imprisoning ones.

And let us remember that goods help destroy stereotypes. Every protest group in our society creates new constellations of clothing to repudiate old meanings and establish new ones. The history of feminism in North America represents, among other things, a continual repudiation and reinvention of our material culture as women refuse sexist clothing and create outfits that give voice to a new view of gender. Goods are both the prison and the keys to the cell.

Let us also grant that our love of goods is sometimes wasteful. Certain patterns of consumption must change, and they will. But those who suppose we will become a society of plainness and simplicity are simply wrong. The abundance, the diversity, and the obsolescence of consumer goods are not driven by marketing deception or our own giddy disregard for the state of the planet. They are driven by the objectives of our culture. Some of the reductions we are now contemplating are necessary and possible. Others are simple pipe dreams that misunderstand the nature of the consumer society, our society.

And let us remember that goods will propagandize for the green society. "Green" meanings are even now being loaded into goods, and it is in this form that they will help to colonize consciousness and achieve a more ecological society. This is a bitter irony for some of the green enthusiasts, but it is as it should be. This is what our culture does.

Let us also grant that materialism relates to selfishness. This too must change, and it will. But it cannot change until we understand why goods mean so much to us. Simply to say that we are driven by selfishness, vanity, and greed is not useful or illuminating. It is time to take a more intelligent view and to see that consumer goods capture us because they capture the meanings with which we construct our lives.

Should goods be vilified? Hippies, intellectuals, and ecologists think so. But why is it that hippies always have to wear very particular jeans and sandals to engage in this hostility for material objects? Why is it that intellectuals must flaunt their affection for tweed coats and peculiar headgear? Why is it that the greens must wear Birkenstocks to declare their good intentions? All of this is plain enough. These anti-materialists are using materials to define the group and the self. They are using consumer goods to fashion an identity. They depend upon material culture to make their culture material.

Consumer society is not an artificial and catastrophic social invention. It is a culture with its own systematic properties. And we are not devouring beasts who treat with the devil. We are creatures who depend on the meanings contained in the material world.

2   On Oprah

My article "Homeyness" (the article in Part Two of this book) was published, as most things academic are, to expressions of polite interest and an abiding silence.

Then one day the phone rang. It was Amy, a staff member for the *Oprah Winfrey Show*. Was I the author of "Homeyness" and would I like to come to talk about it on the show?

"Yes," I said reflexively, "sure I would."

I say "yes" to everything of this kind, and at this point, I did not fully appreciate what a gift this was. Certainly I had heard of Oprah. But I did not grasp that she was by this time in the American scheme of things already a little like a god. The call was brief and I was told that arrangements would be made, that I would fly out to Chicago and do the show.

I wandered down the hall at my university to see the department assistant, Barbara.

"You'll never guess what just happened."

"What?"

"Well, I got this call from the Oprah show, you know, Oprah Winfrey, and they want me to come and talk about my research."

Barbara's mouth fell open.

"Oprah Winfrey?" she said with reverence.

I nodded.

"You?" she said with scorn.

Barbara revered Oprah. She knew me. That the godlike and the all too mortal should have anything to do with one another was, well, unexpected, perhaps even inconceivable. Barbara made further inquiries.

"On the *Oprah Winfrey Show*? In Chicago? On television?"

"Yeah, apparently."

We had both learned something. I had discovered Oprah was a bigger deal than I had guessed. Barbara had discovered there was something very wrong with the universe.

Barbara found the Oprah news hard to fathom because it obliged her, for a moment, to think more of me, but my academic colleagues embraced it because it gave them a welcome chance to think less.

"Oprah!" one of them snorted. "A scholar on daytime television! Good Lord, so you're going Hollywood."

Arrangements went forward. Before long, I had my instructions and my ticket. I was to go to Chicago twice. The first time was to do a taping in the homes of Chicagoans. On this visit, Oprah wouldn't be there; just me, another "expert," and the production team. The second time I would go to tape the show at the Harpo soundstage.

I arrived at O'Hare. There was a limo waiting for me. Inside the passenger compartment was a woman all in blue. She was wearing a Chanel suit with matching stockings. Her hair was pulled back in the socialite manner, held by a little black band in back.

A look of instantaneous dislike passed between us. Conversation inched forward. It turned out that the woman in blue was the other expert, a New York designer and the author of a recent book on design in the home.

"My publisher has printed an extra 50,000 copies," she said, "What about you?"

I had a photocopy.

"Oh, we're still talking about it," I lied bravely.

We made our way to a Chicago suburb and stopped in front of an attractive middle-class home. Taping commenced.

The first shot was to show the experts entering the home. The idea was that we were to climb the stairs, hit the doorway, look to the camera and say, "Hi, Oprah. We're here at the home of the Sullivans, and we're going inside to take a look around!"

The designer dispatched the task with enthusiasm. She hit her mark, belted out the line, the producer said, "Perfect. You're a doll."

My turn came. Over and over.

"Grant, let's do it once more, and this time could you give it a little oomph?"

After a couple more tries, it was clear I was hopeless. I didn't have the wattage. I could see the producer thinking to herself, "Oh, God, what have they done to me?"

"Can't you be a little more . . . vivid?"

"Um," I said finally, "you do realize I'm Canadian?"

No one thought this was the least bit funny.

The next shot was to capture our reaction to the Sullivans' home. The designer strode down the hallway into the kitchen. She said something like, "Well, it's obvious this is a family with no sense of design. None! Look at these curtains. Wrong shape. Wrong size. Wrong color!"

I cast a glance at the poor Mrs. Sullivan, who was cowering against a kitchen wall. She was beginning to have doubts of her own. I couldn't watch. Persuaded that I was that most grievous creature in a celebrity culture, bad television, I slunk into the living room.

And there were Dan, the father, and Danielle, the daughter, doing what they called the "Pocahontas dance." A couple of days before, they had been to see the Disney movie. Danielle, blond, sunny, and about 6, had "memorized" the theme song, and father and daughter, oblivious to the commotion in the kitchen, were now performing it. This consisted of Dan picking Danielle up, threading her across his shoulders and sliding her back down to the carpet. Danielle sang throughout these exertions, and as she dropped to the carpet, she finished with a joyful flourish.

The designer had swept out of the kitchen and was now, it seemed to me, laying waste to the living room.

She said something like, "Oh, look at this furniture. I mean, really. Everything is pushed to the wall. No sense of proportion or placement."

I took this as my cue. I signaled for the camera, and as it swung toward me, I said,

"Well, actually, there's a reason the furniture is pushed to the wall. It's to make room for the Pocahontas dance. Would you like to see the Pocahontas dance, Oprah?"

The producer looked around in panic. She spotted Dan and Danielle and cued the cameraman with a desperate pointing gesture.

Just in time. For Dan and Danielle were already exuberantly lifting and singing. It was perfect. Had Dan and Danielle known they were going to be performing for national television, the performance might have been anxious and labored. As it was, they were merely sharing a private joy. It was about the sweetest thing you ever saw.

The producer glanced over at me with a look of abject gratitude and new regard. I might not *be* good television but at least I could spot something that was. The designer, on the other hand, was staring daggers.

We went to a couple of homes. The designer was by this time predictable. No one in suburban Chicago seemed capable of grasping the simplest precepts laid down by the New York design community. Her job seemed to be to mock and diminish. For my part, I got a little better on camera, and I labored to suggest that these homes represented something remarkable, that they had turned 2,000 square feet of concrete, wood, and drywall into something happy, homey, and theirs. Our contrast could not have been more clear. For the designer, these homes were a scandalous descent from the Platonic perfections of New York design. For me, they were an ascent from a very different alternative: a cruelly anomic room at the Marriott, say. The producers had chosen us well.

Things got unexpectedly tricky on the flight back to Toronto. My appendix exploded at 30,000 feet and I arrived in a state of distress. This was a Friday.

It took them a little while to find a surgeon, but eventually the appendix was removed. (Why had my appendix chosen this moment to act up? I wondered if it wanted nothing more to do with me. No one, not even an appendix, likes bad television.)

I stayed in the hospital through the weekend. Once or twice, I asked the staff whether I might be allowed to return to Chicago on Wednesday. "Absolutely not," I was told, "you are a very sick man. No traveling." As the day approached, I upped the argument.

"But it's to tape the *Oprah Winfrey Show.*"

The doctor looked at me sharply.

"Oprah?"

"Oprah."

"You, sir, are good to go. See if you can mention the hospital."

So back on the plane . . . and back into the jaws of disaster. What I experienced flying back into Chicago was almost as bad as flying out. A sense of complete dis-ease. I was later to understand this was the peculiar effect of (surgery-induced) dehydration at high altitude. At the time, I just thought I was dying.

The limo was waiting for me (no vision in blue this time) and the driver was a little alarmed to see my state of misery. As we drove into Chicago, we consulted with the Oprah production team, and it was clear that I should be taken once more to the hospital. The traffic was terrible, and I suggested to the driver that he might use the shoulder. He was good hearted but horrified —"Driving on that is against the law!" "There is," I said finally, "a reason they call it the emergency lane." And with this permission, we barreled to the nearest emergency ward.

No, I wasn't dying, the doctors said, after several tests. "You're just dehydrated." They hooked up an intravenous drip. And one of them said, "It's your job to drink as much water as you humanly can. You have to rehydrate, ok?"

Released finally from the ward, and now three hours behind schedule, I staggered into the hospital parking lot. The driver, bless him, was still there. I climbed into the limo, disoriented and disheartened. I was not going to make the taping. I had let the team and myself down. I looked down at a bottle of water on the seat beside me, and thought, "Well done, Grant."

"Well, we're here," said the driver, finally.

I looked out and wondered which of these buildings might be my hotel. All I could see was a very large white box with a sign that read, "Harpo Productions." My faithful driver had completed his mission. No one had told him otherwise, so he had delivered me to the Oprah show.

They greeted me at the front door with astonishment.

"Grant! You're here! Ah, well, you're on!"

I was frog-marched through a maze of corridors, a team of anxious producers quizzing me as we went.

"How bad are you?"

"Um, I am fine. No, I'm fine." I could see the producers looking at one another.

"He's not going out there!" said the makeup man.

"Frank, he's here. He's on."

"But he looks . . . he looks like he's been dead for a week."

"Frank, shut up and do what you can. Slap it on."

Suddenly, we were there. A vast soundstage, brilliant in the television lights, stacked with cameras and monitors, roped everywhere with cables. I was directed to a row of seats. There was the designer. Same Chanel suit and matching stockings, this time all in red. She looked, I thought, a little edgy. I could tell, I thought, what she thought of me.

Informed of my condition, a staff member pressed a bottle of water into my hand.

"Keep this under your chair. You can take a sip during the commercial breaks."

I sat down and looked up. There was the Oprah audience. And they were splendid. If, by this time, I still had any doubts of the majesty of Oprah Winfrey, they were now erased. I was looking at a couple of hundred people who had, apparently, spent a lot of time and money preparing for their moment "in the presence." Clearly, this was not for them "another TV show," but a high moment to be remembered, retold, revisited as the time "I saw Oprah." They gave off an adulation that was frank, exuberant, and complete.

And there was Oprah. It was, as they used to say in another time, astonishing to look upon her. Illuminated by the lights and the adulation, she was, and I use this poor, weary word with some care, charismatic. Effortlessly so. She dispatched the complexities of the show, asking questions, setting up clips, with what seemed to me a flawless self-possession. All the while, she was directing production traffic. "Jimmy," she said at one point to a cameraman, "you were a second slow coming back from the break."

Oprah seemed a very long way away. Actually, everything seemed a very long way away. I listened hard for my cue and tried to step up with remarks that were clear and cogent. But as the show went forward, I began to detect a new discomfort from a body that had, in the last week, turned itself into a production house of unfamiliar sensations.

No, this one was not so unfamiliar. This feeling I knew. And finally, a dreaded last message. A little red light began flashing in my brain. It read:

"Empty bladder immediately." After three hours of intravenous drips and bottled water, I was rehydrated. Okay.

"Oh, good," I thought, "I am going to have 'an accident' on national television." Every grade-schooler's worst nightmare was going to happen to me in middle age before millions of viewers. I imagined a little voice drawing attention to what everyone else wished to ignore.

"Mom, why is there a puddle under that man's chair?"

We still had half the show to go. Now the challenge was to listen for my cue over the urgent instructions sounding in my head. "Situation critical. Empty bladder now. This is your final warning."

Finally, the show was over. I was grateful and a little surprised to see that there was no puddle under my chair, and we all congratulated ourselves on a great show. I nodded, grinned, agreed, congratulated, and finally asked, "I wonder, is there a washroom I can use?" (Canadians!)

Reactions to the show were varied. My mother had received a call from a friend. "I think your son's on Oprah." She only saw the last half of the show, but she thought it had gone pretty well. She did have one quiet question, "The woman in the Chanel suit, do you think she might have been on drugs?"

Barbara was amused. "I thought you looked kind of pale and kind of restless. It was a really weird combination."

And my academic friends were unmerciful. "How you could expect to say anything intelligent about a suburban home is beyond me," one of them exclaimed. "I mean, this is the heartland of anomie, consumerism, selfishness, and aridity. And you and Oprah made it all seem somehow okay. It's not okay. It's the heartland of . . . "

"Thank you," I said, "that will do."

But it won't do, not at all.

Thoughts on Oprah

The first conclusion that presses upon you when you undertake an anthropology of contemporary culture is that it bears so little relation to the things we have been told about it. The more you learn, the more you feel that you have stumbled onto a "lost continent," a world excised from maps, unacknowledged by the scholars, perhaps deliberately concealed from view. The scholars have made their map of contemporary culture, but it rarely serves us well. What should be worthy of Rand McNally turns out to be about as reliable as a placemat from Denny's.

My Oprah experience was an ethnographic opportunity. It was a chance to see that when you stand in a living room in a Chicago suburb and glimpse a joyful Pocahontas dance, you are looking not at drudges or drones or simple-tons blinded by the white light of the media, but at people who had found in a Disney film a little family ritual that may someday stand as one of Danielle's fondest memories and one of the things that seems to capture the man her father was (or might have been).

In Barbara and the Oprah audience, I saw something more substantial than the addled adoration of a celebrity culture; a mark of gratitude for some-one who has systematically investigated the demanding issues of a demand-ing world. Some will say, "But surely experts do this better. Surely, in Oprah, viewers worship a false god." The implication is that people should "just snap out of it" and pay a little more attention to the real authorities in their midst.

And the intellectuals, what have they given us? What have they done to illuminate our lives and our culture? What claim do they have to be better than Oprah? Lewis Mumford called the suburb

> a multitude of uniform, unidentifiable houses, lined up inflexibly, at uni-form distances, on uniform roads, in a treeless communal waste, inhabited by people of the same class, the same income, the same age group, witness-ing the same television programs, eating the same tasteless pre-fabricated foods, from the same freezers, conforming in every outward and inward respect to a custom mould. (1961, 486)

John D. MacDonald picked up the theme:

> The incomparably dull track houses, glitteringly new, were marching out across the hills, cluttered with identical station wagons, identical children, identical barbecues, identical tastes in flowers and television. You see, Vir-ginia, there really is a Santa Rosita, full of plastic people, in plastic houses, in areas noduled by the vast basketry of their shopping centers. But do not blame them for being so tiresome and so utterly satisfied with themselves. Because, you see, there is no one left to tell them what they are and what they really should be doing. (1964, 167–168)

Pete Seeger elaborated in a song called "Little Boxes," composed by Malvina Reynolds in 1962 and performed by him in 1963.

> Little boxes on the hillside
> Little boxes made of ticky-tacky
> Little boxes, little boxes
> Little boxes all the same.
> There's a green one and a pink one
> And a blue one and a yellow one

And they're all made out of ticky-tacky
And they all look just the same.

And the people in the houses
All go to the university
And they all get put in boxes
Little boxes all the same.
And there's doctors and there's lawyers
And business executives.
And they're all made out of ticky-tacky
And they all look just the same.

And they all play on the golf course
And drink their martini dry
And they all have pretty children
And the children go to school.
And the children go to summer camp
And then to the university
And they all get put in boxes
And they all come out the same.

And the boys go into business
And marry and raise a family.
And they all get put in boxes
Little boxes all the same.

From the lordly heights of his Harvard post, John Kenneth Galbraith had this to say:

> The family which takes its mauve and cerise, air-conditioned, power-steered and power-braked automobile out for a tour passes through cities that are badly paved, made hideous by litter, blighted buildings, billboards and posts for wires that should long since have been put underground. They pass on into a countryside that had been rendered largely invisible by commercial art. . . . They picnic on exquisitely packaged food from a portable icebox by a polluted stream and go on to spend the night at a park which is a menace to public health and morals. Just before dozing off on an air mattress, beneath a nylon tent, amid the stench of decaying refuse, they may reflect vaguely on the curious unevenness of their blessings. (1958, 223)

Could this be any more patronizing? This is the treatment we got from intellectuals in the 1950s and the 1960s. It would be nice to say, "Well, this was just their first reaction. Eventually, they were to offer us a more interesting, nuanced, sophisticated view." But we *can't* say that. For they continue to hammer away at the consumer culture with enthusiasm (Baritz 1990; Ewen 1976 and 1988, 217–232; Frank 1997; Holt 2002, 82; Klein 2000; Kunstler 1994; Marcuse 1964; May 1989). Barber refers to "the numbing and neutering uniformity of industrial modernization and the colonizing culture of McWorld" and to the "trivialization and homogenization of values [which are] an affront to cultural diversity and spiritual and moral seriousness" (1995, 9, xii).

This poisonous view has seeped out into popular culture to install itself as one of the pictures Hollywood now gives us of ourselves. The theme of bankrupt suburbs and thoughtless consumers appears in a play by Eric Bogosian (*Suburbia*) and movies by Richard Linklater (*SubUrbia*), Ang Lee (*The Ice Storm*), Sam Mendes (*American Beauty*), Gary Ross (*Pleasantville*), Todd Solondz (*Happiness*), Peter Weir (*The Truman Show*), and Lars von Trier (*Dogville*). It is now something we think about ourselves. A generation or two of Americans accept this view as gospel.

The damage goes deeper than this. Consumers such as the Sullivans can hear the intellectuals and the artists. Sometimes they internalize the message, and it fills them with self-loathing, uncertainty, and unhappiness. How strange this is. Intellectuals insist that they are attacking a malformed, bankrupt culture. Instead, they help create one.

Let's review, shall we? On the one hand, we have Oprah working day after day on the themes she and her staff believe viewers care about. On the other, we have academics, novelists, and songwriters consenting to give us pony rides on the high horse of magisterial disdain. They have conducted themselves with all the grace, generosity, and empathy of a designer from New York City.

Contrary to the lordly view, consumers do more than "reflect vaguely on the curious unevenness of their blessings." They go after their problems and try to sort them out. And Oprah actually helps. She goes after the big issues, and she does so without a trace of the "suffer the little children to come unto me" patronage that the experts find so becoming. (She does so even when the likes of Jonathan Franzen reward her extraordinary efforts to encourage reading with contempt.) Oprah has earned her regard by being clear, timely, thoughtful, frank, and, yes, charismatic. Consumers have been given a choice: a woman who is charismatic versus scholars who are, well, really more numismatic.

The book you hold in your hands is an attempt to map a couple of parts of the lost continent. I hope to show that the consumer culture is a culture after all. In Part Two, I offer the essay on homeyness. This will show, I hope, that homes (and suburbs) are not "ticky-tacky boxes" and that consumers are not "tiresome and . . . utterly satisfied with themselves." They have found a way to turn houses into homes. Not an easy task and certainly not a contemptible one.

In Part Three, I will show that cars are not "mauve and cerise" indulgences but both a private and a public response to the culture of the moment. In Part Four, I will show that there is something more to the celebrity culture than a starstruck response to the media. Consumers choose and use the celebrity culture to a very deliberate purpose. In Part Five, I will show how the old view of the consumer culture, the one constructed by high society and the scholar, continues to haunt one of our most important institutions of public education, the museum. The remaining sections reach out to marketing practitioners and invite them to embrace a new model for the influence they have on culture.

I am happy to report that this book joins with other books. A sole brave voice, Herbert Gans, has always stood up against the scholars who were inclined to treat Levittown, the postwar suburb of Long Island, as an "uneducated, gullible, petty 'mass.'" He dared to accuse these scholars of "upper middle class ethnocentrism" (1967, vi). More recently, Wolfe has noted how little we really know about the American suburb (1998, 33–34). Baxandall and Ewen recently published *Picture Windows: How the Suburbs Happened*. Their study of Levittown could find little that conformed to the standard view (2000, xxi). Several journalists (Fitzgerald 1987; Freedman 1999; Peterson 1999; Postrel 2003), academic writers (Cowen 1998; Dickstein 1999; Kelly 1989, 1993; Marling 1994), and filmmakers (Levinson 1990; Payne 1999) have taken up the theme, and the mood of what Baxandall and Ewen call "antisuburban snobbery" is perhaps beginning to lift (2000, xxi; see also Carrier 1992, 195–196; Le Wita 1994, 6, 22; and Traube 1996).

This book is, then, a small contribution to a growing trend. Plainly there is much to do. A lost continent awaits us. Anthropologists will make their contribution, if exploding appendixes and bladders do not interfere too much. But this is a task for everyone. It is time to take our culture back.

Part Two
Homes

Strategy:

The essay notes that when it comes to homes, we do not act like rational economic actors. In Drew Bledsoe's case, a vast investment was made in home ownership that Mr. Bledsoe could never hope to recover. A great deal of investment in home renovation has this status.

The article, "Homeyness," offers an anthropological account of what we mean by "home" and how we transform houses into homes. By showing the cultural value created by these places, the article offers an answer to the Bledsoe paradox.

3   The Drew Bledsoe Paradox

The Mysterious Home Economics of Homo economicus

When Drew Bledsoe (then the quarterback of the New England Patriots) decided to build a home for himself in Boston, his economic advisors had to explain to him that the millions he was about to spend would never come back to him. This is because the people who would buy his house would be buying it for the land alone. They would knock Drew's palace down and build anew. Everyone who owns this property, in fact, knocks down and starts fresh. None of them recaptures the millions they spend on their homes.

Drew was apparently puzzled. So should we all be. *Homo economicus,* economic man, is not supposed to act like this. To "invest" millions of dollars in a "property" and then have to walk away from it . . . this is not the rational thing to do. (It is especially not rational when you are an NFL quarterback who may discover on any given Sunday that the caprice of an owner or a coach obliges him to pick up and pursue his career on the other side of the country. But almost everyone who spends this kind of money on a house lives a fluid life that can demand sudden relocation . . . and this cataclysmic loss.)

The Bledsoe paradox does not hold for just the very wealthy. It is a truism of home renovation that the renovator will not recapture all (in some cases, any) of the value of the money they spent on renovations. They might regard a new kitchen and deck as an improvement that increase the value of a property. But they're wrong. They are about to sacrifice hard-won savings to the Bledsoe paradox.

How should we think about this? We might say, "Well, no, the money people put into their homes or their renovations is not meant as an investment." People spend this money to make themselves comfortable. They are spending for the moment, not the long term. It is an investment in happiness, not the real estate market.

Let's run the numbers. Let's say that Bledsoe spent three years in his house before moving to Buffalo and that he spent $2 million on house construction. The "happiness fee" here was around $650,000. That's $220,000 a year, $20,000 a month, or $645 a day. Drew, man, get a room. What about the more usual home owner? Let's say the average renovation is $100,000 and that people spend an average of 3.5 years in their homes. Here the happiness fee is roughly $3,000 a month, or $100 dollars a day. (An anthropologist with a calculator is a dangerous thing; better check these numbers.)

The opportunity cost is itself quite high. If the renovators had invested the $100,000 intelligently in the stock market of the middle 1990s, they could have retired by decade's end. The inconvenience cost is high, too. Ask any homemaker what it's like to put up with commotion, dirt, and a missing kitchen for four months, and he or she almost always says, "We will never do it again." That there *is* an inconvenience cost should make us suspicious of the happiness argument. If happiness were truly the objective, this family could treat themselves to lavish hotel life every weekend and leave money in their pockets.

The sociobiologists will no doubt say that we rebuild or renovate to claim the property. The notion here, to put it somewhat crudely, is that this investment is the way our species pees in the corners. As usual, this argument is a blunt instrument which fails to explain most of the data at hand. Are we to understand that the construction of a vast faux Tudor and a split-level monument to modernism have *exactly* the same motive? Are we to understand that the hundreds of little decisions that people agonize over when building or renovating are really just a false consciousness? French drapes, glazed windows, open skylights—it's all really just pee. But there is a simpler question, one that sociobiology cannot reckon with: Why don't we just actually pee in the corners?

Let's imagine we have done our anthropological homework. We have interviewed Mrs. Maison about the new renovation she and her husband just completed on their three-year-old home. They tore off the back of the house and replaced it mostly with glass. Light now pours in. When we ask Mrs. Maison why she went to such great expense and inconvenience, she says, "Well, you see, my husband just loves the light in the morning. Me, I would sleep until noon, if you let me, but Frank's a morning person and he loves to get up and pad around in the first light of the day. It's his quiet time. It's his thinking time."

This is a charming statement of wifely solicitude, but it's wrong. When we talk to Mr. Maison, he doesn't talk at all about morning light. He talks about space and openness and being able to see the garden. When we gently prompt him about mornings, he says, "Oh, that. Yeah, I know. My wife keeps saying that to everybody, and it's partly true. I mean I am a morning person, and the house is way nicer in the morning. But I liked it before. I mean in the winter months, there really isn't any light."

Homo economicus, meet *homo faber* (man the maker). The reason Mr. and Mrs. Maison spent $180,000 on this renovation was to capture an idea Mrs. Maison has of her husband, and, more important, to *create* the idea she has of her husband. He works too hard, she thinks. He has so many demands made of him. If only he had a little more time to himself. If only he could be bathed in the light of the morning, maybe. . . . This is a more-complicated species of wifely solicitude. Mrs. Maison is crafting the home to craft her husband.

The Bledsoe paradox proves not to be a paradox at all. We invest in our homes (when we have the good fortune to have homes and money enough to remake them) because they are transformational opportunities. We make them to make ourselves. This is money well spent . . . when it works. It's badly spent when the idea we are trying to invent of ourselves is implausible or otherwise uninhabitable. It does not fit very well with our notions of economic man, of ourselves as rational creatures who invest for future profit. But that's only because *homo economicus* is defined too narrowly. It would help a little if we would see that some economic activities are also cultural ones (the reverse is also true), that we undertake these activities especially when we want to cast our ideas out into the world in the hopes that they will "discover" us there and take up residence.

In a sense, the paradox comes from a paradigm. Economic man is a robust part of who we are but only a part of who we are. When we cast *this* idea out into the world, we are sometimes puzzled by the creature who turns up at our door.

4 Homeyness

A Cultural Account of One Constellation of
Consumer Goods and Meanings

Abstract

This essay offers a cultural account of the constellation of consumer goods and meanings in North America called "homeyness." It reports ethnographic data collected in and on the modern North American home. This essay considers the physical, symbolic, and pragmatic properties of homeyness, showing its cultural character and consequences.

Introduction

This essay draws on anthropological theory, ethnographic research, and a wide range of social scientific scholarship to consider the cultural characteristics and consequences of a neglected cultural phenomenon. The account is divided into four parts: (1) the scholarly precedents and objectives of the essay; (2) the physical properties of homeyness as these were described by respondents in a recent ethnographic research project; (3) the symbolic properties of homeyness: its cultural meanings and logic; and (4) the pragmatic properties of homeyness: the uses to which it is put by contemporary North Americans and its larger structural consequences.

The research reported in this essay was conducted in an urban area of southern Ontario in the summers of 1985 and 1986. Forty individuals were interviewed. The interview for each respondent took six hours in total. Interviews were conducted in the respondent's home, almost always in the living room. All respondents lived in freestanding houses. The forty respondents were divided into two equal categories by status (blue collar or managerial). The following characteristics were common for all: race (Caucasian), religion (Protestant), ethnicity (British), time their family had been in Canada (at least three generations), and marital status (married). Men and women were almost equally represented.

Research was conducted using ethnographic methods and a four-step method of qualitative inquiry described in McCracken (1988d). The study was designed to investigate the cultural logic, the underlying beliefs and assumptions, of one aspect of consumption behavior in modern North American life. It was also designed to show how the cultural meanings contained in homeyness are put to work in the "projects" of individual North Americans as they construct notions of self and world (McCracken 1986b). In sum, this essay is designed to show what homeyness means, how it means, and with what cultural consequences it means.

Scholarly Context

The present study has its foundations in several of the social sciences. It is designed to address a range of research topics.

Anthropologists have been as prepared as anyone to speculate on their own society, but generally they have been fastidiously unwilling to examine the ethnographic details of mainstream North American life (Gulick 1973; Varenne 1986). The study of homeyness takes anthropology into the domestic heart of North American society to show that the theoretical issues that concern the field can be investigated just as readily in the petri dish of modern life as they can in a more conventional field site. More particularly, it seeks to show that the issue of cultural "construction" may be investigated in modern North America (Bruner 1984a, 2–3). Homeyness is one of the instruments by which some North Americans construct several of their most important concepts of self and family.

The study also is designed to draw from the renaissance now taking place in the study of material culture both in anthropology and American studies (Appadurai 1986; Bruner 1984a; Cordwell and Schwarz 1979; Glassie 1973; Kavanaugh 1978; Lechtman and Merrill 1977; Neich 1982; Prown 1980, 1982; Quimby 1978; Rathje 1978; Reynolds and Stott 1986; Richardson 1974; Schlereth 1982; Wolf 1970). This body of work deepens our understanding of the ways in which material culture makes culture material. The present essay is designed to show how "homeyness" as material culture helps realize certain notions of sociality and rootedness that are otherwise inaccessible to North Americans. I hope to encourage the contention, implied by Prown, that some things about social life can be captured only through the study of material culture (1982, 3).

The essay also draws on historical studies on the origins and development of the consumer society (Braudel 1973; Campbell 1983, 1987; Fox and Lears 1983; Harris 1978, 1981; Horowitz 1985; Lears 1981; McKendrick, Brewer, and Plumb 1982; Miller 1981; Mukerji 1983; Pope 1983; Shi 1985; Williams 1982) in general and the relationship between material culture and the development of the North American home and family (Clark 1976, 1986; Doucet and Weaver 1985; Gordon and McArthur 1985; Handlin 1979; Holdsworth 1977; Leach 1984; Marchand 1985). The study examines how domestic environment serves as a site of individuality, sanctuaries against work, centers of spirituality, and staging grounds for that intensely important bundle of activities, values, and undertakings in Western societies called "domesticity." As Clark has noted, the North American home is a place charged with "symbolic and moral meaning" (1986, 238). This essay will attempt to show that much of this meaning depends upon the homeyness constellation of consumer goods.

This essay draws on the fields of environmental studies, architecture, and geography (Agrest and Gandelsonas 1977; Altman, Rapoport, and Wohlwill 1980; Carlisle 1982; Carswell and Saile 1987; Duncan 1981; Krampen 1979; Rapoport 1982; Saile 1984; Tuan 1982) and their study of household design and furnishing (Forty 1986; Hine 1986; Jackson 1976; Korosec-Serfaty 1976; Kron 1983; Lawrence 1981, 1982, 1984; Pratt 1981) and "home" (Altman and Werner 1985; Giuliani, Bonnes, and Werner 1987; Hayden 1981; Seamon 1979; Tognoli 1987; Wright 1980, 1981). It provides an ethnographic account of the "centering" and "place attachment" characteristics of the home environment, topics that have drawn some interest in the field but relatively little research (Tognoli 1987, 658).

This study will address the sociological study of material possessions. Sociologists have examined the emotional and structural significance of special possessions (Csikszentmihalyi and Rochberg-Halton 1981), the status significance of material goods (Blumberg 1974; Davis 1956, 1958; Felson 1976; Laumann and House 1970; Rainwater 1966), the larger consumer system and its creation of cultural meanings (Gottdiener 1985; Hirsch 1972), patterns of preference (Gans 1974), the use of objects as role models (Rochberg-Halton 1984), the commodification of the body (O'Neill 1978), and the sociology of collecting (Danct 1986).

Interestingly, however, some of the sociologists who have considered homeyness have come away perplexed. In his study of the homes of postwar Detroit, Felson could find no ready explanation for what he called the "bric-a-brac factor" (1976, 414). Candidly, he admits to aspects of the home "beyond the reach of this writer's sociological imagination" (414). Laumann and House in their study of living-room furnishings suffered a similar difficulty and acknowledge "distinctions beyond the untutored grasp of our interviewers" (1970, 338). I would contend that some of the sociological significance of consumption behavior proves less evasive when sought in an ethnographic context.

Attention is also given to the field of consumer research, including its treatments of materialism of North America (Belk 1985), the use of ethnographic methods (Belk 1987a; Deshpande 1983; Hirschman 1985; Hirschman and Holbrook 1986; Holbrook 1987b; Wallendorf 1987), the political implications of consumption patterns (Caplovitz 1967; Firat 1986), the development of consumer pathologies (Faber, O'Guinnard, and Krych 1987; Gromno 1984, 1986), patterns of product symbolism (Hirschman 1981; Holbrook and Hirschman 1982; Holman 1980; Levy 1978, 1981; McCracken 1988a; Mick 1986, 1988), the institutional implications of consumption (Mayer 1978; Nicosia and Mayer 1976), the effect of consumption patterns on family interaction (Olson 1985), the nature of "favorite object" attachment (Wallendorf and Amould 1988), consumption rituals (Bloch 1982; Rook 1985), and consumption folklore (Sherry 1984). By pursing these several objectives ethnographically, the present study hopes to contribute to the study of "macro consumer behavior" (Belk 1984b).

Homeyness: Physical Properties

According to the *Oxford English Dictionary,* "homey" is an adjective that refers to things "resembling or suggestive of home, home-like, having the feeling of home, homish." According to the OED, it first appeared in written English over a century ago, in 1885. But the term "homey" is regarded as a vulgar term, unfit for polite discourse. Commentators on the family, the home, and domestic affairs in this century have eschewed it, preferring the daintier "home-like" (Anonymous 1968; Boschetti 1968; Brenan 1939; Morton 1936; Robinson 1941).

If the term has been avoided by social commentators, it has been embraced with enthusiasm by North Americans. Respondents in the research conducted for this study applied the adjective "homey" to a range of domestic phenomena in modern North America. They considered it a property of many aspects of the home, including its colors, materials, furniture, decorative objects, arrangement, interior design, and exterior characteristics. As these respondents tell it, the creation of homeyness is one of the most pressing objectives of their domestic circumstances and family lives. By their account, homeyness is an "effect" keenly to be sought for virtually every aspect of the home, from its exterior surfaces to the smallest details of the mantlepiece. Let us identify the physical properties identified as homey.

"Homey" colors are the "warm" colors: orange, gold, green, brown. The preferred materials for interior walls are wood, stone, and brick. The only acceptable material for furniture construction is wood. Fabrics for furniture are relatively unfinished natural fibers. Fabric patterns are florals (especially chintz) or conversationals. Furniture styles are traditional, homemade, handcrafted, colonial, or antique. One respondent, for instance, looked forward to replacing an Arborite kitchen table with a round pine table and six caneback chairs.

Objects are homey when they have a personal significance for the owner (e.g., gifts, crafts, trophies, mementos, family heirlooms). A homemade ashtray assembled from shells collected on a summer holiday by the children served one family as a reminder of an important time and place in the history of the family and was therefore considered especially homey. Objects can also be homey when they are informal or playful in character (e.g., the novelty ashtray, a pillow in the shape of a football, a pillow with verse in needlepoint). Plants and flowers are objects that contribute to the homeyness of a room. Some objects are homey because they support or contain decorative objects (e.g., wooden hutches and what-nots). Decorative objects such as glass or china objects of a very particular character can be homey, but interestingly this class of objects is, on the whole, dangerous to the homey effect (as we shall see below). Objects that mark the season (e.g., corn in autumn, holly for Christmas) are homey. Pictures of relatives, pets, and possessions are also homey. Paintings of certain kinds can have a homey character, especially sentimental treatments of landscapes or seascapes. Books in quantity can "furnish" a room and give it a homey character.

Arrangements are homey when they combine diverse styles of furnishing in a single room. They are also homey when they establish patterns of asymmetrical balance and when they pair and center heterogeneous objects. Homeyness can also be achieved by the judicious combinations of particular colors, fabrics, and pieces of furniture. For many people, the important principle of arrangement is redundancy, and they bring many homey things together into a single arrangement. For others, homey objects are best used sparingly and in isolation.

Homey interior details include bay windows, breakfast nooks, wainscoting, wood-beam ceilings, kitchens, dens, "snug" rooms, low ceilings, and fireplaces. Exterior characteristics include a low-slung "bungalow" roof, well-enclosed and well-treed backyards, paned and mullioned windows, shutters, porches, lawn ornaments, ivy-covered walls, plants and shrubs close to and encompassing the house, mock-Tudor timbering, brass lanterns and other lamps, an asymmetrical front, and a small front door.

Respondents used a very particular set of adjectives to describe "homeyness." A favorite characterization of the homey place was to say that it looked "as though someone lived there." The terms "informal," "comfortable," "cozy," "relaxed," "secure," "unique," "old," "rich," "warm," "humble," "welcoming," "accommodating," "lived in," "country kitchenish" were all used as glosses. The terms "private" and "nice and bright" were also used, though less frequently. Respondents said that homeyness is a feature of the home that is immediately and intuitively obvious. As one respondent put it, "I can go into a hundred homes and I can tell in a second whether it's homey or it isn't, just by the feel of it."

This indeterminacy is apparently characteristic of homeyness. As the historian Handlin notes, "Authors like Catherine Sedgwick [b. 1789] and John Howard Payne [b. 1791] never specified the particular characteristics of an ideal home but claimed only that the quality they admired was a feeling, a spirit, or an atmosphere that was indefinable and indescribable" (1979, 15). As we shall note below, homeyness is no simple sum of material parts but an intangible, illusive quality that can be difficult to define and achieve.

But if respondents sometimes found themselves unable to capture what homeyness is, they rarely suffered any difficulty in saying what it is not. The enemies of homeyness, that is to say, were easily characterized. One respondent described an ornately formal living room as "cluttered up with a whole lot of fancy stuff" and therefore unhomey. The terms used to characterize unhomey homes were "pretentious," "formal," "stark," "elegant," "cold," "daunting," "sterile," "showpiece," "reserved," "controlled," "decorated," "modern," and even "Scandinavian."

Homeyness: Symbolic Properties

The term "symbolic property" refers to the meaning and the logic that gives a physical property its cultural significance. In the case of homeyness, more particularly, "symbolic property" refers to the kinds of meanings that inhere in homey phenomena, the assumptions on which these meanings rest, and the strategies by which these meanings are actuated.

Homeyness as a cultural property is an intensely prescriptive and intensely elusive meaning. It represents a domestic condition that is highly valued by North American culture-bearers but is not easily achieved by them. The difficulty is that many forces work against the realization of homeyness. Sometimes the notion, like any ideal moral condition, is simply more than North Americans can sustain. It is better than their best efforts. Sometimes it is contradicted by other cultural principles that work to shape the family and the home. Sometimes it is, due to an evanescent character, difficult to capture, to make actual, to realize. While North Americans know homeyness when they see it, they do not always have a clear idea of how it is accomplished. Furthermore, there is no simple formula for the creation of homeyness. Like all really important cultural achievements, homeyness is most compelling when it somehow transcends itself, when it is greater than the sum of mechanically prescribed parts.

These several factors and the difficulty they present in realizing homeyness in the world have a profound effect on its character. They cause it to assume a deeply processual nature. "Homeyness" as a cultural phenomenon is of necessity constantly under construction by those who would make it present in their lives. It is constantly in need of refreshment and recreation if it is to survive and succeed in the world. In order to capture the cultural character of a phenomenon with these characteristics, it is necessary to go beyond its meaning and its grammar and to capture the logic and the strategies, the symbolic properties, by which it operates.

For the purposes of exposition, I have distinguished eight symbolic properties of homeyness. I review these properties below, characterizing how each is intended to act upon the individual and the cultural logic by which it does so. I examine, in turn, the diminutive, the variable, the embracing, the engaging, the memorial, the authentic, the informal, and, finally, the situating properties of homeyness. These properties are rehearsed here in order of their primacy. Each property helps to support every subsequent one. Each property helps to extend all previous ones. The following eight properties have a "telescoped" relationship to one another.

The Diminutive Property

Homeyness has a diminutive aspect. Ceilings are low, doors and windows are small, space is divided and filled, lines are broken and repeated, and shapes are little and sometimes organic. Homeyness cannot survive the bleak expanse of an off-white wall. It cannot tolerate sparse furnishings, clean, uncluttered lines, or "elegance" of any kind.

This property of homeyness helps give the domestic environment manageable proportions. As Levi-Strauss suggests in *The Savage Mind,* that which is "quantitatively diminished . . . seems to us qualitatively simplified" (1966, 23). The diminutive aspect of homeyness has a simplifying power; it makes an environment more graspable, conceivable, thinkable. It gives an environment the "human scale" that has preoccupied postmodern architecture. It stands in opposition to the monumental and brutalist aspects of modern built form and represents habitable space that is "manageable" both as a place to use and as a place to grasp. In the language of anthropology (cf. Levi-Strauss 1963), the diminutive property helps to make these places "good" to think because it makes them "easy" to think (Tambiah 1969).

The Variable Property

Homeyness has a variable aspect. It appears deliberately to eschew uniformity and consistency. This property is most clearly illustrated by the preference respondents showed for local houses made of "rubblestone" rather than cut stone. Rubblestone is highly variable in shape and size and must be piled "higgledy-piggledy," whereas cut stone, being consistent in size and shape, is laid in uniform rows. Confronted with this concise choice between the variable and the uniform, respondents declared their preference for the variable. In their view, variable rubblestone made a home more homey.

This variable property of homeyness is also evidenced by the preferred patterns of fabric, furniture arrangement, exterior design, and what-not collections, in all of which variability is highly prized. It is this property of homeyness that explains its hostility to classical patterns and definitions of order. Homeyness is seen to be inconsistent with symmetry, balance, and visibly premeditated order.

Variableness is calculated to make homey environments appear more particular and therefore more "real" than nonhomey environments. The logic of this association is this: variability makes things appear more contingent, contingency makes things appear more individual and authentic. Homey phenomena are supposed to be relatively haphazard, highly contingent, the particular outcomes of particular intentions, desires, and events. They are not supposed to be the work of premeditation, routinized processes (e.g., mass manufacture) or anonymous calculation. This makes the homeyness ideology vulnerable to several ironies and contradictions. For instance, the very woodwork and "gingerbread" that gives certain surfaces the appearance of contingency (and homeyness) exists only because of the invention of new sawing technologies and the mass manufacture this made possible. Just why this property of homeyness should succeed in making homey environments appear more "real" is not entirely clear. But it is worth noting that Miller (1972, 364) has observed a very similar pattern for the theater. Miller notes that stage performances have greater veracity when they contain signs that run against the semiotic grain of the play.

The Embracing Property

Homeyness has an embracing aspect. This is partly a function of the smallness and variableness of homey space. But it is also the result of the way in which the homey environment is filled, organized, and contained. The surfaces of the homey environment exhibit a pattern of descending enclosure. Each surface is enclosed by a greater surface and in turn encloses a lesser one. This hierarchical chain of enclosure creates the embrace of the homey environment.

The first act of encompassment begins with the neighborhood and yard. Some neighborhoods, especially, for instance, the cul-de-sac, have a strongly encompassing character (Brown and Werner 1985). The presence of trees on public streets and fences, shrubbery, and ornaments in private yards also contribute to a sense of enclosed space.

For some homes, the first enclosing surface is the ivy (*Hedera helix,* var. *Hibemica, Angularis,* or *Dentata Variegata*) that climbs and encompasses the exterior wall of the house. This has the effect of embedding the exterior of the house in a still greater exterior, adding a layer to the encompassing folds of the house and obscuring the hard and manmade surfaces of the house in a surface that is not only organic but also evocative of benign pastoral images and cloistered institutional ones.

The next potentially embracing surface of the home is the roof line. When a home has an overhanging hipped roof, it is seen to be embraced by it and made more homey. This roofline appears in several architectural styles common to nineteenth- and twentieth-century North America (e.g., mock-Tudor cottage, pitched Gothic house, California bungalow, and some of the domestic architecture of Frank Lloyd Wright). A variation of this encompassing effect is repeated in the canvas awnings that are sometimes placed over windows. These awnings serve in a sense to "roof" the window and give the house a homey appearance by adding to its embracing surfaces.

The next potentially homey surface of the house is the external wall. Respondents argued that this surface is especially homey when it consists of small and variable units (the diminutive and variable properties at work in a larger one). The wall of a mock-Tudor home therefore qualifies, as does brick, stone, and any wooden surface with Gothic or "gingerbread" ornament. Respondents felt that massive walls with unbroken spaces and lines were incapable of the homey embrace, and one respondent was moved to compare these external walls to those of a prison compound, the least homey of environments.

Another interior surface is the books that sometimes line the walls of a den, study, or library. Here we see the creation of another layer, interior instead of exterior, manmade instead of natural. This layer, like the one before it, helps, in a visual sense, to buttress the outside and fortify the inside. But additional symbolic resources are deployed. This layer of books is the real and potential source of the layers of knowledge and understanding with which the individual mediates his or her relationship to the world and constructs the self, a point to which we shall return below. It is therefore the source of additional encompassing materials. But just as important, a wall of books represents ports to an extraordinary intellectual and imaginative geography in which the individual is free to "lose" or "find" (and so construct) the self. Books supply encompassed material as well.

The other furnishings of the wall of the homey environment help to extend its embrace. The sheer abundance of pictures and hangings for the wall creates another layer, this one of objects of the family's own manufacture. These pictures record the family's past and present (e.g., wedding and graduation pictures), its internal and external relationships (e.g., Mothers' Day cards, team photographs, club plaques), and its accomplishments (e.g., diplomas, bowling trophies, stuffed fish). They represent a layer the family has made of itself for itself.

The "memory wall," as we may call it here, appears to have a special relationship to the family. The family, in modern North America, is a highly performative cultural entity. It must make itself a family out of its activities and connections, out of its enacted roles and performed relationships. The "memory wall" appears to capture both aspects of this constructed family's "encompassed/encompassing" logic. As an encompassing surface, the wall of family memorabilia stands for the family as corporation, the larger, containing institution the family has made for itself through its shared activities, accomplishments, and interconnections. As an encompassed surface, the memory wall stands for the smaller, contained, individualized diversity that exists within the family. Using yet another "part-whole" logic, the wall repeats this rendering of the family. The entire body of wall ornaments stands for the corporation, subsuming individual pieces within a larger whole. But every particular piece in the collection stands as an individualized part, representing the personal experiences and achievements of an individual.

The furnishings of the room help complete the process of encompassment. They make up the last ring of material intimacy in the home. One group of these furnishings encircles the wall and a second set creates small pools at the center of the room. Chairs and sofas drawn into a circle, focused on an imaginary center point, are the final surround in this material world. When this circle is occupied, a final human surround is accomplished. The final piece of the encompassing process can be the odor of cooking food that surrounds the individual as he or she enters the home (Classen, Howes, and Synnott 1995).

In sum, the embracing aspect of homeyness demonstrates a descending pattern of enclosure. The structure of the neighborhood, the foliage of the street and yard, the ivy of the exterior wall, the overhanging roof, the exterior wall, the books of the interior wall, the memory wall, the furnishings of the room, the constructed family, and the constructed self all work by graduated stages to create the sense of enclosure. Each ring of intimacy encloses the next, so that the center of a room has a deeply embedded quality. The occupant of such a space is removed and protected from the outside world by an intricate series of baffles and mediators.

The process of enclosure has, from a logical point of view, an active quality that aids in its representation. Each layer of intimacy (except the first and last) is both encompassed and encompassing. Outer layers enclose inner layers which in turn enclose still more inner layers. This logical relationship of encompassing and encompassment, arrayed as it is in a hierarchical series, gives the notion of enclosure a repetitive and shifting quality. The acts of encompassing and encompassment are repeated again and again in the household. Furthermore, what is enclosed at one moment is enclosing in another. These two qualities make the embracing property of homeyness conceptually lively; more active than passive in character, more visible and plain.

But the process of enclosure also has a dynamic quality from a historical point of view. All of the elements of the encompassing hierarchy require time to be established. The ivy takes time to grow, the books take time to collect, the memory wall takes time to create, the furniture time to buy and arrange, the family time to construct, the self time to assemble. There is a strong developmental aspect to the embracing property. It takes time to accomplish; the layers go on bit by bit. This too helps to emphasize the embracing process.

The process of enclosure even has a dynamic quality from a social point of view. It is created by diverse agents, including the forces of a domesticated nature (e.g., the ivy), an anonymous marketplace (e.g., the house), a personalized literary community (e.g., books chosen by the family), a family (e.g., the memory wall), and an individual (e.g., hobby products). The embracing quality of the homey space is a collective accomplishment to which diverse parties contribute. This diversity of contribution gives it a quality of contingency that it could not have were it the work of a single individual or group engaged in a single project.

All of these layers for these several reasons help to give homey space an encompassing character and to iterate and reiterate the room's containing quality. The occupant of such a space is held, almost cosseted, by its contents. This aspect of the homey principle gives it the ability to make the individual feel secure and protected from external threat. In this capacity, the homey space has the same symbolic and psychological value as a parental embrace. It offers security from real but especially from imagined dangers. The psychological satisfactions to be drawn from this protection are, respondents claim, quite considerable. That it is, in the colloquial sense of the term, merely "symbolic" protection does not appear to make it any less comforting, important, or desirable.

The encompassing powers of the homey environment are sometimes felt most acutely and consciously by those who wish least to feel their effect. Children who have recently moved away from home sometimes complain, on their return, of the "stifling" and "infantilizing" quality of the home and its ability to reduce them to old patterns of dependency. This is homeyness at work.

But if respondents understand the encompassing quality of homey phenomena in these psychological terms as an embrace, the ethnographic observer may give another, somewhat more structural account. The embracing property of homeyness appears to take some of its emotional power from its special relationship to the constructed character of the family and individual. For the family and the individual cannot fashion the embracing aspect of homeyness without fashioning the self and family. Cultivating a homey environment, and especially constructing the memory wall, contributes willy-nilly to the construction of the self and the family. Some of the intense satisfaction attached to homeyness, some of its resemblance to the parental embrace, stems perhaps from this special relationship to the processes by which the self and family take shape.

The Engaging Property

Homeyness has an engaging aspect. It appears deliberately designed to engage the observer. This process begins with the "welcoming" objective of homey phenomena. There is no ethnographic study that enables us to understand how, in this culture, it is possible to speak sensibly of a holly wreath, for example, as welcoming. But respondents found this an unexceptional, indeed necessary, adjective for a range of decorative materials. They were able to suggest (but more frequently merely to imply) that the wreath has something in its character that extends an invitation for interaction, promises a warm reception, and represents a certain emotional tone for the interior within. Homey objects, respondents say, are supposed to "draw" the observer in.

Like the embracing property, this engaging property of homeyness has a graduated character. Engagement in homeyness works by stages, becoming more intense as the individual is more deeply insinuated into the homey environment. The holiday wreath on the front door attempts a relatively public and general species of engagement. As the individual moves into the home, he or she encounters increasingly specific and personal gestures. The arrangement of the house, of a room, of the furniture of a room, of the large decorative details in the room, of the small decorative "touches" (as they are called) all can be charged with homeyness, and each draws the individual still further into engagement.

The engaging strategy extends to and governs even the demeanor of individuals within the homey space. By convention, the occupants of a homey space are supposed to be "open" to new arrivals and prepared to "greet" them with generosity and warmth. This notion of "openness" is an important one for respondents, and their insistence on it points to the existence of the engaging strategy as well as the encompassing strategy. Openness is meant to be played out not just in the material culture of the homey environment but even in the behavior of its occupants. The occupant of the homey space, when part of a group, is supposed to greet a visitor by breaking the circle and rising to meet the visitor. The body is itself "opened" as the occupant turns to face the visitor and extends an open hand in greeting. It is most important that the face be, in a sense, open, tilted back slightly with mouth and eyes opened with surprise, pleasure, and recognition. The orientation of the entire room, both its animate and inanimate objects, opens in greeting (and then, when the visitor has been made part of the group, closes again so that he or she too is encompassed).

The process continues with the arrangement of chairs in a manner that invites interaction; the presence of playful, amusing objects that demand a reaction; and the existence of objects such as magazines, knitting, and even games or puzzles. The homey room may also contain homemade furniture, wall hangings, and art objects, all of which seem designed to occasion conversation and the opportunity for engagement. All of these things invite the occupant to become a participant, if only as the close observer of a lively environment (cf. the Victorian precedent discussed by Clark 1986, 117–120). They also invite several occupants to become conversational partners whose interaction with the room prompts interaction with one another and vice versa.

Previous properties have already succeeded in containing and embracing the occupant. This one now demands a more active, autonomous, and self-directed kind of relationship. Homeyness has moved from a passive involvement to active involvement, the great sine qua non of all projects that seek engagement. With engagement, the homey environment has found a powerful way to strengthen its relationship with the occupant.

The Mnemonic Property

Homeyness has a mnemonic aspect. The most striking objects here are the house itself, replete with family association and history, trophies, gifts from children or friends, photographs of the family, tourist mementoes, handcrafted pieces of furniture, and decorative objects. All of these carry an unmistakable historical character. Indeed, they have been called the "family archives" (McCracken 1987). The mnemonic significance of objects is so strong that it can override aesthetic and other "decorator" considerations. One respondent found herself caught between aesthetic and mnemonic considerations and referred to a picture

[that] I really don't like, but someone who I really care a lot about gave it to us as a wedding present. I put it up because I like this woman, [but] I have it on this backside of the wall so you can't really see it as you come in.

These objects are intended to recall the presence of family and friendship relationships, personal achievements, family events, ritual passages, and community associations. Some respondents spoke of these objects not just as a record of their past but even as a kind of proof and enactment of it. In the language of semiotics, these memorial objects "index" the presence of certain aspects of personal and family life even as they play these aspects out in the manner of a performative (Peirce 1932).

This aspect of homeyness has the effect of deeply personalizing the present circumstances. The place that is containing, embracing, and engaging is now very strongly particularized and localized in time. It is made a place in time. This temporal "emplacement," as we might call it, of the homey environment is accomplished by the expressing, indexing, and performance of the family's historical meanings and recollections. The individual is now much more vividly "somewhere" than before because the environment is much more vividly "sometime" than before. The engaging aspect of homeyness helps to substantialize the environment in which the individual finds him or herself.

The Authentic Property

Homeyness has an authentic aspect. Respondents spoke of homey spaces and things as being somehow more "real" and somehow more "natural" than certain alternative styles of furnishing. They spoke of homey things and space as being strongly opposite in character to things that were "contrived," "artificial," and "forced." In their view, inauthentic styles were the product of modern aesthetics, interior designers, showpiece homes, and high-status individuals.

All of the aforementioned cultural properties help homey spaces and things assume this authentic character. The small, variable, intimate, engaging, and mnemonic aspects of homey phenomena all contribute here. But the key to this aspect of homeyness is its intensely personal nature. Homey things and spaces, as we have seen, reflect the particular details of personal lives. Homey things and spaces help distinguish the home from the homes around it and its occupants from other people. It emphasizes the individuality of the individual and the family in a society that insists with special intensity on this discrimination even as it inevitably engages in patterns of materialism that threaten to obscure it. As Forty suggests, "In contemporary Western society, home life is the only effective signifier of personal authenticity" (1986, 152).

Homeyness succeeds in this because it is seen to be untouched by the calculations of the marketplace, the doctrines of politics or religion, the falsehoods of the status system, the impersonations of the fashion world, the contentions of the advertising enterprise, or any of the other meanings that are served up by the meaning-manufacturers of a mass society. Homeyness is the record of a life, a particular life, lived without ulterior motive, creating its own meaning for its own purposes.

The authentic aspect of homeyness helps then to complete the process of emplacement by giving it a spatial dimension. Through the creation of a slew of entirely personal details, it creates a highly centered sense of place. It is this aspect of homeyness that helps to create the impression that, in the valued phrase with which respondents characterized the highest accomplishment of the homeyness enterprise, "someone lives here."

The Informal Property

Homeyness has an informal aspect. Each of the physical properties identified above can be located on a formality continuum, and in every case the homey choice falls at the informal end. Homey colors are the most "warm" and "friendly." The materials are relatively unfinished, almost deliberately unfine. The furniture positively embraces a rustic, relatively crude appearance. Decorative objects are often inexpensive. They are valuable not for their formal beauty or skillful execution but for their humor or sentimentality. Arrangements avoid classical symmetries or modern spareness, and a relative clutter is enjoined. Interior and exterior details of the house design are deliberately rustic, rural, cottage-like, and unprepossessing. The homey look appears deliberately to eschew any stylistic characteristic that is associated with the formal, the ceremonial, the distant, the disengaged, or the decorous. It appears constantly to work to suggest a certain humility and accessibility. As one respondent put it, "My house says, 'Look at me, I'm really beautiful but I'm not pretentious, I'm humble.'"

Homey homes and rooms appear deliberately to seek to "lower the tone" of human interaction. As the same respondent explained, "Here [in the homiest part of the house] you could throw things around and I wouldn't worry about breaking anything. Like you could put glasses on this furniture and I wouldn't care and you can just, you know, really be comfortable and not worry about things." She opposed homey places to places "that make you want to be more careful." In short, homey places are supposed to reassure the occupant that no special formality of dress, posture, demeanor, or conversation is required of them. From the respondent's point of view, one of the great objectives of homeyness is that it "puts people at their ease."

Another respondent reacted to a picture of a grand living room with almost violent dislike for its formal tone. He explained that in a visit to one of the residences of Queen Elizabeth II, he had found evidence of homeyness. He was especially impressed with "the rooms that they [the royal family] lived in where the TV set was and you could tell they sat around and had a few drinks before dinner and watched the news or whatever and it looked like it was lived in and yet by God it is the home of the queen and far more homey than that thing [i.e., the room pictured in the photograph]. That looks like one of the state rooms that they put up to hold a state banquet." According to this impassioned account, even the most formal of social creatures, a royal family, avoids the tyranny of formal surroundings.

The homeyness strategy appears to diminish the formality of the room in order to diminish the formality of the interaction that takes place within it. It is not clear how this transformation is accomplished but it is perhaps the case that the homey environment presents a face that is deliberately without defenses or pretenses in order to reassure the occupant that he or she may forgo defenses and pretenses of their own. Homeyness serves as a vital cue to the rules that govern a particular domestic universe. It says, in effect, "You may be yourself without risk of embarrassment or ridicule." It appears designed to ease participation, to reassure the individual that the involvement is, from an impression-management point of view, almost entirely riskless.

The Situating Property

Homeyness has a situating aspect. The occupant of homey space is not just contained, embraced, engaged, reminded, emplaced, and reassured, he or she is also deliberately situated within it. In this final stage of the homeyness enterprise, the occupant of homey space becomes, in effect, part of the arrangement. This aspect of homeyness is accomplished by all of the aspects that have gone before, especially the smallness, intimacy, embracing, engaging, mnemonic, emplacing, authenticating character of the phenomenon. Once all of these properties have worked their dramatic effect upon the occupant, the occupant is situated within the homey field as an integral part of it. In this final stage the individual ceases to be an observer, ceases to be a participant, and becomes finally simply a part of the surrounding homey environment.

As we have noted, the largest objective of the symbolic properties of homey objects and their arrangement is involvement. This process is advanced and completed when the occupant is drawn into the configuration of objects and their meanings in such a way that he or she is, in a sense, claimed by it. Homey objects and their arrangement seek to make the individual a homologue of the environment, an integral part of the whole. Successfully situated in homey space, the occupant of homey space becomes a homey creature. He or she appears to take on the properties of the surrounding space and objects. A kind of meaning transfer has been achieved.

This is homeyness in its most powerfully transformative, performative mode. It is homeyness as an active agent of culture working to metamorphose the individual. In a sense, the material culture circle is completed. For homeyness represents an ideology with which the individual invests material culture with very particular cultural meanings. Once in place, however, these meanings then turn back upon the individual in such a way that he or she is claimed by them. Individuals create homey material culture and, eventually, homey material culture returns the favor.

Symbolic Properties in Sum

These are the chief (but not the only) elements in the cultural enterprise homeyness represents. Individually and in combination, these eight symbolic properties of homeyness work to create the involvement of the occupant of a domestic environment and finally to claim them in a thoroughgoing sense. Homeyness seeks to make the occupant fully occupy homey space and so to claim his or her full attention and affect. The diminutive property makes the homey environment thinkable, the variable property makes it real, the embracing property makes it cosseting, the engaging property makes it involving, the mnemonic property makes it emplacing in time, the authentic property makes it emplacing in space, the informal property makes it reassuring and riskless, and the situating property makes it fully capturing. The cumulative affect of these persuasive properties can be very powerful. It can situate individuals in the world as few other cultural devices can. Homeyness is for many people the adhesive that attaches them to self, family, time, and place.

Homeyness: Pragmatic Properties

The term "pragmatic properties" refers to the objectives of a cultural phenomenon, the work it is capable of accomplishing in the social world. The distinction intended here between symbolic and pragmatic properties treats symbolic properties as the *internal* objectives of homeyness and the pragmatic properties are its *external* objectives. In the case of homeyness, more particularly, "pragmatic properties" refers to the ends to which homeyness is used as individuals work to construct certain kinds of meaning in their lives (Bahktin 1981, 270; Bruner 1984b; Mertz and Parmentier 1985; Shweder and

LeVine 1984; Silverstein 1976, 18; Singer 1984; and Tambiah 1977). There are indeed many pragmatic properties of homeyness, many ways in which it is pressed into service in the creation of the social self and world. Only four of these are discussed here. These include the use of homeyness as an enabling context, as a status corrector, as a marketplace corrector, and as a modernity corrector.

Homeyness as an Enabling Context

The first pragmatic property of meaning is its use as an "enabling" context. Here homeyness has as its objective the creation of a meaningful context within which other meanings become possible. It deploys its various symbolic properties to enable the creation of these meanings. It is a necessary condition of these meanings.

Cultural phenomena are now widely understood to have a performative or processual character (Austin 1965; Sapir 1931; Tambiah 1977). The assumption here is that these phenomena must be continually performed, enacted, or (re)produced in social life in order to have a clear, credible, and fully "actual" existence for the individual and the collectivity. As Bruner puts this, "Self and society [can] not be taken as given, as fully formed, fixed, and timeless, as either integrated selves or functionally consistent structure. Rather, self and society are always in production, in process" (1984, 2–3). Many species of symbolic activity serve to produce the self and society. They include language; the drama of everyday life; ritual and ceremony; art; narrative traditions in the form of stories, proverbs, and myths; and all of the categories of material culture (built form and its furnishings not least among them). All of these activities rehearse the self and society in a manner that makes them more transparent to reality, actual, and obvious.

My contention here is that homeyness has a very particular role to play in the domestic version of the production process. Its larger purpose here is to create the stage on which all of the various domestic enactments of self and family can be undertaken. These enactments cannot be successful (or, in Austin's phrase, "felicitous") unless homeyness has endowed the house with its particular symbolic properties and powers of engagement.

Homeyness serves as an enabling context in three ways. First, it "drenches" the home environment with properties (smallness, realness, particularity, risklessness, etc.) that help the individual successfully to enact their conception of the family and the roles they play within it. Families who live in environments without homey meaning can no more enact their notions of what a family is than a theater company can perform Gilbert and Sullivan's *Pirates of Penzance* without the aid of costumes and scenery. They do not have access to the vital companion meanings that are necessary to give their performances credibility and power. For instance, the family deprived of its homey breakfast nook is deprived of a vital prop for a ritual activity important to creation of family solidarity (Saile 1984). The family deprived of the "memory wall" loses a key dramatization of its collective past and individual achievement (cf. Boschetti 1968). Fathers and mothers deprived of their dramatic props lose badges of office, symbols of power, assurances of solicitude, to name just a few. A family deprived of all homey meanings must encounter insuperable difficulties in the process by which the family is created and sustained.

But if homeyness is profitably compared to the stage and sets of a performance, it may also be compared to the "prompter" who gives a performance direction and continuity. In this second capacity, homeyness creates an environment dense with symbolism from which the actors of the family take their cue. To take one example, the cosseting character of a homey environment helps to remind a family of one of the values by which its relationships are supposed to be oriented. To take another, heirlooms can evoke one of several notions of family continuity and the individual's responsibility thereto (see McCracken 1988b), while craft and handiwork can stand for the preferred modes of family participation and contribution (see McCracken 1987). The homey environment helps continually to prompt the actors in the home, reminding them of the roles and larger objectives of family life. Without these cues and prompts, the family is bereft not just of the stage and scenery of their performance but also of the instruction and reminder that gives it consistency and continuity. It is, incidentally, precisely this cuing ability of homeyness that can help the home imprison the individual in sex-role stereotypes.

Third, the homeyness enterprise of engagement works upon each individual to bind him or her to the family and ensure his or her participation there in good times and bad. In this capacity, homeyness exercises its gravitational powers to sustain the commitment and conviction of family members. It helps ensure that the dramatic company will continue to participate and perform with enthusiasm.

It is noted above that homeyness has its own strongly processual character, and it is appropriate here to observe how this compares to the processual character of the family itself. Both homeyness and the family are constantly under construction through the scripted and innovative efforts of the members of the family. But one takes precedence over the other. Homeyness must be created before the self and the family can be created. And it must be created continually. In other words, it is only if and as homeyness is fully realized that the performative efforts particular to the family can be undertaken felicitously. As more than one respondent put it, "You just can't have a family without a home."

From a general theoretical point of view, this is a phenomenon of some interest. Increasingly, attention is being given to the context-dependent nature of meaning (e.g., Mertz 1985, 4; Silverstein 1976). In this case, the context is not the surrounding linguistic material or the other elements of a ritual but the carefully manipulated material environment, an inanimate world. Homeyness gives us an opportunity to see how the context provided by material culture can be used to create and manipulate meaning. It shows us an enabling context that consists not in words or actions but in things.

For the theoretical perspective more particular to material culture studies in anthropology and American studies, this pragmatic aspect of homeyness is also of interest. For here is an instance of material culture on which other kinds of culture, especially in its performative and processual mode, especially depend. We have witnessed material culture simply reflecting cultural categories and principles (Adams 1973; McCracken 1982), we have seen it serving as performatives (Kavanaugh 1978) and as operators (McCracken 1985), but we have yet to see it, as we do here, serving in something like a metaperformative role. This is a neglected species of material culture to which we may wish to be more sensitive.

From the point of view of the study of the ethnography of North America, the "culture and built form" perspective within environmental studies and consumption behavior, this aspect of homeyness is also of some interest. This understanding encourages attention to the pragmatic as well as the more traditional cultural properties of the home. The study of homeyness encourages us to reflect with new energy on how people are the users of the meaning with which their homes are endowed. It encourages us to see how the meaning in the built environment is put to work. The study of homeyness allows us to glimpse people making contexts that then make them.

Homeyness as a Status Corrector

The second pragmatic property of homeyness may be called the "status corrector" use. As the social sciences have noted since the work of Veblen (1953/1912) and Simmel (1971), much of the person-object relations of modern North Americans are devoted to the creation and communication of status messages. It is less well noted that this symbolic strategy has, of necessity, given rise to countervailing strategies. Homeyness is one of these. Homeyness allows the individual to defend against status strategies. It allows for the containment, management, and repudiation of these strategies. Homeyness performs this work in two quite different ways for two quite different social groups.

High-standing groups have a decidedly ambivalent attitude about homeyness (Seeley, Sim, and Loosley 1956, 52). As a prevailing tone for home furnishings, it is carefully avoided. My expert respondent on this and other issues, an interior decorator, remarked that the adjective "homey" is never used by her clients to describe their wants and needs. This was echoed by the ethnographic data collected for the project. Respondent testimony reveals that homeyness is regarded as having the power to "ruin" the beauty, formality, and calculated charm of an interior and to embarrass, perhaps even disqualify, the high-standing individual. This potent and dangerous power is rewarded with the contempt of high-standing individuals who mock homeyness as overstated, sentimental, and "noisy."

It is entirely possible that homeyness is something that upwardly mobile families must dispense with as they begin their upward climb. Observing the value of homeyness in the construction of the family and the self, it is worth wondering here what the consequences of the repudiation of homeyness might be. My expert respondent offered the astute suggestion that the current popularity of the color "peach" stems from the fact that it resembles (without reproducing) the warm homey colors that families must relinquish as they move up. This is one way of "smuggling" homeyness into new material circumstances.

Those of high standing do nevertheless depend on homeyness to relieve certain of the burdens created by their status strategies. The chief of these burdens is the difficulty that some individuals experience living in environments that are fully dedicated to status symbolism. Interiors that are "perfect" from a status point of view are sometimes also perfectly uninhabitable. The Crestwood Height dwellers of 1940s Toronto claimed that they found their club more homey and inhabitable than their homes. They preferred to stay at the club for fear of "marring the theatrical arrangements prescribed [for their home] by the decorator" (Seeley, Sim, and Loosley 1956, 53).

For these individuals, carefully controlled access to homeyness is exceedingly valuable. The Crestwood Height dwellers chose the safekeeping of a distant club, but one respondent in the research project chose instead to "permit" a number of homey objects in his home. These included a piece of tourist art, two reminders of his summer cottage, and a den. Unlike the rest of the home, where "everyone has to be on their best behavior," the den and the homey pieces were seen to be engaging, informal, playful, and relaxed, and a valued refuge from the exacting demands of the family's status strategy.

High-standing individuals use homey objects both as a status strategy and a status corrector. In the first capacity, homey, attention-getting objects are placed in the living room to provoke the curiosity of the guest and to give the host the occasion to tell a self-aggrandizing story about his or her recent trip to a "fascinating little country in Asia." In the second, homey objects are used deliberately to "lower the tone" of an otherwise daunting room and put the guest at his or her ease. Hosts often use these objects as conversational opportunities to tell stories against themselves.

Homeyness has a very different pragmatic significance for middle-standing groups. Research results suggest that these groups embrace homeyness without ambivalence. For these groups, homeyness is an unalloyed good—difficult to achieve, challenging to sustain, but always and unambiguously desirable. For this group, the accomplishment of homeyness is one of the great objectives of family life.

Homeyness is embraced in this manner in part because of its first pragmatic property. Middle-standing families like homeyness because it is the necessary condition of their successful enactment of their concept of the family. But it is also true that homeyness serves this group as a status corrector. Respondents suggested that homeyness was their bulwark against status competition. They described their homey environments as safe domains impervious to the demands (and the taunts) of the status system. Without homeyness, it appears, they would be the helpless captives of this system, constantly prone to "buying up" in a ceaseless battle for prestige (McCracken 1988c). A homey environment turns the occupant's attention away from this battle and provides satisfactions and solidarities against which the battle dwindles into unimportance. For many of the middle-class respondents, homeyness is homemade meaning, whereas all of the meanings of the status game are market-made meanings. By using homeyness as their bulwark against the status system, individuals protect themselves from the intrusions and demands of the designer, the marketer, and the showy neighbor, some of whom, respondents said, create homes of beauty but precious little joy.

The social sciences have for too long imagined that status is the chief meaning carried by the material culture of a consumer society. They have just as glibly supposed that when consumer goods carry status significance, they do so in a simple positive manner. It is time to see that goods carry many meanings additional to those of status and that some of these meanings are very deliberately at odds with the status system and the objectives of conspicuous consumption.

It is worth emphasizing here that homeyness has a kind of multivocality, assuming one meaning for those of high standing and another for those of middle standing. The variability of the meaning of cultural phenomena in complex societies is a topic of some special interest for the semiotic and symbolic anthropologist (Berstein 1975; McCracken and Roth 1985; Schatzman and Strauss 1955). The study of homeyness suggests that this diversity of meaning is present in the very construction of the domestic world and that it may be driven in part by diverse status strategies.

Homeyness as a Marketplace Corrector

Respondents suggested that the homeyness aesthetic was especially useful as a means of stripping their possessions of their commercially assigned meanings. Consumer goods enter the home complete with class, gender, role, and age meanings as these have been transferred out of the global cultural structure of North American society into the material culture of the marketplace (McCracken 1986b). Some of these meanings are welcome ones for the consumer and the family, but others bear little relationship to the present constellation that organizes these lives, and still others come bearing profoundly disruptive potential. The efforts a family must make to create a homey environment help to strip and transform these meanings. The coffee table that leaves the store teeming with the market meanings (i.e., status symbolism, fashion currency, and pretensions to elegance) fast becomes a somewhat plainer, more companionable piece in the company of homey objects and homey creatures. Homeyness is so powerful in this respect that it can even transform goods that are charged with a bogus "homeyness" (e.g., those with a false wood-grain finish) into genuinely companionable objects.

The best illustration of this function of homeyness is brought out by the dislike of interior designers that was voiced by several respondents. These designers stand accused of introducing into the home whole assemblages of consumer goods that remain impervious to the meaning-manipulation efforts of the home owner. Designers are seen as preventing the creation of a homey environment and as leaving the individual defenseless against the alienating power of the unreconstituted commercial goods.

This aspect of homeyness is of special theoretical interest because the social sciences have on the whole been inclined to accept the popular view that North Americans are necessarily the passive recipients of commercial manipulated meanings. There is reason to think, on the contrary, that North Americans are for some purposes entirely capable of judiciously selecting and manipulating the meanings of the marketplace. Far from being the vulnerable playthings of the forces of marketing, they are possessed of their own culturally constituted powers of discrimination. The study of homeyness helps us to see one of the mainstays of this culturally endowed (and endowing) ability. More research is needed here to tell us which social groups have these powers of discrimination and whether their distribution varies with class, age, and sex.

Homeyness as a Modernity Corrector

The fourth pragmatic property of homeyness is its ability to contend with modernity. Respondents indicated that they regard modern styles of house design and furniture as unattractive, inhospitable, and severe. The unkindest thing one respondent could say about interior furnishings was to call them "Scandinavian." Respondents complained that modern design made the home cold and unforgiving. This position is nowhere better illustrated than in the comments that appear in Creighton and Ford's *Contemporary Houses Evaluated by Their Owners* (1961). This wonderful ethnographic document shows some thirty-six houses designed after the modern style and provides the comments of their occupants. In the words of one family, "The major lack that we have begun to feel . . . is some place to retreat to from the very openness that we like so much. We need a small cozy, den-like room to sit in sometimes as a change of pace" (219). In the words of another, "We like the open planning, but there are times when human beings have a need to feel closed in and comfortable. At such times we use the library" (195).

Modern homes with the undifferentiated, multifunctional, open-plan spaces; long lines and smooth unbroken surfaces; and lack of ornament violate the tenets of homeyness. They especially contradict the intentions of the diminutive, the variable, and the embracing aspects of homeyness. But the modern aesthetic also contradicts the mnemonic, authentic, informal, and situating properties of homeyness. So thoroughgoing is the opposition between homeyness and the modern aesthetic that the latter appears almost to have been created in contradistinction to the former.

The discomfort of North Americans notwithstanding, the modern style has prevailed as the motif of exterior and interior design and it will be some time before postmodern developments loosen their grip on the domestic home. In the interim, homeyness has served as a kind of corrector here. It has allowed families to give more habitable meanings to environments that are otherwise potentially forbidding and even "Scandinavian."

Conclusion

From a general perspective, homeyness appears to play a curious and vital part in the larger cultural system of modern North America. I have tried to argue that there is a continuity between the properties of the family and the properties of its material circumstances. Both the family and the home are supposed to be diminutive, contingent, embracing, engaging, backward looking, authentic, informal, and situating. This continuity is not the simple shadow of cultural ideas on the surfaces of the "real" world. As I have tried to argue, when individuals and families undertake the creation of homeyness, they are engaged, willy-nilly, in the creation of the family and the self. The symbolic properties of the family, in other words, follow from the creation of the symbolic properties of the homey home. Homeyness, as a set of interior design ideas, is also a set of cultural specifications for the creation of a social group and a cultural domain. Homeyness supplies the template for the construction of an environment and a family.

But we may go farther. The construction of homeyness also aids in the construction of a system of relations in which the home is situated. For homeyness supplies some of the meaningful coordinates according to which the family and the home are to be discriminated from other domains, especially those of work and public life. When the home and family are given homey symbolic properties, when they are made diminutive, contingent, embracing, engaging, backward looking, authentic, informal, and situating, they are made to exist in contradistinction to other meanings and domains contained within the North American cultural system. They come to exist in opposition to meanings and domains that are deliberately comprehensive, systematic, rational, instrumental, individualistic, disengaged, forward looking, contrived, and formal. To this extent, the ideology of homeyness enters into the processes by which we fashion the distinction between "private" and "public" domains and "personal" and "anonymous" ones. It helps us to construct and mark the distinctions between the affective and the instrumental, the natural and the artificial, and the authentic and the contrived. In short, homeyness is intimately caught up in and an organizer of some of the symbolic properties by which certain of the most crucial cultural categories and distinctions are known in modern North America. Homeyness helps fashion the architecture of the home, the family, and the culture all at once.

But if we shift from a collective to an individual point of view, it is possible to observe homeyness in a still more dynamic performative mode. The pragmatic properties of homeyness give individuals a means by which to fashion their relationship with the larger institutions of modern society. It lets them reckon with the intrusion of alien meanings from the marketplace, the distracting competitive impulses of a mobile society, and the unwelcome aesthetics of changing fashions. Homeyness helps the individual mediate his or her relationship with the larger world, refusing some of its influences and transforming still others. It plays its role here by empowering the individual to select and refuse the cultural meanings, to be a discriminating consumer in the culture of the consumer society. The process also happens in tandem. It is in creating the homey home that the individual fashions his or her relationship with the outside world. Here, too, homeyness creates the template for the architecture of both material and social circumstances, this time from the individual's point of view.

This essay offers an account of the physical, symbolic, and pragmatic properties of homeyness. It has attempted to show why this neglected and perplexing cultural phenomenon should prove so preoccupying for the North American householder. The anatomy of homeyness offered here identifies eight symbolic properties by which homeyness pursues its conspiracy to capture the thought and affect of the individual and four pragmatic properties according to which homeyness is pressed into service in the accomplishment of vital social and cultural work. Several of the social sciences have been evoked in this analysis and it is hoped that the essay will reciprocate these contributions and stimulate further interdisciplinary exchange.

Part Three
Automobiles

Strategy:

This pairing begins with a "real life" encounter with the cultural meaning of cars. "Calling grease" was a game my friends and I used to play. The game turned entirely on the extent to which "greasers" blurred the boundaries between their '54 Chevys and themselves.

The article looks at another aspect of the cars of the 1950s. Specifically, it looks at the way in which mid-century modernism and certain notions of social mobility were played out in the 1954 Buick and subsequent car designs. The article opens with a glimpse of the famous Raymond Loewy, a man who, with John Kenneth Galbraith, scorned these cars.

5   Calling Grease

In 1962, I was 11 and inclined to acts of daring. I look back on these escapades with embarrassment. They were stupid, dangerous, and cruel. They did, however, teach me something about cars.

In 1962, I used to play a game called "calling grease." This game took place on Saturday nights around dusk. My friends and I would stand on a street corner and wait for the boys (so-called "greasers") from the valley to bring their Fords and their Chevys into town. It wasn't hard to spot these cars. They gleamed with wax and polish. They announced themselves with a deep-throated rumble. We could see them, and hear them, a long way off.

The game was this. We stood on a corner. We waited till one of these gleaming monsters came to stop before us. We caught the eye of the driver and, as we held his gaze, one of us leaned out over the car and spat on the hood.

We followed three rules: (1) run for your life, (2) wait until drivers and occupants were out of the car before "taking off," (3) never take the same escape route twice. Rules 2 and 3 were designed to give the occupants a fighting chance. Rule 1 was designed to give us a hope of surviving.

As I say, it was not the brightest or kindest thing anyone spent their childhood doing. But it proved to be relatively harmless fun. By this I mean they never caught us. They had the disadvantage of being surprised, angry, and badly dressed. Tight pants and funny boots made it hard to run.

Well, not always. I remember sprinting through a backyard, my All-Star Converses snapping their way through a rhubarb patch. Suddenly, behind me, came the thundering sound of Cuban heels on a concrete carport. I scaled a fence and sprinted through the next yard, but the sound of Cuban heels stayed behind me. Another fence, another yard, more heels. Converse All-Stars, do not fail me! Finally, I did the sensible (and cowardly) thing. I waited flush against the next fence and watched as my pursuer flew through the yard and disappeared. Some All-Star.

"Calling grease" said something about car ownership. The thing depended upon drivers taking violent exception to a little moisture on the hood of their car. And they always did. More than once, they left these magnificent cars unattended in the middle of an intersection in order to give chase.

This impressed and puzzled an 11-year-old. Plainly, there was something deeply, violently intrusive about that spit. Somehow this insignificant gesture got into the relationship between the car and its driver and profaned it.

Smoking our victory cigarettes (in the manner of all men of combat), we talked it over. Mike McDermott, our best spitter, summed things up by saying, "They don't see any difference between themselves and the car. You spit on the car, you spit on them."

This explanation was greeted by sagely nodding heads. Mike spoke as truly as he spit. But secretly, I had my doubts. I remember sitting there looking at the tip of my cigarette and thinking, "What do you mean they don't see any difference between a person and a car?" Mike's "answer" seemed only to deepen the mystery. How could anyone fail to distinguish between themselves and 3,000 pounds of metal? How was a confusion of this order possible?

Wiser, older reflection tells me Mike was right. People do identify with their cars. They do, sometimes, have difficulty telling the difference between the "who" of the self and the "what" of the object. For the young men from the valley, waxed and rebuilt Fords expressed toughness, virulence, power, and style. They expressed mastery of the world, mobility, independence. They were about potency and sexuality. They were about "getting" girls. They were about extracting the last few liberties from a vanishing youth. They were about tearing autonomy away from grownups. They were about getting ready for adulthood. This is what Mike and I were spitting on. I see that now.

What follows is an essay about another aspect of the car culture of the period. It's a treatment of the cars the greasers' fathers drove. Here too there was a deep connection. Here too Mike's wisdom applies. The fathers of the 1950s also blurred the boundaries between themselves and their cars. "When Cars Could Fly" is an attempt to answer this mystery.

6 When Cars Could Fly

*Raymond Loewy, John Kenneth Galbraith,
and the 1954 Buick*

Abstract

This essay examines the Forward Look created by Detroit designers and advertisers for the cars of the postwar period, particularly the 1954 Buick. There are three sections to the essay. The first reviews the Forward Look itself. The second reviews some of the ways intellectuals responded to the Forward Look in the 1950s and early 1960s. The third offers an anthropological account of the Forward Look. Mostly, this essay is about how the automobile industry, responding to consumer taste and preference, defied elite tastemakers and intellectuals to create an extraordinarily robust economic event.

The ads for the 1954 Studebaker were enthusiastic. They ran a third-party endorsement: "In the style department, Studebaker is 50 miles ahead of any other American car." They showed the car's designer, Raymond Loewy, sitting thoughtfully at his desk beneath the title "the world's most famous designer." They declared the 1954 Studebaker "the only really modern car in America" (Anonymous 1954a, fig. 6.1).

As it turned out, Studebaker lost $29,000,000 on the 1954 model, and the corporation responded swiftly. It renounced Loewy at a press conference (Anonymous 1955a). It repudiated his design. The new Studebaker, the 1955 model, appeared with a model plane on the hood, more chrome, and something called "flightomatic" transmission (Anonymous 1955c). Predictably, Loewy was unhappy with this treatment of his reputation and his car. He delivered his rebuke before the Society of Automotive Engineers (later reprinted in *The Atlantic Monthly*), railing against the "bulk," "flash," and "wastefulness" of Detroit's "sad parade of the 1955 models." The new models, he said, were an act of "vulgarity and blatancy . . . an orgiastic chrome-plated brawl" (Loewy 1955, 36).

While Loewy's Studebaker was losing millions, other 1954 models were selling well. "Sales Acceleration Leaves Detroit Auto Men Breathless" read a headline in *Advertising Age* (Anonymous 1954b). An astonished Knoxville dealer got 10,000 visitors on the first day of the new season. In Los Ange-

Figure 6.1. Studebaker "Styled by Raymond Loewy"

les that year, 750,000 people visited Ford dealerships alone. Detroit, overwhelmed at first by the new demand, turned out more than 7 million vehicles the next year to respond to it (Anonymous 1954b; Anonymous 1954c; Anonymous 1955a; Anonymous 1955b; Anonymous 1955i; Brean 1954; Rae 1965, 199; White 1971, 73).

Why did Loewy's Studebaker lose $29 million while competitors were setting sales records? Why did consumers refuse Loewy's car so emphatically when they were prepared to embrace his other design work? Loewy himself was surprised, as his tirade before the Society of Automotive Engineers shows. He believed himself "an arbiter of taste," charged with the right and the responsibility to shape what consumers wanted. That they should want a "chrome-plated brawl" instead of his immaculately modern Studebaker puzzled and irritated him (Loewy 1955).

To be fair, he was not the only one. Titans of social commentary John Kenneth Galbraith (1958), Ralph Nader (1972), Vance Packard (1959), and Philip Riesman and Eric Larrabee (1964) all found something odd and, finally, ludicrous in the cars of the 1950s. They heaped scorn on the product-design and advertising industries that created them. Thanks to this work, there is now a consensus about the cars of the mid-1950s. They are seen as tokens of a consumer culture at its most wasteful, irrational, and ridiculous (Flink 1975, 194). They are called "vulgar," "crude," "gaudy," "childlike," and "grandiose" (Guillory 1983, 392). They have been called a false desire provoked by an "excellent selling job" (Handlin 1992, 111). Most provocative, they have been accused of "trappings [that were] purely for show [having] nothing to do with improving the vehicle's qualities as a medium of transportation" (Rae 1965, 209).

Loewy and Mid-Century Modernism

In the late 1940s, design historian Sigfried Giedion said that he believed the hero of the emerging consumer culture of the period would be not an architect (as in Ayn Rand's famous choice) or an engineer but an industrial designer (1948, 610). He might have been talking about Raymond Loewy, and he probably was. Loewy was conspicuous, influential, and highly regarded. With commissions from Gestetner, Sears Roebuck, and the American Tobacco Company, Loewy marked the American "brandscape" repeatedly (Sherry 1987). His 1940 redesign of the Lucky Strike package is now called "very minor" (Forty 1986, 243). But at the time, the package and the designer were acclaimed. In 1949, Loewy's standing in popular culture won him a place on the cover of *Time* magazine. In 1954, *Life* magazine featured him in full-page co-promotions.

Loewy appears to have grasped some of the secrets of self-promotion, and his apotheosis was, in part, self-created. A French national, he fought in World War I and distinguished himself both by his bravery and his inclination to redesign corners of the battlefield with stolen furniture and an implacable sense of style. As his wealth and reputation grew, Loewy lived well, indulging himself in grand cars, country estates, and a succession of conspicuous blondes (Meikle 1979, 60).

It is not hard to identify the origins or the character of Loewy's design practice. He was a part of the "streamline" movement that shaped commercial design from the 1930s onward (Bletter 1985, 97; Bush 1975). The narrow definition of the term was clear enough: "Streamline form is the shape given to a body (a ship, an airplane) to the end that its passage through a material (water, air) may meet with the least possible resistance." But the term grew in its range until one could speak of "streamlining" many things, even a business or a government. Eventually, the term was interchangeable with the word "modern" (Giedion 1948, 607).

Loewy helped streamline the ferry, the train, and the automobile. His early work for Studebaker, which began in 1933, helped raise sales of the 1939 Champion from $43 million to $81 million (Bayley 1979, 175). In keeping with the new breadth of the term, he streamlined the Gestetner duplicating machine, "enclos[ing] everything that could be enclosed" (Forty 1986, 135). He made the Coca-Cola fountain dispenser look like an Evinrude outboard motor (Meikle 1993, 185). He produced a pencil sharpener that communicated "a sense of speed" (Sparke 1998, 121). Streamlining had come to things that didn't actually stream (Craig 1990).

By the 1950s, the streamline aesthetic was finding its way into the consumer world. "Mid-century modernism," as it is now called, had several characteristics (Greenberg 1984). It opposed ornament, decoration, and anything that consisted of post hoc beautification (Meikle 1979, 136). The aesthetic character of the object was to be integral, not something added on. As Lewis Mumford said in what became a statement of the movement, "[The modernist aesthetic] strips off from the object all the barnacles of association, all the sentimental and pecuniary values . . . and focuses attention upon the object itself" (1934, 353). In one of the slogans of the movement, "form follows function." In another, "less is more."

In the case of architecture, this meant removing moldings and cornices from interior spaces and classical or gothic treatments from exterior ones. The American designer (and Loewy's teacher) Norman Bel Geddes called for the removal of "the overornamental and elaboration of the past" on the grounds they no longer suited "forthright" people (Meikle 2001, 135). It meant giving kitchens and their objects a new simplicity. The Kitchen of Tomorrow at the General Motors Motorama of 1956 featured a "sheer look" which "discarded the clutter of applied baroque decoration on appliances and virtually eliminated the use of metal stampings and glass enamel" (Pulos 1988, 138).

In the case of cars, mid-century modernism meant getting rid of gratuitous size and shape. In particular, this meant making cars lower, less bulky, and, especially, reducing their chrome highlights, or "brightwork," as chrome on cars was called. When Loewy crafted his "evolution of the automobile," he showed it moving steadily away from brightwork (in Bush 1975, fig. 99). Loewy stripped 150 pounds of chrome from the Cadillac he bought his daughter for her grand tour of Europe (Loewy 1979, 178). He scorned bright-

Figure 6.2. 1954 Lincoln, the Newest Trend in Modern Living

work; he called the front grille a "dollar grin" and a "great chrome fence" (1951, 312, 315). Chrome offended against the "less is more" principle.

Perhaps inevitably, the modernism of the period found its way into the marketing of the period (Wernick 1994). Lincoln used the theme aggressively. In one ad, it evoked the larger design revolution: "If you see a house that is low and glass-walled, a country club whose buildings fit the terrain, people whose living is up-to-the-moment, you'll become aware of a new trend in modern motoring—the growing trend towards Lincoln" (Anonymous 1954d). Here and elsewhere in the advertising world, split-level domestic architecture and International Style office buildings were used as symbolic companions for the brand in question. In another ad, Lincoln laid claim to the movement's key term, reassuring the consumer that "Lincoln makes your driving as modern as your living" (Anonymous 1954e). In a third, it appeared to take advertising copy directly from the streamline handbook: "Gone are bulging lines, the hard-to-see-over hood, and chrome-for-chrome's sake" (Anonymous 1954f, fig. 6.2).

Loewy was gifted, influential, and, as we have seen, successful beyond the dreams of most commercial designers. By 1954, he had distinguished himself with some twenty-five years of accomplishment. This included several years of design for Studebaker which helped it capture market share and establish a corporate profile. It is probably fair to say the losses suffered by the 1954 Studebaker were not the result of the deficiencies of this particular model or the diminishment of Loewy's talent or influence. It is more likely that Loewy's 1954 Studebaker was eclipsed by the Forward Look.

The Forward Look

The year 1954 marked the introduction of what the head of the Automobile Manufacturers Association called "the most sweeping model changes in years" (Anonymous 1954b). This new style is sometimes called the "new look," sometimes the "swift look," and sometimes the "Forward Look" (Anonymous 1954b; Anonymous 1954dd; Marling 1994). (Chrysler adopted "Forward Look" as a styling descriptor in 1955 in its struggle to catch up to the industry trend. But "Forward Look" was in general use throughout the 1950s, and it is used here in this generic sense.) The 1954 version of the Forward Look was introduced by an omnibus advertisement from General Motors:

> Here are the smart new sweep of line—the low, swift look—the arching new expanse of backswept windshield glass—and a host of advanced new engineering features—that were found in GM's "dream cars" only a few short months ago. But they are dreams no longer. Today they are real. For even as people looked with longing at those "cars of the future," the toolmakers and the diemakers were busy on the tasks which turned them into production models for 1954. (Anonymous 1954dd)

A Buick ad showed consumers gathered in the showroom. They whisper: "Can we really buy them? Are these production models—or more of those tantalizing 'car of tomorrow' examples of what future styling may be?" (Anonymous 1954hh).

An ad for the 1954 Oldsmobile declared "More than any model, this new 'Ninety-Eight' for 1954 expresses Oldsmobile's forward looking and forward thinking. It's Oldsmobile's dream car—the pinnacle toward which Oldsmobile stylists and engineers have been working since the introduction of the 'Rocket' engine. You'll know it as a car of the future by its distinctive panoramic windshield and the long, low, forward look" (Anonymous 1954h, fig. 6.3). A Chrysler ad, in its belated attempt to claim the industry trend as its own brand, said, "You can always look to the Forward Look first—for the features of the future" (Anonymous 1956a).

The characteristics of the Forward Look were clear and surprisingly consistent across competitive models (Brean 1954, 82). The Forward Look was

Figure 6.3. Oldsmobile's "Dream Car"

not very streamlined, forsaking the "least possible resistance" for the greatest possible show. The Forward Look was substantial, imposing, dramatic, and heavy with chrome. Consumers might be embracing modernist simplicity in their homes, offices, clothing, and appliance designs. But when it came to cars, they wanted something else. What they wanted, Horn tells us, were "cruel-looking tail fins, grinning front grilles, tensed wrap-around windshields, and splendid bodies lashed with chrome highlights" (Horn 1985, 12).

The Forward Look came, mostly, from General Motors, largely in the design of Buick, Oldsmobile, and Cadillac, chiefly through the design work of Ned F. Nickles and Harley Earl, who had been planning it for some years (Brean 1954; Sparke 1998). The oral tradition in Detroit has conflicting versions of the origins of the Forward Look, but a credible account comes from Alfred Sloan, who said that Earl drew part of his inspiration from the planes he saw while visiting a friend in the air force during World War II (1963, 323; Hillier 1983, 146). Earl's 1954 models were a culmination of his work on the 1948 Cadillac, the 1949 Oldsmobile, and the 1951 Le Sabre (Basham, Ughetti, and Rambali 1984). All three players—Cadillac, Buick, and Oldsmobile—had released variations on the theme from the beginning of the decade. It was in 1954 that the Forward Look made a systematic bid for consumer attention.

New '56 Cadge Cuntra Royal Lancer with Magic Touch Control.

BORN OF SUCCESS TO CHALLENGE THE FUTURE!

Presenting: New Push-Button Driving! New Trend-Setting Style! New Break-Away Power!

The day of push-button driving is here! And it returns its true in a new '56 Dodge so dramatically beautiful, so daringly advanced in style and power, so dramatically poised, that no other car can match its miles.

This is the Dodge of destiny—born of success, born for success.

It brings you the feel of success in its revolutionary Magic Touch Push-Button Control. You "turn on" the range of PowerFlite automatic driving with a touch of your finger.

It brings you the look of success in the sweeping distinction of new Forward Flair styling: Proud, graceful, refined.

It brings you the power of success—surging break-away power from a new 230 h.p. Super Powered Super Red Ram V-8 engine, sparked by 1-in-1 lightning 12-volt electrical system.

Your Dodge Dealer invites you to share the strength of the great Dodge program. See the '56 Dodge today!

New '56
DODGE
VALUE LEADER OF THE FORWARD LOOK

Figure 6.4. Forward Look Dodge

The Forward Look "extracted value" with some success. In 1950, when the look was nascent, the industry retooling costs attributable to model changes (i.e., expenditure for the new tools, jigs, and dies needed to produce new models) were relatively small. The cost to the consumer was a scant $19.6 million. By the launch of the Forward Look in 1954, this figure had risen to $263.5 million, and the year after, as competitors struggled to catch up, it rose again to $469.2 million. To put this another way, the retooling cost per car in 1950 was around $3. By 1955, it was $75. Consumers were paying a premium (Fisher, Griliches, and Kaysen 1962, 440, 450).

The competitive effects were marked. Plymouth had no claim to the Forward Look in 1954, and sales that year were slow. Traditionally in third spot, Plymouth was supplanted by Buick and Oldsmobile and fell to fifth. By February of 1954, sales were down 40 percent. Desperate, Plymouth launched its "powerflite" automatic transmission halfway through the 1954 calendar year (Redgap n.d.) and made substantial styling changes for the 1955 model (fig. 6.4). That year Plymouth produced the "Forward Look Plymouth."

The journal of a Plymouth dealer in Florida described the result:

> This [1955] has been the best year ever. . . . Plymouth just seems to keep
> going. I have never seen anything like it. No matter how many I get in,
> the demand for them still exceeds the amount I have. I got a back log now
> of over 100 customers. I hope they will take 1956 models, or I may get
> skinned alive. What a business! Last year I couldn't seem to give 1954 Ply-
> mouths away. Now, I don't have enough 1955s to make everyone happy. I
> just hope Exner [i.e., Virgil Exner, hired by Chrysler in 1953, eventually
> vice president of style and design, and the man who hired Maury Baldwin,
> who designed for the 1955 Forward Look at Plymouth] keeps his head and
> doesn't go the way of those other striped pants boys in Highland Park. I
> swear they seem to forget who they were building cars for! (Redgap n.d.)

The Forward Look theme was suddenly everywhere. Model names evoked space ("Pontiac Strato Star"), space technology ("Oldsmobile Rocket"), and flight ("Hudson Jet"). Free at last of Loewy's tepid modernism, Studebaker introduced "flightomatic" transmission. Oldsmobile had had a head start with its "rocket" theme, but now it moved emphatically in the direction of the new motif, featuring "new Jetaway hydra-matic." For those who failed to grasp the metaphor, the Oldsmobile ads showed a picture of a plane streaking through the heavens. Buick evoked the theme coyly, "True, this Buick won't Fly—but it does have variable pitch propellers in its Dynaflow Drive." Another Buick ad was more forthcoming. It was entitled "Flight Into Any-where." Plymouth showed their 1956 model against the profile of a fighter plane (Anonymous 1954g; Anonymous 1955c; Anonymous 1955d; Anonymous 1956b).

Hood ornaments, including those of Buick, Pontiac, Oldsmobile, and Ford, took the shape of a plane. For many years, Pontiac had favored the chieftain's head consistent with its brand name. But in 1953, the head suddenly came with wings. In 1954, the wings were more marked. By 1955, the hood ornament was wings only (figs. 6.5–6.8). Against the usual logic of marketing, an enduring brand icon was displaced by a mere category one. Oldsmobile had used a flight theme from the 1930s and moved in the late 1940s to rocket imagery. The first unambiguous plane appears in 1950, the year after Earl's debut at General Motors. The plane theme held for the remainder of the decade and disappeared by decade's end (Anonymous n.d.a). Even the Packard Clipper had a plane on its hood, while the luckless Kaiser did not (Anonymous 1954g). Many of the 7 million people who bought cars in 1955 now drove with a tiny airplane tucked into the base of their peripheral vision (White 1971, 73).

The trend was so pronounced in the 1956 models that *Time* magazine finally took note: "[M]any new cars borrowed from the shape of swept-wing

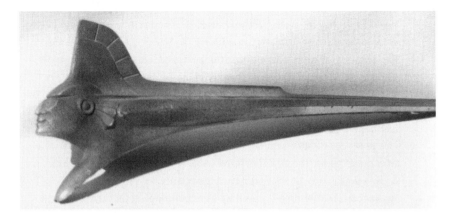

Figure 6.5. Pontiac Hood Ornament, 1952

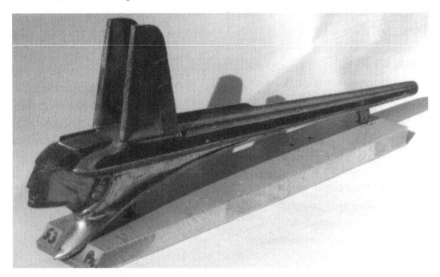

Figure 6.6. Pontiac Hood Ornament, 1953

Figure 6.7. Pontiac Hood Ornament, 1954

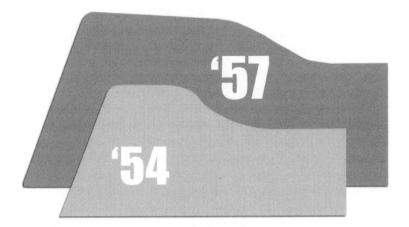

Figure 6.8. Cadillac Fin Diagram. Courtesy Cherrysoda.com.

aircraft to give autos a jet-propelled look" (Anonymous 1955f). The General Motors Motorama introduced the 1955 models by making them soar through clouds of flash powder over a large pool of water. Lincoln introduced the experimental Futura, a Plexiglas version of a car-jet.

A General Motors "dream car," the Firebird designed by Harley Earl and shown as early as 1954, was perhaps the most exaggerated instance of the trend. It looked remarkably like a fighter jet, wings, cockpit, and all. Only wheels revealed its true vehicular nature. In their efforts to make cars appear capable of flight, car shows became increasingly dramatic, and a wag at *Advertising Age* mocked them with a headline: "GM's Motorama to be Lavish Spectacle; Will Also Show Cars" (Anonymous 1955f; Anonymous 1955g; Pulos 1988, 373–374).

It is sometimes possible to discern the parentage of the Forward Look. The 1954 Buick, for instance, descended from the Skylark, the most successful of GM's limited-edition "image cars" for 1953 (Vance n.d.). The Skylark, in turn, descended from two General Motors dream cars of 1951: Harley Earl's Le Sabre and the XP-300, which Earl designed with Charles Chayne, Buick's chief engineer and a GM vice president. The Le Sabre, in turn, was inspired by the F-86 Sabre swept-wing fighter jet.

The XP-300 also evoked the fighter jet (Bonnafous n.d.). The initials "XP" stood for Experimental Pursuit, the air force designation for a fighter plane in development. The 1954 Buick, it turns out, came from an air force family.

The Oldsmobile also found inspiration in the world of fighter jets. At the Motorama of 1953, it showed a prototype called the "Starfire" that was modeled after the Lockheed F-94B (Russell n.d.).

The fins of the 1948 Cadillac, which grew throughout the decade, appeared first on Lockheed Lightning P-38 bombers of World War II (Sloan 1963, 323; Sorensen n.d.).

But the connection was not always with fighter jets or other military aircraft. Sometimes Detroit was evoking merely planes and sometimes merely flight. When Buick showed the new model cruising into a large urban airport (Anonymous 1955i) and especially when it showed it drifting past a little country one (Anonymous 1956f), cars were equated with humbler players in the aviation family.

It would be wrong to suggest that the themes of flight and fighter planes were the only meanings that Madison Avenue sought to invest in 1954 models. Status, the thing that Packard (1959) and others believed to be the obsession of this period, is in evidence. Ads show the doormen of swank hotels and resorts staring in open-mouthed admiration at the arrival of the new Buick, Cadillac, or Dodge (Anonymous 1954f; Anonymous 1954i; Anonymous 1954j; Anonymous 1954k; Anonymous 1954l). But this was a diminished theme. Packard's noble musings aside, status meanings were no longer the most potent kind of meanings to invest in cars. So said Pierre Martineau, one of the real experts of the period, to the readers of *Advertising Age* in 1954 (Martineau 1954, 1958).

The world of fashion is in evidence, too. (Detroit was seeking to sell some American families a second car, and it may be that the fashion motif was thought appropriate for housewives.) Several advertisements took the form of an invitation to visit the "Spring Fashion Show" of automobiles. Ads begin to dwell on interior details of color, shape, and texture as if they were fashion accessories. A Fisher Body advertisement featured clothing fashions by the designer Schiaparelli. Plymouth presented its visuals in the manner of a fashion sketch. The most patronizing of these efforts appeared in a Chrysler ad which asked, "What kind of 'hat' does your horsepower wear?" The Chrysler V-8 engine is shown wearing a spring bonnet (Anonymous 1954m; Anonymous 1954n; Anonymous 1954o; Anonymous 1954p; Anonymous 1954q; Anonymous 1954r; Anonymous 1954s; Anonymous 1954t; Anonymous 1954u).

Other strategies were ventured. Pontiac, for instance, offered itself as an automobile with a special affinity for the "moon-lit drive." Hudson offered an increasingly urban American an idealized country landscape. For a culture struggling with the demands of postwar parenting, Ford featured a father and son walking hand in hand. Chevrolet showed a father (looking like Bing Crosby) taking his daughter on a fishing expedition (Anonymous

1956c; Anonymous 1954v; Anonymous 1954w; Anonymous 1954x; Anonymous 1954y).

The Forward Look was merely one of several strategies in evidence. But the Forward Look was perhaps the most generative. It was hard at times to tell whether the theme was flight, space, rockets, planes, military planes, or fighter jets, but the range may tell us how fecund the theme was proving. Another measure might be the ingenuity and exuberance with which it was used. The instrument panel of the Buick took on the look of fighter controls (Anonymous 1954z). Plymouth announced "control tower visibility" for the wraparound windows of the period (Anonymous 1954p). Oldsmobile claimed "all the flow of fluid, all the go of gears, liquid-smooth and lightning-quick" for one of its transmissions (Anonymous 1956d). This sort of thing is greeted with ridicule in the present day. That it was plausible and, indeed, compelling in 1954 tells us something about the power of the theme.

Detroit had found what came to be thought of in the 1990s as the "killer application," and the timing was felicitous (Downes and Mui 1998). By the early 1950s, the U.S. auto market was facing saturation. For the first time, there were more passenger cars than households (Rothschild 1973, 42). In the Forward Look, Detroit had found a way to recruit new consumers and inspire existing ones to quicken their purchase cycle or add a second car. The Forward Look helped drive the automobile industry to new growth. What's more, it helped sustain the "cargo cult" explosion of the postwar economy (Ross 1995). Truly, what was good for the general motorist was good for the country.

The Forward Look: The Intellectual's View

When we last looked in on him, Raymond Loewy was bitterly haranguing the Society of Automotive Engineers about his treatment at the hands of the Studebaker Corporation. Still, he can hardly have been surprised. Twenty-nine million dollars (nearly $200 million today) is a lot of money for a company to lose, especially in a year when competitors were flourishing (McCusker 2001).

Loewy did not go quietly. With his ready access to the press, a public declaration was inevitable. The question was merely where and how he would deliver it. In the event, Loewy chose the high horse. He declared himself an arbiter of taste. He called the new Studebaker a "Jukebox on Wheels," leaving no doubt as to the audience he believed worthy of the new 1955 Studebaker, those crazy, hepped-up kids who ran amuck in soda fountains consuming sugary food and popular music. And he accused the industry of "vulgarity" and "blatancy."

These are telling words in most Western conversations. They suggest that Loewy was embarked upon a strategy of status diminishment. Loewy was evoking a long-standing social logic. When he called these cars "blatant," he proposed that we think of them as "obvious," as great, unsubtle bricks incapable of subtlety, authenticity, or grace. Low-status parties typically announce their standing and betray their pretensions with artifacts and performances that are badly wrought and insufficiently refined. Class will out, the notion goes. By their errors, we shall know them. When Loewy called these cars "an orgiastic chrome-plated brawl," he redoubled the attack. The new cars from Detroit were lawless and chaotic, outside the civilizing power and standards of good design and polite society. They are lawless in the way that low-status parties are always lawless, a mob without the capacity for self-rule (Major 1964).

It appears that Loewy was embarked upon an effort to repudiate the Forward Look. These cars, he insists, do not connect to anything of substance, interest, or larger cultural import. They are merely a species of aesthetic error and a social failing. They failed social criteria as much as design ones. Loewy evoked the authority and the weight of a social judgment (Bourdieu 1984).

Here again is John Kenneth Galbraith in *The Affluent Society* (1958):

> The family which takes its mauve and cerise, air-conditioned, power-steered and power-braked automobile out for a tour passes through cities that are badly paved, made hideous by litter, blighted buildings, billboards and posts for wires that should long since have been put underground. They pass on into a countryside that had been rendered largely invisible by commercial art. . . . They picnic on exquisitely packaged food from a portable icebox by a polluted stream and go on to spend the night at a park which is a menace to public health and morals. Just before dozing off on an air mattress, beneath a nylon tent, amid the stench of decaying refuse, they may reflect vaguely on the curious unevenness of their blessings. Is this, indeed, the American genius? (223)

What may we say about this? Let us note particularly what Galbraith says about the car. He paints it mauve and cerise. There are three anthropological questions. Why give the car any colors? Why give it these colors? Why use these terms for the colors?

Galbraith begins with the colors "purple" and "cherry red." In the American pallet, these were vulgar colors. In Matthew Arnold's still-active notion of culture, high culture is fine, refined, and usefully difficult. Low culture and color, by contrast, seduce by being easy and obvious (Arnold 1993, 59; cf. LeMathieu 1988, 106). Galbraith gives the colors grandiose names. He calls them "mauve" and "cerise." Western status hierarchies are hostile to social counterfeit, to "mutton dressed as lamb." They devise a special penalty for those who pretend to be above their station. Galbraith appears to wish to inflict this penalty. He paints the car to show its vulgarity and then repaints it, as it were, to show its pretension.

But color is not the only object offered to our scorn. Galbraith describes a family confined to a tent, dozing on air mattresses, inhaling the stench of the decay of the park. But they have only a "vague" response to these "blessings." They find their circumstances merely "uneven" and this unevenness merely "curious." In all, they barely notice their misery. Once more, they suffer the aesthetic impairment of their class. Galbraith would intervene and disabuse them of their color sense and show them their "blessings" are, really, a man-made hell. But they could not hear him, so Galbraith thought. He later said, "One of my greatest pleasures in writing has come from the thought that perhaps my work might annoy someone of comfortably pretentious position. Then comes the saddening realization that such people rarely read" (1981, 30–31).

These remarks mean to create an asymmetry. By rhetorical strategy and his own declaration, Galbraith places himself above the car, the culture that produced it, the people who own it, and the would-be beneficiaries of his intervention against all three. We can only guess at the grounds of this asymmetry. We know by autobiographical confession that Mr. Galbraith comes from a small farming community in Canada (1964). He may have been trading on the prestige of his field (economics), his university (Harvard), or his subculture (the elite of the liberal eastern seaboard), and probably all three. But the real source of his superiority may be that he had found a victim, a hapless family on an air mattress. It is, perhaps, by declaring these creatures vulgar, unworthy, and insensate that he appoints himself a man of taste and standing. It is, finally, a hall of mirrors. The social critic pursues his social mobility by criticizing the vehicle by which others seek theirs.

As it turned out, the intellectual class would recover from the rude shock of the 1950s automobile and the consumer culture it represented. They would muster a more penetrating and intellectually formed response. We may treat David Riesman as a transitional figure. Riesman wrote about driving as an aimless activity relieved only by "quiz-bits, frequent commercials and flatulent music of AM radio." He compared the suburb to "a fraternity house at a small college" (1964, 242–243). This is the old strategy at work. Riesman is using the language of diminishment. He too seeks to construct an asymmetry between the observer and the observed.

But we also hear in Riesman another, more potent, strategy—what we might call the "conformity" argument. In *The Lonely Crowd*, he argued that the individualism of American society was at risk; he believed that Americans had forsaken inner life, creativity, and independence for peer acceptance. Plainly, these were better grounds for the counteroffensive, and the theme took wing. Four years later, we find Lewis Mumford calling the suburb

> [a] multitude of uniform, unidentifiable houses, lined up inflexibly, at uniform distances, on uniform roads, in a treeless communal waste, inhabited by people of the same class, the same income, the same age group, witnessing the same television programs, eating the same tasteless pre-fabricated foods, from the same freezers, conforming in every outward and inward respect to a custom mold. (1961, 486)

Clearly, this treatment of contemporary culture is not unique to the 1950s intellectual. Brantlinger (1983) observes the lapsarian logic with which democratic cultures are sometimes criticized. After the fall from elite control, certain abuses and shortcomings are inevitable. Brantlinger also says there is a "negative classicism" that holds that the more a society depends upon mass culture, the more likely it is to decline. It would also be wrong to suggest that it was only an American invention. Carey observes the twentieth-century English discomfort with culture that comes from commerce. He finds it in the work of writers as various as F. R. Leavis, George Bernard Shaw, Ezra Pound, D. H. Lawrence, E. M. Forster, Virginia Woolf, Evelyn Waugh, W. B. Yeats, and especially T. S. Eliot (1992; cf. Hebdige 1882). Docker (1994) offers us a treatment of the influential critiques constructed by F. R. and Q. Leavis (1930) and the Frankfurt School (Adorno 1991). But it was in America that the critique took deep and lasting root (Long 1985).

How deep and lasting we may judge if we return to this quote from *The Quick Red Fox,* a detective novel published in 1964 by John D. MacDonald.

> The incomparably dull track houses, glitteringly new, were marching out across the hills, cluttered with identical station wagons, identical children, identical barbecues, identical tastes in flowers and television. You see, Virginia, there really is a Santa Rosita, full of plastic people, in plastic houses, in areas noduled by the vast basketry of their shopping centers. But do not blame them for being so tiresome and so utterly satisfied with themselves. Because, you see, there is no one left to tell them what they are and what they really should be doing. (1964, 167–168)

By this time, there is a rhetorical convention. It uses extension (the whole suburb), intension (the many parts of the suburb), and repetition (Mumford's "uniform" and "same" and MacDonald's "identical"). The repetition helps to "prove" the claim of uniformity by reproducing it. Look, it demonstrates rhetorically, all the parts of the whole *are* the same. This is a life, we are told, flattened by conformity and commercial interest. That there is a convention suggests that intellectuals have agreed upon a way to talk about the problem and that, increasingly, they work from this convention as much from their own observations.

That this should come from a *novelist* is itself noteworthy. The ideas of Galbraith and Mumford are now so well understood and widely circulated that they are within the grasp of a popular writer and, through him, the reader of popular fiction. Indeed, the conformity argument is now something popular culture is beginning to think about itself. The seeds of self-loathing have been planted.

The Forward Look: An Anthropological Account

The intellectual account, still popular, still flourishing, is not perhaps exhaustive. In the anthropological convention, we are obliged to go beyond the native's point of view, beyond what the intellectuals of the moment insisted on, beyond the accounts of the advertiser and designer. It is probably no more useful to say that the Forward Look was the work of vulgar and conformist commercial society than it was to say that it came from the breakthrough of "control tower visibility," the stylistic genius of Earl, the euphonious promise of "liquid-smooth and lightning-quick" transmissions, the spectacle of the flash-powder Motoramas, or those lavish two-page spreads in *Time* and *Life*. To understand the success of the Forward Look, we might examine its connection to the moment, the industry, and the consumer. There are three "connections" in particular.

Mobility as a Private Objective in 1954

The language of everyday life at mid-century gives some clue to the values, preoccupations, and concerns of the moment. A visiting anthropologist in the 1950s would have remarked in particular on how Americans talked about their lives. It was not unusual to hear them refer to themselves as "getting ahead," "really going somewhere," "traveling in the fast lane," "on the way up," and "heading straight for the top" (Dundes 1980).

This sort of language is, in the larger ethnographic scheme of things, exceptional. In most cultures, the assertion "He's really going somewhere" would be taken literally, and the response "Is he really? Where?" would be an acceptable reply. But in Western cultures, especially in the 1950s, "He's really going somewhere" had metaphoric force. It was a way of talking about social movement as physical movement. More exactly, it was a way of thinking about life prospects as traversable space and lives themselves as vehicles of transport within this space. As Susman put it, "To many Americans, movement in space was the equivalent of social mobility" (1984a, 263).

"He's really going somewhere" was an ordinary and useful contribution to speech because, in the "physics" of this world, it was helpful to know an individual's location and velocity. The metaphor was (and remains) so well established in the Western view that it didn't always present itself as a figure of speech (cf. Chinoy 1955, 126). "He's really going somewhere" often worked as a statement of fact, the metaphor made invisible by the familiarity of constant usage (Sapir and Crocker 1977). That it *was* a figure of speech is indicated by how powerfully unacceptable was the response "Is he really? Where?" In the 1950s (as today), this would be regarded as an act of conversational mischief.

It was a characteristic of America at mid-century that some part of the definition of the individual was seen to come from temporary location in social space, from what we still call "social standing" (Coleman and Rainwater 1978). The word itself, "standing," suggests something achieved, relative and momentary. Everyone had social standing. Especially in the 1950s version of this scheme, everyone competed for it in what was thought to be a zero-sum game (though "zero-sum" is not, of course, a 1950s turn of phrase). Standing was not fixed. At any given moment, it located the individual relative to everyone else in a fluid configuration. Finally, standing came from something. It came, in part, from family origins, class, ethnicity, race, and gender. It came, in part, from the choices, initiatives, accomplishments, and even the affectations of the individual (Bellow 1987, 13; Cawelti 1965; Kant 1990; Merelman 1984, 30). Standing was, to this extent, something to be variously accomplished, asserted, and negotiated by the individual and inferred, constructed, and, finally, conferred or denied by the spectator and the collectivity (Berger and Luckmann 1964; Goffman 1951).

Social standing presupposes social movement. To achieve standing, the individual will engage in what we still call "social mobility." When we speak of this mobility, we do so usually as if it were movement in *vertical* space (Lakoff and Johnson 1980, 16). Desirable status is seen, usually, as *higher* status. Desirable movement is therefore seen as *upward* movement. This view of the social world and actor have been active in the West for many hundreds of years, however much the particulars have been reworked for, and by, the historical moment at hand (Elias 1983; Guazzo 1586; Lovejoy 1950; Shils 1970). The twentieth century appears to have accepted this organization of social space ("He's headed right for the top") and to have added a modernist inclination to see status movement as movement "away" ("He's really going somewhere"). In this case, movement is not vertical transport. It is movement from a present location "out," "away," or "beyond" to some new one.

Writing within earshot of the 1950s, Berger and Luckmann noted how important the notion of mobility was, even when it was unaccomplished: "While practically everybody feels committed to upward mobility as a central life-goal, a majority fails to achieve it" (1964, 340). That the life-goal was something more than an idle hope was noted by Smelser and Lipset: "Movement to upper-middle or intermediate positions or from working class to middle class, or from the slums to the suburbs in one generation [was] attainable for millions" (1966, 278). When Americans talked about "getting ahead," "going somewhere," "traveling in the fast lane," and "heading straight for the top," these were not cavalier remarks or empty metaphors. They were reflections of an important aspiration and reality in American life in the 1950s (Lipset and Bendix 1959; Shumsky 1996; Warner and Abegglen 1955).

Mobility as a Public Objective in 1954

Interestingly, this kind of language could be heard in another conversational domain. When Americans discussed the state, aspirations, and ambitions of the country, they would sometimes speak of America "forging ahead," "moving upward," and "advancing to meet its destiny." The nation was imagined to be propelling "forward" into the "future" because, in a favorite sentiment, the future was thought to "belong" to America.

The notion of progress has a distinguished intellectual and cultural lineage stretching back to its roots in the classical world (Nisbet 1969). It was given new significance by the political, economic, and intellectual revolutions of the eighteenth century (Spadafora 1990). Several nation-states were seen to qualify as opportunities for the realization of progress, but the honor was generally supposed to belong to America (Marx 1964; Passmore 1970; Pole 1980; Williams 1966). The New World was where the perfectibility of the individual and the collectivity was most likely to be achieved. But before the idea of progress could find its way into American life, it would have to make itself manifest by stages: the world's fair, science, technology, and the gadget.

Progress as a notion was especially visible and formative in the world's fairs of the late nineteenth and early twentieth centuries. As demonstration of what the future held, they served as great advertisements for the idea of progress. Rydell says that the expositions from the nineteenth century onward were deliberately constructed as "road map[s] to perfectibility" (1984). Here too it is now customary to mock these events as naively optimistic. That they were credible and compelling should give us pause. An international exposition in Chicago in 1933 was called "Century of Progress." The World's Fair of 1939 was also dedicated to the theme (Rydell 1993). The General Motors exhibit there, *Futurama,* designed by Norman Bel Geddes, showed an

America made glorious by better transportation, asserting that "the progress of civilization has run parallel to advancement in transportation." But the demonstration of progress was something more than dumb show, a civics lesson, or propaganda. For many people, the fair was useful notice. Dickstein says, "The Fair was a stunning piece of Science Fiction for an age poised at the brink of an economic and technological leap" (1989, 22).

Those unimpressed by world's fairs had a second opportunity to glimpse America's connection to progress. In the form of science, the idea of progress was something Americans knew and cared about. Science was revered in this period (Kluckhohn and Kluckhohn 1946, 111). It promised a future shiny with optimism and opportunity. But even as science, progress remained somewhat remote, the domain of MIT "brains" and other world-renouncing creatures with tape on their glasses. Besides, science was the perpetrator of the terrifying laboratory accidents that became a staple of the Hollywood B movie. This made it revered but not quite trustworthy. As science, progress could win funding from the American taxpayer, but it was not yet quite approachable, not quite ready for mass consumption.

The next step helped fix this. Progress descended from science to technology. It was now distinctly more visible, intelligible, and practical. It could count the Army Corps of Engineers among its supporters and the Tennessee Valley Authority among its accomplishments. Universities and institutions such as Bell Laboratories devoted money and talent to the translation of science into technology. Progress was now bridges, dams, highway systems, telephone networks, "miracle" chemicals, skyscrapers, and a succession of inventions. Still daunting (gigantic Gulliver, barely restrained), it was now unmistakable and manifestly useful.

From here, it was no distance at all to the consumer marketplace. A stream of products were entering the 1950s home, including the television, the hifidelity record player, the dishwasher, and, that period favorite, the blender. Many of these came with that mark of technical prowess and scientific solicitude, the push button. Now the tiniest investment of effort could release the utility of the machine, dispatching the most laborious of chores: cleaning clothes, chopping vegetables, mowing lawns. We take this order of convenience for granted, but there was a generation for whom the push button was astonishing. It demonstrated something about the state of the world. "Progress," as General Electric put it, "is our most important product."

But there was one consumer category that could claim place of pride: the gadget. Americans of this period have been called "gadget crazy" (Anonymous 1954gg; Erikson 1968, 31; Marias 1972, 36). The ads of the 1950s are ecstatic about the "sheer" ease, convenience, and efficiency product designers now made available. Gadgets were progress writ small and effortlessly at hand, prosthetic extensions that passed their properties of ease and efficiency along to the owner. The idea of progress was now within the nation's grasp.

Detroit participated in the cult of progress. Between 1936 and 1956, General Motors sponsored a "Parade of Progress," which traveled throughout the U.S., visiting hundred of towns and small cities. The idea came from Charles F. Kettering, GM's vice president in charge of research. Kettering was inspired by GM's science and technology exhibit at the 1939 World's Fair in New York (Williams 1977). One year, probably 1953, Mrs. George J. Witenko attended with her husband and three children, and the next day she wrote a letter of thanks to General Motors: "Last night we drove to Dayton to see the 'Parade of Progress.' I want to thank you for making it possible for us to get a better understanding of how so many things work and of how our America is going forward" (Witenko n.d.).

Descended from on high, progress was now both obvious and indubitable. It was there as the "hi-fi" in the living room, the picture windows of the split-level home, the miraculous plastics of the kitchen, the Technicolor of the movie screen. So much of the American world of goods spoke of progress, who could doubt that America was its favorite child, best hope, and true beneficiary (Giedion 1948; Hine 1986)? In progress, the nation had a found proof of, and a warrant for, a mobility of its own.

The notion of progress took new urgency from the presence of a foreign challenger. Soviet ideology and aggression threatened the American agenda. Progress was not merely the responsibility of civilization; it was now a cause of the "free world." And science was not merely a disinterested inquiry into nature. It was the demonstration of America's "just cause" and a resource in the struggle with the Soviets. Technology was not merely the gadgetry of better toasters and telephones; it was now the machinery of international competition and the very instrument of war, the fighter plane (Anonymous 1956e).

Horn calls the jet a "fitting symbol of the 1950s," noting that it was not unusual to hear the decade called the "jet decade" (Horn 1985, 34). This extraordinary flying machine was simultaneously an affirmation of the American command of science, a glorious example of its technology, and the deadly apparatus by which the Soviet threat would be subdued. The F series fighter planes became media stars in the mid-1950s. The readers of *Time* magazine were treated to passionate studies of its military abilities. *Life* magazine called these planes "wondrous weapons" and spoke with pride at the "billions" that were being spent in their development and production. Flyboys such as Chuck Yeager were the heroes of the day (Wolfe 1979). For many Americans, the fighter plane represented an essential American accomplishment. It was the triumph of progress, science, and technology and was now the great hope of international competition. It was the very symbol of a constellation of values (Anonymous 1954gg; Anonymous 1956e). Those who had failed to glimpse progress in the World's Fair or its several manifestations could find it played out in the Cold War.

An anthropologist can hardly ignore the homology here of mobility happening in two domains, one personal, the other public. For the individual American, it was a "life-goal," something to be constructed and negotiated as the individual struggled to "get somewhere." For the American collectivity, it was a national objective to be fought for in competitive space. Borne on the wings of scientific advancement, technological achievement, and national destiny, America was "getting somewhere" too.

The Future as a Temporal Orientation in 1954

The language of everyday life at mid-century contained a third set of revealing phrases, and these did manage to capture the attention of a visiting anthropologist. Doing fieldwork in a small town in Texas in the early 1950s, Harvard anthropologist Evon Vogt recorded a townsperson saying, "Why, I'd say we live in the future. We're always looking forward to the future. Once in a while some of us gets together uptown and talks about the past, but everybody is for the future. What's done is past, I don't care a thing about that" (Vogt 1955, 93).

How members of a culture reckon time will decide (and reveal) a great deal else about them. One question to be asked: Do respondents "lean backward" toward a "past" or forward toward a "future"? Vogt found his American respondents leaning emphatically forward. "To look forward to the future, to forget or even reject the past, and to regard the present only as a step along the road to the future, is a cherished value in American culture and a conspicuous feature of life on the frontier. This future-time orientation, and associated value emphases on 'progress,' 'optimism,' and 'success,' have had a profound influence on the settlement and development of Homestead [Texas]" (Vogt 1955, 93).

But a concern for the future was not only a preoccupation of the small-town American frontier. It was there in the world's fairs dedicated to progress. The theme of the 1939 World's Fair was "Building a World of Tomorrow." The General Motors exhibit was called *Futurama*. The administration building of the fair featured the "bridge of tomorrow." The food displays and exhibits had a futuristic theme, with "Mrs. Modern" as its presiding muse (Kirshenblatt-Gimblett n.d.). (Plainly, the temporal orientation in question was active in the idea of progress. I have separated them for sake of exposition. Ideas of mobility encourage a future orientation. The reverse may also be true. But one does not presuppose the other.)

This temporal orientation is not, in fact, peculiarly American. It is part of the larger Western cultural development now called "modernity." The Israeli sociologist Ariely wondered whether the modern era was not "one [that] created a new awareness of, and orientation to, time, a new historical sense, an expectancy of the future" (1966, 11). Habermas calls modernity a "changed consciousness of time," an "anticipation of an undefined future and the cult of the new." It revolts, he says, against the "normalizing functions of tradition," giving new importance to "the transitory, the elusive, and the ephemeral" (1983, 5). Calinescu says, "[M]odernity came about as a commitment to otherness and change, and . . . its entire strategy is shaped by an 'anti-traditional tradition'" (1987, 66). He says, "The art of the modernist" always contains "the revelation of the new" (1983). Osborne calls modernity "a form of historical time which valorizes the new as the product of a constantly self-negating temporal dynamic" (1995, xii).

Octavio Paz says that modernity is "cut off from the past and continually hurtling forward at such a dizzy pace that it cannot take root, that it merely survives day from one day to the next: it is unable to return to its beginnings and thus recover its powers of renewal" (in Berman 1982, 35). Others have suggested that the modern sensibility prized the future over the present, that it encouraged an amnesia that removed the present from memory almost instantaneously (Huyssen 1995). Jameson believes he may have discovered the very processes by which this amnesia is made to happen. "One is tempted to say that the very function of the news media is to relegate such recent historical experiences as rapidly as possible into the past. The information function of the media would thus be to help us forget, to serve as the very agents and mechanisms for our historical amnesia" (1983, 125). There is, in sum, an academic consensus about the ways in which the Western concept of time was reshaped by and in the modern era. This sense of the world as a place that continually supplants the "now" with the "new" is enough to move Nye to suggest that Americans, particularly, crave discontinuity (1994, 285). To adapt the language of Martin Jay, modernity created its own temporal regime (Jay 1988).

Western cultures, much more than traditional ones, have been inclined to think of time as open ended (Boorstin 1978; Eliade 1954; Priestly 1964; Quinones 1972). Modernist cultures played this out to a daring conclusion. They invented a culture that warrants its own continual replacement. Modernist cultures are concerned less with order, memory, and tradition (and the agencies that see to their reproduction) and more with the creation of forgetting, variety, discontinuity, and innovation (and the agencies that make these possible). It is as if the presiding genius of a culture, once best represented by the government bureaucrat, was now a reckless, relentless, irrepressible entrepreneur. Modernist cultures are devoted to their own continual thoroughgoing reformation.

There was a moment when the sheer optimism of the modernist moment promised a "soft landing." After all, in the modernist view, the future glistened with promise. This much of the unspecified *was* specified. Whatever happened, surely things would end more or less well. (In the words of a Ford ad from 1951: "On that road the nation is steadily traveling beyond the troubles of this century, constantly heading toward finer tomorrows. The American Road is paved with hope" [in Pollei n.d.].) Many traditional cultures would find this optimism odd, reckless, even unimaginable. Forty years after the fact, we are inclined sometimes to think so too. But generally, even knowing that our "constantly self-negating temporal dynamic" will sometimes end badly, we persevere. Soft landings and hard, the temporal orientation of modernism persists as perhaps the chief way that time is conceptualized in the West.

The Forward Look

The Forward Look helped summon ideas out of the ether into the world. It managed to connect cars to a larger ideological enterprise: notions of mobility in social and international space on the one hand and notions of time on the other. Just as the postwar consumer boom was beginning to peak, the "boys in striped pants" found a theme that would connect them to the moment, the consumer, and the marketplace. As we have seen, the Forward Look was conceptually diverse, referring sometimes to space travel, sometimes to fight jets, sometimes to civilian planes, sometimes merely to flight. It was variously invested in cars, sometimes with grand stylistic gestures—the majestic fins of the Cadillac—and sometimes with the smallest gesture—the tiny swept-wing icon of a Pontiac advertisement. It existed cheek by jowl with many other themes, those of status and family particularly. It emerged in the late 1940s, taking shape fitfully and competitively over the course of the decade. Then it disappeared. In these few years, it managed to put cars at the center of things Americans cared about. As a cultural phenomenon, it was, in short, noisy, complicated, various, variable, conspicuous, and evanescent. It was also extraordinarily successful. The production figures for Buick tell the story: 444,609 in 1954, 738,814 in 1955, 572,024 in 1956, 405,098 in 1957, and 241,908 in 1958. In its moment, the Forward Look was extraordinary—and the moment was brief (Anonymous n.d.b).

Cars as Cars

Cars hardly needed outlandish metaphors. Comparisons aside, they endowed the driver formidably. To take the wheel in 1954 was to control three and a half tons of metal and glass and to gain dramatically in the speed, grace, and power with which one moved. Drivers would no doubt have risen to this occasion in any case. There was, after all, something in the experience of driving, something in the emotional, visceral, interactive nature of the activity, that blurred the boundary between the driver and the car. Unable (or unwilling) to see exactly where driver leaves off and car begins, drivers were inclined to take credit for properties that belonged to the car. *They* were now large, gleaming, and formidable. The speed, grace, and power of the car now belonged to them. With or without aviation metaphors, cars were a prosthetic enhancement, something that gave new properties to the individual. Aeronautic allusions or no, cars enhanced human mobility.

The cars of the 1950s enhanced the owner particularly. They were dramatically larger, more powerful, and faster than the cars of the 1930s and 1940s. They gleamed with chrome and color undreamed of in the Model T. The cars of the 1950s looked fast. They accelerated quickly. They moved nimbly. They went fast. They went far, crossing continents with relative ease. The owner prepared to see the properties of the 1954 Buick as her own was magnificently augmented. Surrounded by the exoskeleton of Detroit design, the consumer was light bearing, sleek, aerodynamic, powerful, formidable, and mobile.

There were several ways for the upwardly mobile American at mid-century to voice their aspirations and accomplishments as social competitors. We know that entertainment, vacations, clothing, and houses were all used this way (Martineau 1958). But the automobile was a consumer good that didn't merely claim or show or seek to prove mobility: it *was* mobility. Moreover, cars had all the things that clothing and houses did—currency, style, visible expense—but they also gave the consumer what status would give them—mobility. What cars could do as vehicles of spatial mobility were both the means and the ends of social mobility.

The ethnographic record is mostly blank here, but anyone who lived through the 1950s (baby boomers plus their parents, some 160 million people) has their own personal experience of the phenomenon. Families in the 1950s were peculiarly sensitive to the automobile in the driveway. In the months that passed between the placing of the order and the arrival of the car, families would rustle with anticipation. (Some families of the middle and lower middle classes were prosperous enough to make this anticipation a yearly event.) Children would quiz their fathers on the model he had ordered. Did it have whitewalls? Had a convertible truly been out of the question? Then there was an interminable wait. Finally the call would come: "Your car is ready, Mr. Montgomery." And then the car would arrive, sending a bolt of joy through the household and a ripple of interest through the neighborhood. "Oh, the Montgomery's Buick is here." A maiden voyage would ensue, and the neighborhood would have a chance to take stock of this spanking-new status claim and status performance.

Neighbors would see the new Buick sail majestically by. Some of these might remark, with some combination of interest, envy, admiration, and spite (but probably not irony), "That Montgomery. He's really going places." This car, symbol of other, still-more-majestic vehicles of transport, showed how movement in physical space could be made into a statement of movement in social space. The Montgomerys really were getting somewhere, even when it was just around the block. In 1950s America, on new-car day, the Montgomerys' progress was a kind of victory lap. In the world of track and field, no one seems to think it's odd that the reward for winning is more running. But, in this case, the lap was apt. It was spatial mobility to demonstrate status mobility. "That Montgomery, he's really getting somewhere."

But the work of the Buick was not over. With its victory lap of the neighborhood complete, the Buick now became a surveillance vehicle on a reconnaissance mission. It embarked upon an investigation of other neighbors in that other urban and suburban ritual, the Sunday drive. Where might mobility take the family? Everyone had a pretty good idea which neighborhood was "next" in the great hierarchy of city neighborhoods. A Sunday drive let the family reconnoiter. Is this our future? How did people live there? Most pressing, could *this* family live there? Now it was spatial mobility scouting social mobility.

Children, sitting in the back seat, were slow to see the point of the exercise. What could be less interesting than "driving around" with one's parents? Parents would engage them in laborious conversations in which the status agenda was prosecuted mostly by implication.

Parent 1: "I like those shutters."
Parent 2: "Too old fashioned."
Child: "Are we going to live here some day?"
Parent 1: "Well, we might. You know. Would you like to, do you think?"
Child: "Um, sure. What about my friends?"
Parent 1: "You'd make new ones. Oh, what a lovely garden."
Child: "Snobs, you mean?"
Parent 1: "No, I'm sure they're very nice. Your friend Ricky lives here some-
        where, doesn't he?"

The General Motors cars of mid-century may even have helped Americans address a paradox of their time. Competition in the social sphere was, in the short term, invisible. How could one know whether one was "getting ahead?" Where did one stand, at this moment, relative to other Americans? Had the family moved ahead a little, a lot, not at all? Surely some of this could be worked out by a laborious process of inference. "I see the Joneses are taking a two-week holiday this year. Let's see. We went only for one. That must mean . . . " But in a culture obsessed with mobility, relative social location, and the pursuit of social standing, there was never enough clarity. No one actually knew in any precise way where he or she stood.

Out on the road you could tell. You were wrong. But you could "tell." The act of driving was an act of competition, a drama on the highway. On the highway, you could see who was closing in, who was getting ahead, and who was "acing" whom. Youngsters on board followed these motorway competitions with interest. After all, they had good seats and no need to pretend indifference. From time to time, in the heat of the moment, they might shout something like, "He's getting ahead! *Dad*, he's getting ahead!" Dad was obliged, for a moment, to drive judiciously and then to say, "This is not a race." But of course, it was a race. Quite clearly, it wasn't *the* race. In a sense, everyone knew it was a pretty bad rendering of *the* race. But in the absence of a clearer rendering of this most important social matter, it would have to do.

Cars as cars augmented the consumer, and so augmented they gave the consumer a physical mobility that played out their social mobility. For the luckiest families, the vehicle in question arrived new each year, evidence that progress was happening, a way of marking what that progress was, and an opportunity to investigate new neighborhoods, those stations of the cross on the mobility trail, with a sharpened sense of what was possible, of what was next. Surely, this was one of the burdens of that eternal question from the back seat: "Are we there yet?"

Car as Planes

The power of cars to augment the consumer was itself augmented by the metaphor of mid-century. Cars as planes worked as a simple social metaphor (Sapir and Crocker 1977). It helped transfer the properties of planes to cars. We may take this to be the deliberate, self-conscious, and competitive objective of the product design and advertising initiatives reviewed in this essay. Detroit understood the symbolic and the competitive opportunities before them. As Sloan remarks, the point of styling had always been to make cars look faster (1963). In proposing and then engaging the plane metaphor,

Detroit sought a new device for the metaphorical transformation of car and consumer. What was possible was promising, and what was promising was productive.

The cars as planes of the 1950s enhanced the owner even more. Cars as planes were dramatically larger, more powerful, and faster than cars as cars. The owner who took on the properties of the car as plane was augmented again. Surrounded by the exoskeleton of aviation design, the consumer became *still more* light bearing, sleek, aerodynamic, powerful, formidable, and, apparently, mobile.

Aviation was a powerful source of cultural meanings in the 1950s. As Corn notes (1983), it had taken hold of the American imagination. Decades before, figures such as Charles Lindberg and Amelia Earhart apparently stepped straight from the pages of the heroism handbook. They worked alone in highly publicized, suspenseful, coveted acts of daring. The media followed every detail. For sheer little-guy pluck, it was hard to beat Calbraith Rogers, who without much training or experience left Sheepshead Bay, New York, in 1911, in a Baby Wright to seek the $50,000 prize William Randolph Hearst had promised the first person to cross the continent in thirty days. It was understood that Calbraith would have to land several times en route to repair and refuel, and, as it turned out, he put down seventy times. The press noted that nearly a quarter of these landings were actually crashes, and the world began to suspect that while Calbraith was pretty good at the flying part, he was still working on his landings. If Lindberg and Earhart were mythic in their standing and accomplishment, creatures worthy of awe, Rogers was the little guy with whom anyone could identify.

By the 1950s, aviation had moved well beyond the delicate, implausible machines that had taken Lindbergh, Earhart, and Rogers into the heavens. Indeed, planes may have come farther than cars. Flying across continents and oceans was now routine. Airspeeds had doubled and tripled. Passenger and cargo capacities were vastly increased. The sophistication of instruments, navigational equipment, and landing gear was improved. Even without the advancement that took place as a result of World Wars I and II, planes had become formidable pieces of technology. It was this technological robustness that Detroit tapped with the aviation metaphor. Cars impressed as cars. They wowed as planes.

But aviation contained another cultural charge. Some readers will remember a time when flying was a "special occasion." Airports and flying stock were shiny and new. Consumers dressed up to fly. Children were obliged to be on their best behavior. Pilots and stewards had a certain glamour about them. Air travel appeared in the movies as a token of excitement and worldliness. In the present day, when air terminals resemble bus stations and air travel can feel like kidnap, this is hard to remember. But in this historical moment, cars as planes could evoke a certain social tone. In an odd way, airports had become portals to the future.

It is true that cars as cars put real enablement at the disposal of the consumer in a way that cars as planes did not. Cars as planes did not actually change the speed, distance, or agility with which a consumer could travel. What the metaphor supplied was what we would nowadays call a virtual enhancement (Jones 1997; Turkle 1995). It may be that some of this was anticipatory. In the 1950s, Americans still hoped that sometime planes would replace cars as the typical means of travel and that there would be "a plane in every garage" (Corn 1983). But even when cars as planes served as a virtual enablement, they were genuinely transforming.

It would be wrong, in other words, to dismiss this as Walter Mitty's "pocketa-pocketa-pocketa" fantasy (Thurber 1941), the compensatory gesture with which ordinary people tried, desperately and incredibly, to give their lives new drama and importance. The metaphor was more than make-believe. Drivers who were invited to think of themselves as enabled by automobiles began eventually to change, not just in their self-concept but the very manner of their lives and their experience of the world. It became part of the process of self-completion. The physical person didn't need this, but the social person did (Belk 1988b; Carrithers, Collins, and Lukes 1985; Elliott and Wattanasuwan 1988; Glover 1988; Kleine, Kleine, and Allen 1995; Sapir 1931; Wicklund and Gollwitzer 1982, 31–47).

Eventually, the car moved from the optional to the necessary. This was perhaps true too of the metaphor. It may have begun as a fancy, a way of imagining oneself for "pocketa" purposes, but eventually it installed itself in the sense of self and the practice of daily life. Where once its presence was enabling, now its absence was disabling. It became, in a word, a presupposition. (Our contemporary equivalent is electronic mail, which began as a convenience and is now the necessary condition of certain acts of communication and kinds of relationship.)

There is evidence of a growing interpenetration of humans and machines. The boundary between the two was blurring. Americans of this decade would have been horrified at this idea. They thought of machines and humans as mutually exclusive categories. But the signs were emerging that this distinction was coming undone.

An anthropologist is interested to note, for instance, that the exam for the driver's license in the 1950s had assumed extralegal significance. Passing the exam became a cultural marker more important in some ways than sexual maturity, the ability to vote, or the right to be treated as an adult. Americans made a great fuss about the occasion. Before completion, the teen was a mere child, reliant on adults, housebound, immobile, denied an adult ambit. After the exam, he or she was changed, transformed. Why? Because he could now be fitted with the machine, as his parents had been. This was a society enamored of technological enablements, where the individual was surrounded by machines on which communication and transport depended. Americans insisted on the distinction between humans and machines, but the line was blurring.

There was another, more telling, symptom of the "cyborg driver": the powerful sense of disablement experienced by drivers when stripped of license or car. They complained not of inconvenience but of violation, as if they had lost something essential to themselves. What was at the age of 16 a glorious empowerment came to feel, eventually, like a feature of the essential self. Auto enablement was so taken for granted that few drivers could see it. Only a mechanical breakdown, towaway, or theft could show how deep the transformation had gone.

It is as if we are looking at the creation of a secret cyborg. And it is only thus that we may use Haraway's now-famous term (1991). The conflation of human and machine had slipped into the world, transforming the understanding of self and society. But no one was prepared to name or acknowledge the elephant in the living room. No one was prepared to admit how far the transformation had gone, except perhaps privately and secretly, in those moments when one was engaged in a "race" on the highway or pushing a gas pedal to the floor. The man-machine conceit was something for those "nutty" copywriters and art directors, something to fill the pages of *Time* and *Life*. It was not to be embraced, honored, or acknowledged in any formal way. It was not to be acknowledged at all except in those moments of purchase and driving and racing and pulling away and getting ahead. But there it was. When the consumer was making the second-most-important allocation of the household budget. When people were going to work, to Thanksgiving dinners, to summer vacations, on victory laps, something happened to Americans behind the wheel.

Cars as Jets

Lindbergh, Earhart, and Rogers were early heroes of the world of aviation, but they were in some ways dwarfed by the flyers of the American military and World War II. These were flyers of such expertise and resourcefulness they treated planes like Wells Fargo ponies. Shot down in one, they'd go up in another. The undisputed celebrity was Chuck Yeager. Yeager began his military career as an air force mechanic. His rise to greatness was, among other things, a demonstration of the American inclination to honor talent wherever it appeared. (In England, for instance, the air force continued to have a vaguely chivalric character and to prefer gentlemen over commoners as flyers.) One of the men who spotted Yeager's talent attested to his "cyborg" character. Yeager flew an airplane, he said, "as though he was an integral part of it" (in Anonymous 2002).

Securing his heroic status, Yeager was shot down over France in World War II and managed to return uncaptured. After the war, he broke the sound barrier in the rocket-powered X-1 Bell jet, a task the English had tried and abandoned. Yeager was by this time so well known and so loved in the world of aviation, Wolfe (1979) tells us, that the pilots of domestic airplanes imitated his drawl when communicating with control towers. His name was branded in the public consciousness, the first name blending seamlessly with the last. "Charles Yeager" was unthinkable. So was "Charlie Yeager." "Chuck Yeager" stood for something in the American mind, a symbolic resource that aviation made available to the men in striped pants.

Yeager helped train the next generation of flyboys, the ones in the NASA space program. And when threatened with immobility in a flight capsule ("spam in a can," they called it), the new generation asserted the self-control and control of machines that defined the jet pilot (Wolfe 1979). Despite the fact that this technology was now vastly more complicated than most pilots could fully fathom or manipulate, these pilots helped sustained the image of the pilot as the boy from the Midwest who could keep his plane in the air with his native ingenuity, a screwdriver, and a stick of gum. They helped define the prevailing notion of Americans as can-do creatures who were not merely the occupants of their technology but superbly in control of it. They helped encourage the American conflation of man and machine, the triumph of the secret cyborg, to new heights. In this flowering of the machine age, there is no trace of the anxiety Kubrick was to summon with "Hal," the computer run amuck (Kubrick 1968). In this period, machines always amplified Americans. They did not ever obscure, diminish, or tyrannize them.

The cars as jets of the 1950s enhanced the owner yet again. Cars as jets were dramatically larger, more powerful, and faster than cars as planes. The owner prepared to see the properties of the car as jet as her own was, once more, augmented. These were metaphoric endowments, but, as I have labored to suggest, the social person was quick to take them up and eventually to presuppose them.

As we have noted, Harley Earl's 1951 concept car was modeled on the F-86 Sabre. The F-86 was the central fighter jet of the Cold War. It was active in Korea, winning its engagements with Russian-made MiGs by a ratio of ten to one. It was also the most important jet in mainland defense. Its evocation by Detroit designers is easy enough to dismiss as capitalism at its most fanciful—designers reaching, implausibly, for effect. But it may well be that people in the 1950s drove fighter-like cars for the same reason some people wore NYFD caps following the terrorist attack of September 11, 2001. In an anxious time of air-raid shelters and duck-and-cover drills, this car was, possibly, a gesture of solidarity. Some Americans may have driven the '56 Plymouth or the '57 Dodge because in the trying circumstances of the Cold War, "everyone's a flyboy now."

Millions of Americans now drove with model planes in their peripheral vision. This, too, may have been more than lapel-pin patriotism. These peripheral planes made a plane of the car and a pilot of the driver. They created an act of imitation that was perhaps also a gesture of deference and support. It is possible to dismiss this, too, as Mitty's "pocketa-pocketa-pocketa" fantasy, but we could just as well think of these peripheral planes as a kind of "heads up" display, instrumentation from which navigational information flowed. These were ideological coordinates more than spatial ones, but then this was a culture that specialized, as we have seen, in confounding the two.

There was a third way in which fighter jet might serve Detroit and the driver as a useful metaphor. As an instrument of international competition, it spoke to one of the faces of postwar mobility. America was alive with inducements to mobility, but not just inducements. Sometimes the call to mobility was fearful, coercive, obligating. In the bid for new career opportunities and a place in the suburbs, it was "race ahead or be left behind." In this atomistic world, there was no guarantee of movement, no "ratchet effect" to protect one's gains. It took a certain effort just to stay put. In fact, the individual and the family were living in a social space slick with opportunities for disappointment and regress. A relative in need, an economic downturn, another world war, any of these exogenous factors could undo the bid for prosperity. A wrong career decision, a cataclysmic illness, lost optimism, family disarray, these were the endogenous, equally debilitating, possibilities.

In 1955, members of the Washington Advertising Club were addressed by a doctor who told them of the hidden costs of mobility. "Moving up in the world brings not an easier life but a more exacting one. Social demands multiply. Each rise obligates you to heavier responsibilities. You are judged by stricter standards. Your chances for success increase, but so do your chances of failure. . . . Think of yourself as a highly complicated piece of machinery. Your capacity for tension has a limit beyond which it isn't safe to go. That limit is fixed, not by your ambitions, but by the weakest part of your body" (Anonymous 1955k).

No doubt stress reduction was the best advice for hardworking advertising executives. But when the demands of the mobility game induced fear or faintheartedness, it may have helped just as much to "suit up" in the machinery of a 1954 Buick, to dress oneself in its formidable appearances. The car that demonstrated "arrival" and achievement also proved reassuring, perhaps, when the contact sport of status competition went badly. It gave inward and outward "evidence" that mastery and mobility were unimpaired and at least still extant. In a world turned against you, somehow the prosthetics of three and a half tons of metal and glass acted like a balm (cf. Levinson 1987, 1990). To evoke the warrior accomplishments of a Chuck Yeager was no small thing.

Cars and the New Mobility

Cars were caught up in a second kind of mobility, what we might call a modernist mobility. If social mobility was marked in conversations with the phrase "He's really getting ahead," modernist mobility was marked with phrases such as "He's really going somewhere." In this case, movement was no longer vertical, upward, or downward in social space; it was now movement from present location "out," "away," or "beyond" to some new one. This mobility was required of every American whatever their social aspirations. It was the obligation of everyone who lived in the dynamic, changeable world that was 1950s America.

This may have been the decade in which America was beginning to glimpse what it meant to live in a culture where change was no longer episodic but continuous, where the individual could no longer hope to respond with the characteristic stop-and-go pattern of response and reprieve. This may have been the decade where advantage was shifting to people and organizations that could engage in continuous adaptation. It was going to those who were prepared to adopt the modernist posture, to cantilever themselves out over the moment, poised to reconfigure themselves in the blink of an eye. The future had grown more demanding *and* more near. It was necessary to pay close attention to the demands of the moment and then to give them up immediately when the world moved on.

Change was everywhere. The cascade of technical and product innovation continued to pour into domestic life. Plastics were a case in point. This one product changed the appearance, texture, sound, and functionality of the near world. Television had arrived as a domestic technology, changing leisure time and tastes. The move to the suburb changed patterns of association, entertainment, child-rearing, and married life (Gans 1967). Popular music was changing with the fuller admission of an African American influence (Marcus 1995). Youth culture was growing (Palladino 1996). The civil rights movement was challenging the way some people thought about race. Psychologists and existentialists mandated the search for the essential self (Fromm 1994/1941). It was no longer enough to be the perfect father and husband. Now the individual had to have plumbed the depths of his own individuality.

Experts, as scientists, were given a free hand to repudiate time-hallowed traditions. Dr. Spock questioned child-rearing conventions, and Margaret Mead questioned sexual practices (Mead 1928; Spock 1946). Especially as parents, suburbanites struggled to keep family practice within the shifting circle of official approval (Katz 1992). Intellectuals such as John Kenneth Galbraith, Dwight Macdonald, Paul Goodman, and C. Wright Mills hammered away at the shortcomings of the corporation, popular culture, and the suburbs (Pells 1985). Novelists such as Mary McCarthy and John Cheever did the same, though in the latter's *Bullet Park,* the protagonist says "it makes me sore to have people always chomping at the suburbs" (1969, 5–6). It is customary to treat these people as critical voices from the margin. But their skepticism found its way into the lives of middle-class Americans. When we see it as the theme of Nunnally Johnson's 1956 film *The Man in the Gray Flannel Suit,* we know this must be so. This "searing critique" of mainstream society was itself a mainstream entertainment. Galbraith became an intellectual celebrity in the period, and the beat poets became cultural heroes. Far from being creatures of the margin, they were assuming oracular status. As Katz's ethnography demonstrates very well, average Americans were embracing the new critique (Katz 1992).

The American corporation began to think in formal ways about management and strategic planning (Drucker 1954). This is hard to fathom now, but until Peter Drucker, corporate America did not think about management as management at all. It struggled to make cars or sell insurance. That this was the moment in which management was brought to self-consciousness as a professional practice is a measure of change. And it was a change that made for more change. Once the corporation was awakened from its slumber, it could intensify the speed with which it moved.

It is now not unusual to hear the 1950s as a "containment" culture designed to enforce conformity and control things that stood at odds with the prevailing order (May 1989; Nadel 1996). Others treat the 1950s as the dread, glassy calm that precedes the 1960s storm. But we might also say the 1950s were an atelier in which the 1960s were being designed and tried out. This world was dynamic not so much by modernist fiat but because America had embraced the fact (and so many agents and instruments) of change. Americans could feel the world breaking away beneath their feet.

This is another way of saying that the lived reality of American life was now consistent with the modernist concept of time. The citizens of the 1950s appear to have found themselves in possession of what Habermas calls a "changed consciousness of time," an "anticipation of an undefined future and the cult of the new." They were newly exposed to and obliged to be responsive to "the transitory, the elusive, and the ephemeral" (1983, 5). They were now living in "a form of historical time which valorizes the new as the product of a constantly self-negating temporal dynamic" (Osborne 1995, xii).

How to live in such a world was not obvious. The individual needed new skills and instincts. But he or she also needed the courage to enter a world that was still forming, to proceed without the benefit of full intelligence. There was a concern in the period that postwar prosperity had created a personality that was compliant and conformist. Whyte said the "organizational man" was preoccupied with getting along with the team, of putting process ahead of creativity, of sacrificing his individualism for the dubious benefits of corporate life (1956). Curiosity, independence, and innovation, Whyte said, were endangered. But was this the craven bid for security that Whyte insists it is? The organizational man appeared peculiarly well suited to a society changing as quickly as 1950s America. He left his options open. He listened carefully for the new arrangement in the works. He responded instantaneously. Perhaps Whyte's new species of social life is interesting less because it is organizational and more because it is, to borrow a phrase from complexity theory (Kauffman 1995), self-organizing.

David Riesman's *The Lonely Crowd* (1961) was another condemnation of the period. Riesman was persuaded that America was now "other directed," that Americans had abandoned their inner life, their creativity, the pursuit of an essential self and an independence of mind, for the approval of their peers. He accused them of "an exceptional sensitivity to the actions and wishes of others" (38). But the qualities that offended Riesman did confer a certain aerodynamism. For the creature forced to enter a world that was structurally unspecified (and unspecifiable), remaining genial, open, and "exceptionally sensitive" was perhaps not such a bad thing. Perhaps it was a sensible thing to do and a new model of self and action.

We may judge a time partly by its heroes. And the 1950s was particularly enamored of spies, the object of 1950s film and fiction (Drummond 1986, 1996). Some of this no doubt reflects the role spies played in the Cold War. But when Ian Fleming began the James Bond franchise in 1953, he helped invent a character who was effortlessly at home in any circumstance, however unpredictable, opaque, or dynamic. It would be wrong to think of Bond as "exceptionally sensitive" to anyone but himself, but as a paragon of adaptation, he hardly needed to be. He could awaken injured and dazed in a damp castle keep in Czechoslovakia and within hours have commandeered the one nuclear submarine that threatened Western interest. And he did not do this unaided. He bristled with gadgets: watches that worked as buzz saws, lighters that worked as cameras . . . objects that came from relatively high up the progress cascade. Bond was as much a machine as a man, a cyborg in Saville Row tailoring. Like the outer-directed organizational man, he was a marvel of preparedness. It is assumed that spy fiction sold millions of copies in the 1950s because it fed "pocketa-pocketa-pocketa" fantasy. This is the diminishing view; it is not clear that it is the illuminating one.

Perhaps the greatest single challenge to be brought against middle-class America in the 1950s was the accusing presence of the "beats." These were American writers who took shape as a group in the 1940s and came to prominence in the 1950s (Watson 1995). They included William Burroughs, whose novel *Junky* appeared in 1953; Allen Ginsberg, whose poem *Howl* appeared in 1956; and Jack Kerouac, whose novel *On the Road* appeared in 1957. The term "beat" was chosen because it was street language for "broken down" but also because it resonated with "beatific." The beats sought the visionary with the understanding that wisdom was to be reached through self-impoverishment, by breaking down the conventional categories of seeing and being. They were persuaded that there was nothing to be learned from the mainstream of a bourgeois society and insisted on life at the margins, with the dispossessed. Ginsberg, looking back, said, "The new vision assumed the death of square morality and replaced that meaning with belief in creativity" (in Watson 1995, 39). This was the real opportunity for illumination.

Certainly the beats in their fastidiously anti-bourgeois attitude appeared to differ markedly, perhaps systematically, from their brothers and sisters in the middle class. Strangely, though, they appeared to have one or two things in common (Dickstein 1999). The beats, for instance, believed strongly in movement as the path to wisdom. This showed in a literary sense in Jack Kerouac's ceaseless passage back and forth across the country. It also shows in his conviction that the best prose came from direct experience. In these moments, we see him trying to outdistance culture, to get words on the page before culture could form them with literary convention. Kerouac and Burrows advised Ginsberg to stop making rule-bound poetry, to capture "what the eye sees" unmediated by culture (in Watson 1995, 128). In a strange way, both the middle class and their sworn enemies had struck upon the same temporal strategy, the same inclination to leave the moment and enter the future pell-mell (Casey 1997, 110–111).

When Mrs. Witenko and her family drove from Fairfield to Dayton to see the General Motors Parade of Progress, she prized the experience, as we have heard, because it helped the family understand "how our America is going forward." In the larger, literal scheme of things, a car show is an odd place to learn about national destiny. But this was not so in America at mid-century. For this national destiny was not merely, and of necessity, located in the future, it *was* the future. And this was not the future as defined by the dictionary: "a time that has yet to come." It was the future as defined by ideas of progress and modernism, something like "the moment when the improvement of the human condition is, if briefly, realized." GM cars were both the means and the end of this progress, the vehicle the ordinary consumer could use to find their way.

Cars were the gift of progress and proof of it. With three and a half tons of particular steel and glass wrapped around them, consumers could travel at great speeds for great distances. The improvement wrought by the automobile had remade consumers, endowing them with powers of movement they did not have before. This prosthetic enhancement may have started as a will-o'-the-wisp in the mind of an MIT egghead, but the boys in striped pants made it real. It was now so tangible that it could be "mine," so actual that it could be "me."

Cars had actually changed the capacity of the human being. There is a good deal of talk these days about virtual realities and how these give the player/consumer new powers and properties. These are remarkable, but every time someone sings the praises of flight simulation or Doom-type combat, one is entitled to wonder whether this experience can truly equal the experience of traveling sixty miles an hour down a newly constructed highway that connected one coast to the other.

But these were something more than physical enablement; they were also, as we have noted, metaphoric ones. They gave the consumer new properties with which to enter the future and protect them from it. In such a car, the consumer was psychologically and conceptually prepared for a world that was constantly reinventing itself. They were faster, sleeker, speedier. This was no small cultural gift for someone who was not only keen to participate in America's great rush into the future but obliged to move at speed to keep up. Arrayed in the chrome and glass of Detroit design, the consumer was made fit for transit.

Conclusion

Progress as planes, planes as cars, cars as people, people as citizens and occupants of the American future: these were symbolic equations that linked the maximal values of American culture with the most prized possession in the driveway by means of an interlocking cultural array. The 1954 Buick was science and technology "come down to earth," proof of what the cascade of progress could do for the consumer. The consumer moved in the opposite direction; up the array, as it were, from the mundane world of everyday objects into contact with the compelling issues of the day. Detroit had devised a cyberdevice on the drawing board, in the factory, in advertisements, and finally (as if prosthetically) "in the flesh." To make these cars conform to Loewy's notion of design (form following function, less is mysteriously more) was to miss the point altogether. These cars, it turned out, had much larger cultural responsibilities.

We might think of the Forward Look and the Loewy-Galbraith response to it as a contest between two meaning-makers, marketers on the one side, intellectuals on the other. It is clear that in the Forward Look the marketers had invented a symbolic device of some power. It combed the heavens. It brought power to what is otherwise simply a means of transportation. It ignited the postwar economy at the very moment it was beginning to dwindle.

But there were costs and consequences. In *this* zero-sum game, the rise of Detroit meant demotion for someone else. In Loewy's case, the demotion was obvious, public, and cruel. He was displaced and embarrassed. In Galbraith's case, the exclusion was less vivid, but it was, perhaps, just as intensely felt. As *The Affluent Society* shows, Galbraith had plenty of ideas about the way the economy should be run, but it wasn't until the Kennedy era that anyone cared to solicit them (and then, of course, Kennedy was so keen on Galbraith's domestic advice that he made him ambassador to India). Loewy might have been an arbiter of taste and Galbraith an intellectual deity, but popular culture had other ideas about what mattered, and in this scheme, our gallant twosome were also-rans.

Part Four
Celebrities

Strategy:

Ours is a culture in which celebrities play a large and influential part. We are not always comfortable with this influence, but this doesn't mean we have worked very hard to understand it.

The essay for Part Four looks at the career of Marilyn Monroe and attempts to show the ways in which Monroe invented a new form of femaleness (in the face of several kinds of opposition) and then succeeded in investing this cultural meaning in the color of her hair (in the face of a cultural tradition that treated blondness very differently).

The article for Part Four seeks to show how the cultural meanings invented by (and for) celebrities enters the commercial system and through it, the efforts of the consumer to engage in self-invention. This paper takes particular aim at a competing model of celebrity endorsement and seeks to show that it fails to take account of its part in the cultural invention and transmission of meanings.

We begin to shift into a more-pragmatic modality. We are now looking at the mechanics of marketing, and this theme will grow in the sections to follow.

7 Marilyn Monroe, Inventor of Blondness

Eli Wallach watched in astonishment one day as Marilyn Monroe, on the street, suddenly began to walk and talk with new emphasis. The effect was electric. Heads turned, traffic stopped. Wallach asked her what she was doing and she replied, "I just felt like being Marilyn for a moment" (in Steinem 1988, 206). "Marilyn" was an aggregate of symbols and meanings that suddenly took life and walked from the laboratory of Hollywood into our culture.

Monroe was not the only one trying to create "Marilyn." The moguls, for instance, wanted to play the star-maker. The public had its own idea of who "Marilyn" was. (Manifestly, she was "one of them," a little person who had made it big.) Husbands had demands to make. Joe DiMaggio wanted his Monroe wifely and demure. Arthur Miller wrote dumb-blonde parts for her (Steinem 1988, 206). The press was (and remains) a relentless inventor of "Marilyn" (Guiles 1984; Zolotow 1960).

Monroe was not the only Marilyn-maker, but she was probably the most sophisticated and cunning of them. This surprises us a little. Monroe gave us the dumb-blonde routine and we fell for it. It's hard for us to believe that a "bimbo" invented one of the arresting identities of our century. But as the biographies make plain, this was a woman who knew what she was doing and went about the business of self-invention with determination and skill.

How did she do it? With all the resources at her disposal. She began by changing her name from Norma Jean Baker to Marilyn Monroe. She got a nose job and a new chin. She gave up gingham sundresses. She changed her voice, facial expressions, and body movements. Monroe even reinvented her history, claiming to have been a "little orphan girl," which did not quite tell the whole story. And she changed her hair, from curly brunette to wavy blond.

All this careful invention got her somewhere. Leon Shamroy, the camera-man who shot her first screen test, said, "I got a cold chill. This girl had something I hadn't seen since the days of the silent pictures; this girl had sex on a piece of film like Harlow had. Every frame of that film radiated sex" (in Steinem 1988, 47–48).

There's a temptation to suppose that this sexual charisma was somehow a force, and a gift, of nature; that Monroe was a passive vessel for something beyond her control. Even Gloria Steinem (who does more than anyone to let us see Monroe as a real person) stumbles on this point. She speaks of Monroe's "extraordinary luminescence" as if this quality were somehow an accident of birth. Norman Mailer, who can be relied upon to mythologize, talks as if Monroe were the witless recipient of extraordinary sexual powers.

This is wrong. The same biographies are filled with evidence that "Marilyn" was no gift of nature but a creation of Monroe herself. One of her photographers saw this clearly. He could tell that even her white-light sexuality was a deliberate creation:

> I'll focus on her and then looking in the finder, I can actually see the sex blossoming out, like it was a flower. If I'm in a hurry and want to shoot too quickly, she'll say, "Earl, you shot it too quick. It won't be right. Let's do it again." You see, it takes time for her to create this sex thing. (Mailer 1973, 68)

Monroe worked hard to cultivate her persona. We are told that she routinely took photographs home at night and examined them for hours. This might have been a young girl's vanity. More probably, it was a young actress's craft. Monroe returned each morning to ask why some shots worked and others didn't.

Monroe tells us she sought charisma deliberately.

> My God, how I wanted to learn! To change, to improve! . . . I sneaked scripts off the set and sat alone in my room reading them out loud in front of the mirror. And an odd thing happened to me. I fell in love with myself—not how I was but how I was going to be. (Steinem 1988, 90)

Monroe wasn't born with sexual charisma, nor did she have it thrust upon her. Husbands, producers, and the public all wanted a hand, but "Marilyn" was largely a creature of Monroe's own making.

To invent herself, Monroe needed to reinvent blondes. In the late 1940s, blondness was not yet *the* color of Hollywood. The movie stars of the period were mostly brunettes or redheads. In the silent movies, blondes were the exception, not the rule. The two greatest stars of the day, Lillian Gish and Clara Bow, were not blondes. Jane Russell, the reigning star of the pre-Monroe period was a brunette. So was Katharine Hepburn. Joan Bennett began her career as a blonde but rose to stardom as a brunette. Rita Hayworth and Maureen O'Hara were both redheads. True, there were a few blondes with influence: Veronica Lake, Mary Astor, and Joan Crawford, for instance (Anonymous 1941). But blondness was not then, as it became in the 1950s and 1960s, the starlet's choice.

There was, in fact, something slightly outré about blondness in the 1930s and 1940s. It was associated with frank sexuality in an era when any kind of sexuality made people a little nervous. Mae West bears some of the responsibility here. She helped to make blondes stand for sex on the sly. Her character came straight out of vaudeville, designed to radiate the stripper's coyness. Mae West's vamp helped to make blondes stand for sex as a naughty secret (Eells and Musgrove 1982, 26).

Jean Harlow was not so different. She was, in Molly Haskell's words, "one of the screen's raunchiest inventions . . . sluttish and smart, cracking gum and one-liners simultaneously" (Haskell 1974, 113–114). She too helped to make blondness stand for a provocative brand of sexuality. Under the influence of West and Harlow, blondness became a declaration of wantonness.

Monroe's self-invention called for something different. At first, she didn't want to become a blonde at all. She had to be persuaded by her agent, the improbably named Emmeline Snively. Monroe was afraid blondness would look "artificial." She was looking for a different version of sexuality. And because it was not available, she had to make it up herself. She set about doing so in the movie *Gentlemen Prefer Blondes*. By the time the film entered popular consciousness, no one would think of sexuality or blondness quite the same way again.

There's an irony here. After all, the title *Gentlemen Prefer Blondes* was meant to be paradoxical. Gentlemen, everyone knew, preferred brunettes. Blondes were for the dance hall, the burlesque house. Blondes, in the tradition of Harlow and West, were creatures that gentlemen did not date, marry, or, strictly speaking, even talk to.

Monroe managed her triumph right under the nose of the preeminent star of the period, Jane Russell. Russell came to *Gentlemen Prefer Blondes* as the acknowledged lead. She got bigger billing and more money (more than five times Monroe's fee). But the movie slipped away from her. She had the satisfaction, toward the end of the film, of donning a blond wig and doing a crude satire of Monroe's breathy innocence. But it was a fleeting pleasure. *Gentlemen Prefer Blondes* belonged to Monroe. By the time Monroe was finished with it, *Gentlemen Prefer Blondes* no longer had an ironic ring. It's true, the nation thought, gentlemen do.

People have called Monroe's part in *Gentlemen Prefer Blondes* a dumb-blonde role (Steinem 1988, 96). What they are complaining about are the mannerisms of Monroe's Lorelei Lee character. Lee is breathy, pouting, wide eyed, prone to grammatical error, constantly surprised by the world, and unsophisticated in everything she does. These are, no doubt, markers of stupidity in some people. They are also markers of submission, and these days we cringe to see them in the character of any woman, on screen or off.

But Monroe intended them for another purpose. What she sought in *Gentlemen Prefer Blondes* was a form of femaleness that was unguarded. Her Lee is open and unmediated. This is the famous "vulnerability" that people remark on. Despite the fact that Lorelei is on the "millionaire trail," she is with everyone, from captains to waiters, a creature without boundary. Everyone has access to her emotions.

What the critics take for dumbness was, I think, a carefully cultivated access. And this was the quality that Monroe most sought for her invented self. "Marilyn" was charming because there was nothing measured about her, nothing calculated, nothing manipulated. Even the pretensions were transparent.

What was extraordinary about "Marilyn" as a cultural artifact was that she gave so much and demanded so little. This counts as a deliberate violation of the rules of reciprocity. The viewer was, apparently, given access to the entire person. This was, apparently, a person we could see right into and possess completely.

Naturally, we are, in an era reconfigured by feminist understanding, uncomfortable with this. We see now how dangerous the posture is, especially when it is practiced by women, and, most especially when it is demanded of them. From a feminist perspective, it is now hard not to see Monroe's "generosity" as something coerced. Any "gift" that is extorted from the viewer is clearly no gift at all. "Marilyn" was, and remains, an invitation to exploitation.

Liabilities aside, this persona was not something America had seen before. "Marilyn" was about access of every kind: sexual, emotional, intellectual. And the nation was smitten. People were drawn to this selfless creature like moths to the flame. They came driven by many motives, some sexist, some not. They responded to the free gift of access as they do to any gesture of extraordinary generosity—with a generosity of their own. They gifted Monroe with stardom.

It is hard to reconstruct the power of Monroe's transformation. In the 1950s, popular culture still felt the repressive thrall of Victorian sexuality. It still believed sex was supposed to acknowledge its "danger" with a smirk or a leer. In a culture of this sort, Marilyn's generous sexuality was remarkable. Norman Mailer feels its effect still: "Marilyn was deliverance, a very Stradivarius of sex, so gorgeous, forgiving, humorous, compliant and tender" (Mailer 1973, 15). In creating "Marilyn," Monroe created a new kind of blondness. Once the color of peek-a-boo sexuality, blondness was now the color of full disclosure.

8 Who Is the Celebrity Endorser?

Cultural Foundations of the Endorsement Process

Abstract

This essay offers a new approach to celebrity endorsement. Previous explanations, especially the source-credibility and source-attractiveness models, are criticized, and an alternative "meaning-transfer" model is proposed. According to this model, the attractiveness of celebrities as endorsers stems from the cultural meanings with which they are endowed. The model shows how meanings pass from celebrity to product and from product to consumer. The implications of this model for our understanding of the consumer society are considered. Research avenues suggested by the model are also discussed.

The celebrity endorser is a ubiquitous feature of modern marketing. Actor James Earl Jones, singer Diana Krall, athlete Tiger Woods, politician Bob Dole, and comedian Jerry Seinfeld have all loaned their names and images to recent campaigns. Unfortunately, this communications strategy has not earned extensive study. Nor has it inspired especially illuminating theoretical accounts. As a result, the received wisdom on celebrity endorsement is modest and imperfect, and existing models fail to capture several of the most interesting and central characteristics of the endorsement process.

This investigation of endorsement addresses these deficits from a cultural perspective. The argument is that the endorsement process depends upon the symbolic properties of the celebrity endorser. Using a "meaning-transfer" perspective, these properties are shown to reside in the celebrity and to move from celebrity to consumer good and from good to consumer.

For present purposes, the celebrity endorser is defined as any individual who enjoys public recognition and who uses this recognition on behalf of a consumer good by appearing with it in an advertisement. We will refine this definition later, but for the moment it is deliberately broad to encompass not just the usual movie and television stars but also individuals from the world of sports, politics, business, art, and the military. The term "celebrity endorsement" is also meant in this essay to encompass a variety of endorsements, including those in the explicit mode ("I endorse this product"), the implicit mode ("I use this product"), the imperative mode ("You should use this product"), and the co-present mode (i.e., in which the celebrity merely appears with the product). Moreover, it includes a range of endorsement roles, such as cases in which the celebrity is also an expert (e.g., Bobby Unser recommending motor oil), is associated with the manufacturer in some long-term capacity (e.g., John Madden for Ace Hardware), or has no special knowledge of, or association with, the product in question (Jerry Seinfeld and American Express) (cf. Friedman, Termini, and Washington 1976). This definition is designed deliberately to exclude the "typical consumer" endorser (Friedman and Friedman 1979). The model presented in this essay applies to all these variations but the last.

The Literature

Two models, the source-credibility and the source-attractiveness models, inform research and reflection on the topic of celebrity endorsement. Both were devised originally for the study of communications and have been applied only recently to the endorsement process. Both are designed to determine the conditions under which the message-sender or source is persuasive.

The source-credibility model rests on research in social psychology (Hovland and Weiss 1951–1952; Hovland, Janis, and Kelley 1953). The Hovland version of the model contends that a message depends for its effectiveness on the "expertness" and "trustworthiness" of the source (Hovland, Janis, and Kelley 1953, 20; cf. Dholakia and Sternthal 1977; Sternthal, Dholakia, and Leavitt 1978). It defines expertness as the perceived *ability* of the source to make valid assertions. It defines trustworthiness as the perceived *willingness* of the source to make value assertions. The Hovland model holds that sources exhibiting expertness and trustworthiness are credible and, to this extent, persuasive.

The source-attractiveness model also rests on social-psychological research. The McGuire (1985) model contends that a message depends for its effectiveness chiefly on the "familiarity," "likeability," and/or "similarity" of the source (McGuire 1985, 264; cf. Baker and Churchill 1977; Debevec and Kernan 1984; Friedman, Santeramo, and Traina 1978; Joseph 1982; Kahle and Homer 1985). Familiarity is defined as knowledge of the source through exposure, likeability as affection for the source as a result of the source's physical appearance and behavior, and similarity as a supposed resemblance between the source and receiver of the message. The McGuire model holds that sources who are known to, liked by, and/or similar to the consumer are attractive and, to this extent, persuasive.

The source models (as we shall call the source-credibility and source-attractiveness models together) have been confirmed by research. The Hovland model has been validated by several parties (Atkin and Block 1983;

Kamen, Azhari, and Kragh 1975; Klebba and Unger 1983; cf. Finn 1980, 779). The McGuire model has also demonstrated its value (Friedman and Friedman 1979), and it appears safe to say that celebrities owe some of their effectiveness as marketing devices to their credibility and attractiveness. The source models are, to this extent, a necessary part of our understanding of the endorsement process. But they do not capture everything at issue in the endorsement process. Indeed, there is reason to think that these models cannot explain endorsement's most fundamental features. The evidence for this skepticism is everywhere. The research itself is littered with puzzles and peculiarities the source models cannot explain.

For instance, the research by the Friedmans produced results that are not consistent with the source models. They found that some product categories were incompatible with celebrity categories (e.g., Mary Tyler Moore would have served as a poor celebrity endorser for vacuum cleaners). The source models are caught flatfooted here. For the purposes of the models, as long as the credibility and attractiveness conditions are satisfied, *any* celebrity should serve as a persuasive source for *any* advertising message. According to this model, the persuasiveness of the celebrity has everything to do with the celebrity and nothing to do with the product.

Kamen, Azhari, and Kragh (1975) suggest that the spokesperson acts as a kind of "core around which the substantive messages are positioned." In this capacity, the spokesperson helps

> [t]rigger the past associations with the sponsor and stimulate the remembering of past messages. He would integrate new messages with the old so as to build a unifying, coherent, sustained, and consistent image of the brand. (18)

This position implies that the celebrity serves the endorsement process by taking on meanings that they carry from ad to ad and that the celebrity somehow serves as a site in which meanings cohere. Plainly, neither possibility is consistent with either source model. After all, these models make assertions only about the credibility and attractiveness of the message-sender and none about the endorser's role as a medium for the message or the continuity of the message from ad to ad. In the language of Kuhn (1962), the paradigm is beginning to accumulate anomalies. Scholars have been compelled either to abandon or transform the source models.

But if the internal evidence for skepticism is strong, the external grounds are even stronger. The scholarly and professional literature is littered with data that cannot be explained by the source models. There are mysteries everywhere. Bill Cosby failed as an endorser for E. F. Hutton despite his evident success for Kodak and Coca-Cola. John Houseman failed as an endorser for McDonald's despite his effective work for Smith Barney (Marshall 1987). George C. Scott proved, mysteriously, to be the wrong choice for Renault, as did Ringo Starr for Sun Country Classic Wine Coolers (Motavalli 1988). The source models, as the present guardians of current endorsement practice, did not forewarn advertising practitioners of the inappropriateness of these celebrity choices. Nor can they, as the received academic wisdom on the endorsement process, help us understand what went wrong. The source models have not served as a practical or theoretical guide.

Consider, for instance, the example of John Wayne as a celebrity endorser for the pain reliever Datril. "Wayne has nothing to do with the product, and sales of the analgesic languished. . . . [It was a] classic . . . mismatch between star and product" (Kaikati 1987, 6). This is offered as a kind of explanation of what went wrong in the Datril case. But what does it mean to say that the celebrity "had nothing to do" with the product? What "mismatch" between celebrity and product is being asserted here? The source models do not tell us. They cannot explain why John Wayne and Datril were incompatible.

Schudson's treatment of James Garner as a celebrity endorser is germane. Schudson (1984, 212) suggests that there is something mysterious about the advertisements in which Garner appears.

> Garner does not play himself, the person, nor does he play a particular fictive character. Instead, he plays what I would call the generalized James Garner role, the type for which James Garner is always case—handsome, gentle, bumbling, endearing, a combination of Bret Maverick from "Maverick" and Jim Rockford from "The Rockford Files."

This thoughtful observation spells real trouble for the source models. If the celebrity endorser represents not himself but his stage persona, the issues of expertness and trustworthiness can hardly apply. After all, it hardly makes sense to impute credibility to a fictional character. But even if we force the issue and insist that fictional characters can, somehow, be credible, Schudson's observation tells us this is a special, role-specific credibility. It is no longer a simple matter of the willingness and ability to make valid assertions.

The issue of source attractiveness is problematic in another way. According to Schudson's account, Garner's attractiveness consists in the "endearing," "gentle," and "bumbling" qualities of his stage persona. We must add to this perhaps the most salient trait of Garner's stage persona, his claim to being the foremost representative of a particular type of American male. As a prototype, Garner is a member of the larger pantheon of actors that helps define this version of gender type in America (e.g., James Stewart, Cary Grant, Kelsey Grammer, Viggo Mortensen, Owen Wilson, Eddie Murphy).

When we observe Garner from this point of view, we see that his attractiveness depends not on his qualities as a person or even on his qualities as a famous persona. For communications purposes, the celebrity is a composite of his fictional roles. This means that when consumers respond to Garner's "attractiveness," they are, in fact, responding to a very particular set of meanings. They are identifying with a bundle of symbolic properties created for, and by, Garner in the television programs *Maverick* and *The Rockford Files*.

This is not "identification" in the ordinary sense. The source models do not capture and illuminate what is going on. Audience response to James Garner is more complicated and interesting than the source models allow. Garner is persuasive as a communicator not only because he is "attractive" but also because he is made up of certain meanings the consumer finds compelling and useful. Garner succeeds as an endorser for Mazda because he represents a bundle of meanings about maturity, Americanness, confidence, masculinity, intelligence, and good humor.

It is here that we begin to uncover the real insufficiency of the source models as an account of celebrity endorsement. The source-attractiveness model can tell us that consumers will like Garner, but it cannot tell us why—nor can it contend with the meanings contained in Garner's persona. Still more important, the model does not allow us to make sense of the meanings contained in a celebrity endorser once they are determined. The source model can tell us only that a celebrity is attractive, not what attractive is.

The implications of this insufficiency are powerful. First, the source models do not allow us to understand the appeal of any particular celebrity. This makes it impossible to understand why a celebrity like Garner should be persuasive for some products but not for others. The source models prevent us from identifying the matches and mismatches. We are left unable to assess how Garner's image interacts with different product and creative themes.

Second, the source models will never allow us to discriminate between celebrities in any useful way. Certainly they allow is to say that James Garner is, perhaps, more credible than Ted Danson. But it does not allow us to say how Garner and Danson differ from a symbolic or communications point of view. The source models might tell us only that David Letterman, Conan O'Brien, Jimmy Kimmel, Craig Kilborn, and Jon Stewart differ in their degree of attractiveness. This is problematic because we understand that their differences go much deeper than this. Hypothetically, the source models might tell us that Sarah Jessica Parker, Kim Cattrall, Cynthia Nixon, and Kristin Davis (all stars of the TV show *Sex and the City*) are equally credible. But we know that this sameness masks profound and thoroughgoing differences. In short, the source models tell us about *degrees* of difference and credibility when what we need to know about is *kinds* of attractiveness and credibility.

Both the internal and external evidence contain anomalies that demonstrate the insufficiency of the source models. If we are to understand the endorsement process, we must build better, more sophisticated models. We especially must come to terms with the meanings contained in the celebrity and give an account of how these meanings serve the endorsement process. The remainder of the essay is designed to suggest such an account.

Cultural Meaning and the Celebrity Endorser

The effectiveness of the endorser depends, in part, upon the meanings he or she brings to the endorsement process. The number and variety of the meanings contained in celebrities are very large. Distinctions of status, class, gender, age, and personality and lifestyle types are represented in the pool of available celebrities, putting an extraordinarily various and subtle pallet of meanings at the disposal of the marketing system.

For example, class and status are presented by the patrician likes of Peter Jennings and the regal likes of Catherine Deneuve. The upper middle class is represented by Pierce Brosnan, the middle class by Ray Romano, and the lower middle class by Kevin James.

Cultural categories of gender and age are also represented in the celebrity endorser. One extreme representation of maleness is established by the likes of Arnold Schwarzenegger, the other by the likes of Eric McCormack. Ranging between them are Vin Diesel, Ice Cube, Sean Penn, Brendan Fraser, Viggo Mortensen, George Clooney, Denzel Washington, John Cusack, Ed Norton, and David Duchovny. For women, Pamela Anderson and Gwyneth Paltrow represent the two extremes of the continuum. Ranging between them are, perhaps, Catherine Zeta-Jones, Halle Berry, Heather Graham, Liv Tyler, Kate Winslet, Elle Woods, Meg Ryan, Julia Roberts, Cate Blanchett, Annette Bening, and Angela Bassett. Age categories range from the youthful Elijah Wood to the prematurely ancient Danny DeVito.

In addition to these demographic distinctions, the celebrity world also contains a range of personality types. The curmudgeon is represented by Ted Danson, the irritable incompetent by Andy Dick, the good-hearted dimwit by Woody Harrelson, the out-of-control guy by Will Farrell, the out-of-control gal by Courtney Love, the irrepressibly good-humored by Cameron Diaz, the sly and long-suffering by Bill Murray, and the shy and bashful by Renée Zellweger.

The celebrity world also offers a range of lifestyle types. The self-important yuppie is perhaps Kelsey Grammer. The perfect dad was once Robert Young, then Bill Cosby, and now perhaps Jim Belushi. The sunny blonde was once Goldie Hawn and is now Brittany Murphy. The trickster-like mischief-maker is Ashton Kutcher. The demimonde habitué is Steve Buscemi. The man of wisdom and experience is Patrick Stewart. Here, too, the range of depth is extensive.

This review oversimplifies celebrity meanings. Even the most heavily stereotyped celebrity represents not a single meaning but an interconnected set of meanings. Sarah Jessica Parker offers a useful case in point. It is possible to locate her on all the dimensions noted. She is middle class in her status meaning, located toward the "hot" end of the gender continuum, and clearly youthful in attitude if not age. The personality is extroverted and outspoken, the lifestyle open, freewheeling, and exuberant. But plainly, none of these dimensions by itself captures the meanings with which Parker is charged or, more what is more important, the essential configuration of meanings she brings to the endorsement process. For this, it is necessary to characterize the whole person. Parker is observant, risk taking, individualistic, sensual, sexual, witty, irreverent, and liberated. It is this larger package of meanings playing off one another that defines her. These meanings enter into the endorsement process when Parker speaks, for instance, for a corporation or a brand.

These, then, are some of the meanings contained in the celebrity world. They are reviewed here in a cursory, undocumented way. An exact assessment of these meanings awaits empirical study and theoretical development. But enough has been said to indicate that the celebrity world is something rich and more complicated than a collection of merely credible or attractive individuals.

It is, I would argue, precisely the meanings of the celebrity that makes him or her so useful to the endorsement process. An endorsement succeeds when an association is fashioned between the meanings of the cultural world on the one hand and the endorsed product on the other. Not all endorsements succeed in this transfer. Indeed, some are too unsophisticated even to undertake it. But the best endorsements take their power and their efficacy precisely from this: the successful transfer of meaning.

For example, James Garner's endorsement of Mazda succeeds when a transfer takes place between his persona and the Mazda line. It succeeds when the qualities of maturity, Americanness, confidence, good humor, and a certain kind of maleness are made the qualities of the Mazda vehicle. The endorsement succeeds, in other words, when the properties of the man are made the properties of the car.

Meaning Transfer: The General Process

Celebrity endorsement is, in fact, a special instance of a more general process of meaning transfer. I have described this general process elsewhere in some detail (McCracken 1986a, 1988) and review it only briefly here. According to this model, there is a conventional path for the movement of cultural meaning in consumer societies. Meaning begins as something resident in the culturally constituted world (McCracken 1988a, 72–73), in the physical and social world constituted by the categories and principles of the prevailing culture. Meaning then moves to consumer goods and finally to the life of the consumer. Several instruments facilitate this transfer. The movement of meanings from the culturally constituted world to consumer goods is accomplished by advertising and the fashion system. The movement of meanings from consumer goods to the individual consumer is accomplished through the efforts of the consumer. Thus meaning circulates in the consumer society.

Advertising serves as an instrument of meaning transfer in a deceptively simple manner. The transfer process begins when the advertiser identifies the cultural meanings intended for the product (i.e., the type of gender, status, age, lifestyle, and time and place meanings). Or, more technically, the advertiser determines which of the "categories" and "principles" of culture pertain (McCracken 1988a, 73–77). In the language of current advertising practice, the advertiser decides what he or she wishes the product to say.

Once this change has been made, the advertiser surveys the culturally constituted world for the objects, persons, and contexts that already contain and give voice to these meanings. These elements enable the advertiser to bring the selected cultural meanings into the advertisement in visible concrete form. However, the advertiser must portray the elements and the product with consummate care and skill. This care is necessary for two reasons. First, elements come charged with more meanings than are wanted for the product, so the advertiser must evoke some, not all, of the meanings of the elements. Second, elements must be presented in such a way that the similarity between them suggests itself irresistibly to the viewer. This precise combination of elements and product sets the stage for the transfer of meaning from the product to the consumer. Imprecise or unsophisticated combinations discourage it.

Note that there is no necessary or motivated relationship between the meanings and the product. It is not the case that chocolates can be given only certain meanings while tennis rackets can be given only others. Any product can carry virtually any meaning. Goods lend themselves to particular meanings (e.g., chocolates and ceremony), but advertising is such a powerful mechanism of meaning transfer that virtually any product can be made to take virtually any meaning. This property of meaning transfer is still another reason for taking special care in the selection of certain meanings.

Which meanings are chosen for the product will depend on the marketing plan and the sophistication of client, account executive, research providers, and creative team. How well meanings are represented in and manipulated by the advertisement will depend in particular on the creative director and his or her staff. But the final act of meaning transfer is performed by the consumer, who must glimpse in a moment of recognition an essential similarity between the elements and the product in the ad. The consumer suddenly "sees" that the cultural meanings contained in the people, objects, and contexts of the advertisement are also contained in the product. Well-crafted advertisements enable this essentially metaphoric transference. Badly crafted advertisements do not.

Once meanings have been moved into goods, they must also be moved into consumers. Consumers must take possession of these meanings and put them to work in the construction of their notions of the self and the world. They must craft and shape these meanings to fulfill the strategies of meaning-manipulation with which they have constructed their lives. Consumers are constantly finding gender, class, age, lifestyle, time, and place meanings in their possessions and using these meanings to fashion aspects of the self. They are constantly taking possession of cultural principles in consumer goods that help define and fashion the home, the family, and other aspects of the world in which they live. Consumers turn to their goods not only as bundles of utility with which to serve functions and satisfy needs but also as bundles of meaning with which to fashion who they are and the world in which they live (Belk 1988b). When this is done, the movement of meaning is complete. The meaning that began in the culturally constituted world has finally come to rest in the life and experience of the consumer. The cultural circuit is complete.

Thus, in general terms, do culture and consumption interact to create a system of meaning movement in contemporary societies. I have given just one account of this process (McCracken 1986a, 1988b). Readers may wish to consult other accounts of this process (Adams 1973; Holman 1980; Levy 1959; Mick 1986; Prown 1980; Stern 1988; Wallendorf and Arnould 1988), how it is used (Ames 1982; Appadurai 1986; Belk 1982; Csikszentmihalyi and Rochberg-Halton 1981; Solomon 1983), how it enters into the marketing system (Douglas and Isherwood 1978; Gottniener 1985; Hirschman and Holbrook 1981), and how it might best be studied (Levy and Rook 1999; Prown 1982; Sherry 1991; Umiker-Sebeok 1988).

Meaning Transfer: The Celebrity Endorser's Contribution

Celebrity endorsement plays a crucial part in the meaning transfer just described. As figure 8.1 shows, the meaning that begins in the dramatic roles of the celebrity comes, in Stage 1, to reside in the celebrities themselves. In Stage 2, the meaning is transferred when the celebrity enters into an ad-

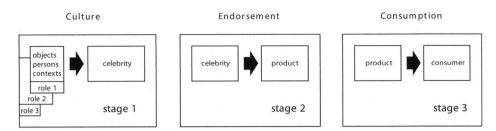

Culture   Endorsement   Consumption

Figure 8.1. Meaning Movement and the Endorsement Process, by Grant McCracken

vertisement with a product. Some of the meanings of the celebrity are now the meanings of the product. In the final stage, the meaning moves from the product to the consumer. Celebrity endorsement makes a very particular contribution to each of these three stages.

Stage 1

Endorsement gives the ad access to a special category of persons from the culturally constituted world. It makes available individuals charged with detailed and powerful meanings. Celebrities are, in this respect, very different from the anonymous models who are normally used to bring meanings to the ad. Celebrities deliver meanings of extra subtlety, depth, and power.

The contrast between celebrities and models is worth developing. It is clear enough that advertisements can undertake meaning transfer without the aid of celebrities. Anonymous actors and models *are* charged with meaning, and, obviously, they are available at a fraction of the cost. For most advertising purposes, the meanings that can be "imported" through an anonymous model are perfectly sufficient. The question, then, is why celebrities should be used for an ad. How does the celebrity "add value" to the meaning-transfer process? What special powers and properties does the celebrity bring to the advertisement, to the product, and, ultimately, the consumer?

Anonymous models offer demographic information, such as distinctions of gender, age, and status, but these useful meanings are relatively imprecise and blunt. Celebrities offer all these meanings with special precision. Furthermore, celebrities offer a range of personality and lifestyle meanings that the model cannot provide. Finally, celebrities offer configurations of meaning that models can never possess. No mere model could bring to Baly-Matrix the properties that Cher delivers, nor could any model have summoned the impatient, time-tested integrity John Houseman gave to the Smith Barney line, "We make money the old-fashioned way—we earn it." Only a man playing Houseman's roles in the way Houseman played them could empower the slogan as Houseman did. Celebrities have particular configurations of meanings that cannot be found elsewhere.

In addition, celebrities are more powerful media than anonymous models. Even when they deliver meanings that can be found elsewhere, they deliver them more powerfully. Celebrities evoke the meanings in their personas with greater vividness and clarity. Models are, after all, merely "borrowing" the meanings they bring to the ad. The celebrity, however, speaks with meanings of long acquaintance. Celebrities "own" their meanings because they have created them on the public stage by dint of intense and repeated performance. Audrey Hepburn delivered "elegance" much more vividly than even the most elegant model. She did so because she had enacted and absorbed this elegance by performing it on stage and screen.

Celebrities draw these powerful meanings from the roles they assume in their television, movie, military, athletic, and other careers. These careers act very much like large ads, as Stage 1 of figure 8.1 shows. Each new dramatic role brings the celebrity into contact with a range of objects, persons, and contexts. Out of these objects, persons, and contexts are transferred meanings that then reside in the celebrity. When the celebrity brings these meanings into an ad, they are, in a sense, merely passing along meanings with which they have been charged by another meaning-transfer process. Or, to put this another way, the meaning that the celebrity endorsement gives to the product was generated in distant movie performances, political campaigns, or athletic achievements.

It is interesting that celebrities appear largely unaware of their part in the meaning-transfer process. Nowhere is this better illustrated than in their concern for typecasting. Actors say they dislike being cast repeatedly in the same role, claiming that typecasting limits their career and creative options. What they do not see is that their careers, their art form, and the endorsement process all depend upon typecasting, at least a mild form of it.

The North American movie demands the participation of actors charged with meanings; it needs actors to bring their own meanings with them to a part. These meanings simplify the movie's dramatic and expository task and give it substance and direction. Bill Murray, John Cusack, Tom Cruise, Susan Sarandon, and Tim Robbins all carry meanings with them from role to role. One of the troubles with unknown actors and actresses is precisely that we are unable to grasp what they stand for.

There are a few exceptions to this pattern. A few actors and actresses are "rinsed" of meaning between roles and, as a result, bring a new persona to each new film. Only an actress of the caliber of Meryl Streep is capable of earning (and exploiting) this privilege. For most, a mild case of typecasting is not just the consequence but actually the very cause of their participation in the Hollywood system. We may expect this effect to diminish as movie-goers become more sophisticated as viewers and Hollywood films become more sophisticated as an expressive medium.

More to the present point, it is precisely this typecasting that makes celebrities so useful to the endorsement process. It is the accumulated meanings of celebrities that make them so potent a source of significance. Meryl Streep has limited value as a celebrity endorser because she is largely free of accumulated meanings. The same might be said of Ian McKellen. Without typecasting, actors are unable to bring clear and unambiguous meanings to the products they endorse. Without typecasting, they have no meanings to give the transfer process.

Stage 2

Ideally, the choice of particular celebrities is based on the meanings they epitomize and on a sophisticated marketing plan. In the best of all possible worlds, the marketing/advertising firm first would determine the symbolic properties sought for the product (having determined which symbolic properties are in fact sought by the consumer). It would then consult a roster of celebrities and the meanings they make available, and, taking into account budget and availability constraints, would choose the celebrity who best represents the appropriate symbolic properties at the lowest possible cost. At present, no roster exists, so advertising firms are forced to rely on a very general rendering of what meanings are available to them in the celebrity world and where these meanings are located.

Once the celebrity is chosen, an advertising campaign must then identify and deliver these meanings to the product. It must capture *all* the meanings it wishes to obtain from the celebrity and leave no salient meanings untapped. Furthermore, it must capture *only* the meanings it wishes to obtain from the celebrity. All celebrities will encompass in their range of cultural significance some meanings that are not sought for the product. Care must be taken to see that these unwanted meanings are kept out of the evoked set.

This will be accomplished by filling the advertisement with people, objects, contexts, and copy that have the same meanings as the celebrity. These elements cue, by the principle of redundancy, the consumer to the salient message. They help select the exact set of meanings that are sought from the celebrity.

The ad will sometimes operate on the meanings of the celebrity and may even modestly help transform them. It is interesting to note, for instance, how novel treatments of Liz Hurley's appearance in the current Estée Lauder White Linen campaign "reposition" her beauty and redefine its meaning (cf.

Wells 1989, 72). This campaign deliberately makes Hurley's beauty more classic, more elegant, and therefore more appropriate to the Estée Lauder White Linen product line. In other words, an advertising campaign can sometimes have the effect of a new dramatic role, bringing the celebrity into contact with symbolic materials that change the meanings contained in their persona. Celebrities have been known to exploit this effect by choosing their endorsement to tune their image. Typically, however, the ad is not trying to transform the meanings of the celebrity. In most cases, it seeks only to transfer them.

Finally, the ad must be designed to suggest the essential similarity between the celebrity and the product so that the consumer will be able to take the last step in the meaning-transfer process. In a perfect world, copy testing is then used to judge whether the ad succeeds in this regard. When assurance is forthcoming, the second stage of transfer is complete and the ad is put before the consumer. The consumer suddenly "sees" the similarity between the celebrity and the product and is prepared to accept that the meanings in the celebrity are in the product. If all has gone smoothly, the properties of James Garner are now the properties of Mazda.

Stage 3

This is the final stage of meaning transfer. How does the process of celebrity endorsement help consumers get meanings out of the product into their lives? How, in other words, does an endorsement by James Garner help the properties of the Mazda become the properties of the consumer?

Consumers are constantly canvassing the object world for goods with useful meanings. They use them to furnish certain aspects of the self and the world. The object world, as we have seen, gives them access to workable ideas of gender, class, age, personality, and lifestyle, in addition to cultural principles of great number and variety. The material world of consumer goods offers a vast inventory of possible selves and thinkable worlds. Consumers are constantly rummaging here.

We know that this final stage of the transfer process is complicated and sometimes difficult. It is not enough for the consumer merely to own an object to take possession of its meanings or to incorporate these meanings into the self. The meanings of the object do not merely lift off the object and enter into the consumer's concept of self and world. There is, in other words, no automatic transfer of meaning or any automatic transformation of the self. The consumer must claim the meanings and then work with them.

We have some general sense that rituals play an important part in this process. Consumers must claim, exchange, care for, and use the consumer good to appropriate its meanings (Cheal 1988; McCracken 1988a; Rook 1985). We know that they must select and combine these meanings in a process of experimentation (Belk 1988b; Wallendorf and Arnould 1988). But this process is still very much terra incognito from a scholarly point of view. Of all the topics in the culture and consumer-behavior portfolio, this one is the most neglected. A cultural understanding of celebrity endorsement illuminates this little-known terrain.

Celebrities play a role in the final stage of meaning transfer because they have created a self. They have done so publicly, in the first stage of the meaning transfer process, out of bits and pieces of each role in their careers. All the world has watched them take shape. From darkened theaters, consumers have looked on as celebrities have selected and combined the meanings contained in the objects, people, events, and drama around them. The self so created is almost always attractive and accomplished.

Celebrities Build Selves Well

The constructed self makes the celebrity a kind of exemplary inspirational figure to the consumer. Consumers are themselves constantly moving symbolic properties out of consumer goods into their lives to construct aspects of self and world. Not surprisingly, they admire individuals who have accomplished this task and accomplished it well. Celebrities are proof that the process works. Celebrities have been where the consumer is going. They have done in Stage 1 what the consumer is now laboring to do in Stage 3 of the meaning-transfer process. Or, to put this another way, consumers are all laboring to perform their own Stage 1 construction of the self out of the meanings supplied by previous and present roles and the meanings accessible to them there.

But this is more than just a formal parallel between celebrities and consumers in Stages 1 and 3. The consumer does not revere the celebrity merely because the celebrity has done what the consumer wants to do but also because the celebrity actually supplies certain meanings in the consumer. Celebrities create a self out of the elements put at their disposal in dramatic roles, fashioning cultural meanings into a practicable form. When they enter the endorsement process, they make these meanings available in material form to the consumer. Consumers are grateful for these meanings and wish to build a self from them. The celebrity is supplying not just an example of self-creation but the very stuff with which this difficult act is undertaken.

Let's return to the James Garner example once more. Consumers have watched James Garner fashion what Schudson (1984) calls the "fictive self" out of the objects, events, and contexts of his screen life. Garner has given them a dramatic example of the very act in which consumers are themselves engaged. Furthermore, Garner has put useful and interesting meanings at their disposal. He has given them a vivid, well-organized, and "performable" self. This film persona (and its successor in the television world, Thomas Magnum) offers a self that is capable (but occasionally incompetent), forthright, and unassuming and almost always the master of his fate (except when conspired against by comically or otherwise imperfectly malevolent forces). The Garner self is diverse, balanced, and, most of all, workable.

But there is a second, in some ways more interesting, way in which celebrities play the role of a "superconsumer." This occurs when the film persona of the celebrity consists not merely of the presentation of an interesting film persona but actually of the creation of a self that is new and innovative. Most film stars bring to the screen a self, cut whole cloth, from the standard American personality inventory. But there are a few who have undertaken a much more difficult and creative innovation in which personality elements are created or dramatically reconfigured.

In this highly creative mode, the celebrity becomes a kind of experiment in self-construction. This makes the celebrity very powerful indeed. He or she has become an inventor of a new self that the consumer can use. An example of such an act of self-invention was the character portrayed by Bruce Willis in the 1980s television series *Moonlighting*. A more contemporary example might be Tony Shalhoub's character in the series *Monk*. Willis helped invent a version of maleness, a way of interacting with others, and a posture toward the world that held appeal for certain consumers. In his creation of the character David Addison, Willis created a character responsive to the feminism of the 1970s and 1980s and in the process put useful meanings at the disposal of the male and female consumer. For his part, Shalhoub invents quite a different posture, one that is nervous and fearful and to this extent equally in tune with his newly anxious times. In a sense, both actors product-test notions of the self for a group of consumers who are themselves engaged in an act of experimentation. The consumer may now identify with both characters. In the Shalhoub case, they may empathize with the neurosis of poor Adrian Monk and note with satisfaction that however neurotic they may be, they will never be quite as bad as that.

The celebrity world is, to this extent, a realm of experimentation in which actors sometimes do more than merely play out cultural categories and principles. Sometimes they also engage in innovations, as when Doris Roberts creates new notions of the elderly, the stars of *Everyone Loves Raymond* work out certain notions of family interaction, and rock stars invent and reinvent the possibilities of the adolescent self. This experimentation makes the celebrity an especially potent source of meaning for the marketing system and a guide to the process of self-invention in which all consumers must engage (McCracken 2001).

Celebrities serve the final stage of meaning transfer because they are "super-consumers" of a kind. They are exemplary figures because they are seen to have created the clear, coherent, and powerful selves that everyone seeks. They are compelling partners to the meaning-transfer process because they demonstrate so vividly the process by which these meanings can be assembled and some of the novel shapes into which they can be assembled.

But who really needs the meanings created by celebrities? We know that certain groups are especially keen on using them. Solomon (1983) observed that anyone undergoing any sort of role change or status mobility is especially dependent on the meanings of their possessions. I (1987) have tried to show the importance of this meaning to those who are moving from one age category to another. O'Guinn, Faber, and Rice (1985) have pointed out that those who are newly arrived to a culture are also heavily indebted to the meanings contained in the consumer society and the celebrity world.

But it has also been asserted that everyone in a modern developed society is underspecified in this sense. As Belk (1984a) and Sahlins (1976) have argued, modern Western selves are deliberately left blank so that the individual may exercise the right of choice. Also pertinent is the relative collapse of institutions that once supplied the self with meaning and definition (e.g., the family, church, and community). Working together, individualism and alienation have conspired to give individuals new freedom to define matters of gender, class, age, personality, and lifestyle. The freedom to choose is now also an obligation to decide, and this makes us especially eager consumers of the symbolic meanings contained in celebrities and the goods they endorse.

This, in broad detail, suggests how celebrity endorsement operates as a process of meaning transfer. We have reviewed each of the three stages of this process, considering in turn how meaning moves into the persona of the celebrity, how it then moves from the celebrity into the product, and, finally, how it moves from the product into the consumer. Celebrities are, by this account, key players in the meaning-transfer process.

The Real Consumer Society, the Real Celebrity Culture

This discussion of the cultural aspects of celebrity endorsements enables us to address one or two larger issues in the field of consumer research. More precisely, it carries larger implications for the debate that now rages about the nature of the consumer society and its celebrity culture. One party to this debate argues that the consumer society encourages low artistic standards, materialistic preoccupations, and an affection for the trivial and unimportant (e.g., Barnouw 1978; Ewen 1976; Lasch 1978; Pollay 1986). The consumer society has been declared the domain of the Philistine.

The North American preoccupation with movie stars is a favorite target (Ewen 1988, 92–100). North America is accused of having a trivially minded fascination with the affairs of the rich and famous. This fascination is cited as evidence of the depths to which popular culture is destined to fall, the bankruptcy of North American life, and the shallowness of the individual who lives therein.

These arguments are, no doubt, very satisfying from a political and polemical point of view, but they do not reckon well with the cultural realities of the celebrity world as described here. These criticisms fail to see that Hollywood, the star system, and celebrity endorsement are all profoundly cultural enterprises and that our fascination with celebrities reflects our involvement in the meaning-transfer system they accomplish.

The celebrity world is one of the most potent sources of cultural meaning at the disposal of the marketing system and the individual consumer. It is, therefore, not at all surprising that we should care about celebrities and the lives they lead. It would be much more surprising if we were indifferent and somehow above an interest in the world of stars. And very much more surprising if we took our lead from the example set by university professors and other culture critics. As all of us labor to fashion manageable selves, it is inevitable that we should cultivate a knowledge of this world. More plainly, North Americans are not "star crazy" but merely active consumers of the meanings that are made available by the celebrity world.

There is indeed a delicate and thoroughgoing relationship between the culture, the entertainment industries, and the marketing system in modern North America. We are beginning to understand what this relationship is and how it works. We must hope that the first victims of this emerging understanding will be the glib assertions that characterize North American society as thoughtlessly materialistic and North American consumers as the narcissistic, simple-minded, manipulated playthings of the marketplace. Celebrity endorsement and the marketing system are cultural undertakings in which meaning is constantly in circulation. As we begin to render a more-sophisticated account of how these systems work, we will begin to see that North American culture and commerce are more interesting and less manipulated than its critics have guessed.

Future Research

The cultural perspective suggests three avenues of research. The first of these is a thorough assessment of how meanings move in the celebrity world. We know that each role, event, or accomplishment in the career of the celebrity changes the meanings of the celebrity, but we do not know precisely how this takes place. We do not know what the precise relationship is between the role, event, and accomplishment on the one hand and the celebrity on the other. Nor do we know how meaning transfers from one to the other. We need a precise idea of how meaning comes to exist in celebrities.

The first avenue of research has a methodological component as well. We need an instrument that allows us to determine methodologically the meanings that adhere in celebrities. We know that the meanings that exist in celebrities are extraordinarily numerous and various, but we have yet to devise an instrument that allows us to detect and survey these meanings. Only some delicate combination of qualitative and quantitative methods will work here.

Once an instrument is devised, certain crucial empirical work can be undertaken. We can determine the meanings that any individual celebrity brings to the endorsement process and survey the meanings that exist in the entire world of endorsement. A typography of the meanings contained throughout the worlds of sports, politics, business, art, the military, television, and Hollywood is possible and will give us a systematic sense of the meanings available.

The second avenue of research should concentrate on a more precise determination of how advertising accomplishes the transfer of meaning from celebrity to product. How do creative directors identify and catalog the symbolic properties contained in the celebrity world? What are the rhetorical and visual devices by which this celebrity meaning is transferred within the advertisement? What celebrity meanings are seen to work best with what products? What is the process by which consumers contribute to the meaning-transfer process? It is also relevant to ask how a celebrity changes his or her stock of symbolic properties by participating in an advertisement.

The third avenue of research deals with how consumers appropriate and use the meanings that come to them as a result of endorsement. How does the consumer take possession of this meaning? How does the consumer use the meaning of the celebrity in the construction of self and world? It may be that some consumers routinely canvass the symbolic meanings of one or several celebrities to take advantage of the experimentation taking place there. Do consumers set up long-term relationships with a single celebrity and systematically "download" all the new meanings this celebrity makes available through new roles and endorsements? Do consumers follow a variety of celebrities from whom they draw a variety of meanings? What happens to consumers when celebrities are transformed by disgrace or new fame? We must begin to chart what becomes of the cultural meanings after they leave the endorsement and enter into the life of the consumer.

These are all questions that need to be answered for us to understand the process of celebrity endorsement in fine detail. They are the research opportunities the meaning-transfer perspective brings to light.

The meaning-transfer approach casts some doubt on the sufficiency of the source models' explanation of celebrity endorsement. But it does not prevent us from asking the questions that have been asked in this tradition. For instance, it is still possible to talk about the issue of credibility or other questions relevant to source research. It is still possible to see that some celebrities are more credible than others and that each celebrity is more credible for some promotional purposes than others.

What the meaning-transfer model does is shift the terms of this debate. When we consider credibility in this new context, we are no longer talking about the manner in which celebrities communicate information but rather about the manner in which they communicate meaning. Credibility now turns on which meanings celebrities make available to endorsements and how well they transfer these meanings to the product. Examples of this cultural credibility are not hard to find. John Houseman was the compelling choice for a Smith Barney advertisement. The actor chosen to succeed him, Leo McKern, carried different meanings in a different configuration. He was, in a word, less credible. The Smith Barney slogan was, perhaps, changed and diminished as a result.

The symbolic or cultural perspective (McCracken 1988a) allows for a new credibility measure of a different sort. There is, for instance, no longer any single kind of credibility. A celebrity can be extremely credible for certain meanings and not at all credible for others. Plainly, this aspect of credibility cannot be captured by the theories and instruments conventionally used. To investigate the celebrity endorsement from the symbolic or cultural point of view, a new set of questions and methodologies must be investigated.

Part Five
Museums

Strategy:

This section opens with a personal confrontation with Uncle Meyer's wallet. It records the character of a curatorial object and its ability to recall the extraordinary events that brought one man out of the Old World into the New.

The article examines the power of objects in a more formal museum context. It notes particularly the contest that takes place in one museum between curators who insist on one set of meanings and museum visitors who insist on another.

What objects mean and how they mean is so little understood that wallets can have mysterious powers and museum curators can fail to engage their visitors.

In this section, we continue our transition into practical meaning-management issues. The article reads as an object lesson, an example of how not to engage in meaning management in the museum world. It also offers a glimpse of what the museum might have looked like if constructed from a more sophisticated meaning-management point of view.

9 The Strange Power of Uncle Meyer's Wallet

Uncle Meyer died in his sleep on August 4, 1990. He was 82 and lived with his wife in a north Toronto high-rise. He worked as a volunteer at an animal shelter. He went for long walks. He was a truly sweet guy, but not a very candid one. He didn't wear his heart on his sleeve. He didn't regale you with the "Uncle Meyer" story.

Except once. One night after dinner, Uncle Meyer brought out his photographs. My wife Judy and I froze. This is the relative's great fear: caught without defenses when the photographs come out.

Uncle Meyer did it perfectly. He just materialized at the dinner table, photos in hand. I saw Judy's eyes widen. I felt myself struggling for an excuse. Weren't we double-parked in a fire zone on a traffic island? Didn't the sitter need a drive home to Rochester? Uncle Meyer had us. We bowed to the hard dictates of good form.

And there it was. Lying under the photographs was a wine-colored canvas wallet, about the size of a paperback. It was stitched together boldly and in place crudely with thick green thread. "What's this?" I asked, already in the object's thrall. Uncle Meyer looked up at me and then back at the wallet. "Oh, that," he said, and stopped.

I picked it up, the anthropologist suddenly on alert. The wallet was what we might call, after Proust, a "Madeleine" object: an object charged with meaning and power.

Madeleine objects have lots of different powers. Sometimes they cut away the present time and place and transport us—in Proust's case to the exquisite embrace of a childhood bed and maternal attentions. But sometimes they have a different influence altogether. Sometimes they come at us like something airborne and night-flying.

Uncle Meyer's wallet was one of these. It reached up and gave me a crack across the snout. The last time I'd seen anything like this, I'd been peering into a museum display case, a Yale University art historian beside me. We had been doing what academics tend to do, parading Ivy League manners, elegant theories, and artful phrases.

We stopped to comment airily on something and an Inuit mask came hurling up out of the case like a shark out of water. The voracious energy of the thing! It consumed our manners, our theories, and our language. Hah! Our pretensions fled in terror, and we were suddenly bewildered little men blinking stupidly. Uncle Meyer's canvas wallet had something of this power. It grabbed at the senses and made the world drain away.

These Madeleine objects are still not much understood. We have all seen them. But they continue to make a mockery of even our grandest theory. Once I thought this was because they had the power of an irreducible object, a sheer "thingness" before which ideas seem empty, mere, abstract. But Uncle Meyer's wallet made me think again. Madeleine objects overwhelm theories because they are more powerfully abstract than any theory could ever be. Uncle Meyer's wallet was an open cut on the surface of our reality, a hole through which culture came spilling into life.

But there was a more tactile power to it, too. Somehow it managed to be both personal and completely traditional. Obviously someone had made it, carefully placing each stitch. But the wallet conformed to a pattern to which generations had contributed. It let you see both the person and the tradition from which it came.

All this was nothing compared to its intimacy. This little canvas envelope somehow transmitted the emotions that were present at its making. You could sense the care taken to create something beautiful and the comfort it gave its maker.

And there was anxiety. The wallet had not been easy to make. It told you that the maker was in the clutches of a terrible emotion that drove the stitches in one direction and then another. In short, the wallet howled because it was charged with rich and difficult meanings that it somehow conveyed as a single sensation. To see the object was to be invaded by its meanings.

Uncle Meyer was slow to tell the story, but eventually he did. The wallet was stitched sixty-five years ago by his mother. She made it to hold his passport and the Canadian visa that would see him safely out of a land of terror, pogroms, and state-sanctioned antisemitism.

Meyer was then 17. He could leave Russia. His family could not. His father died of natural causes, he told me. "My mother, well, the Nazis . . . I don't know what happened."

He arrived in Canada in 1925, going first to Montreal and then to Edmonton to work for a relative. He spent the early years moving back and forth across the country, a member of a team of Jewish roughnecks who worked on the construction of large buildings from Victoria to Kingston.

There was, after all, nothing dreary or domestic about Uncle Meyer's photographs. They were taken from the dizzying heights of construction sites: the Banff Springs Hotel, the Vancouver Medical-Dental Building, grain elevators across the prairies. He recalled painting those elevators. He and his pals liked to ride the wooden platforms when they banged around in high winds.

Meyer's canvas wallet brought him to another country and another life. He lived, despite his roughneck heroics, safe from harm. He escaped the holocaust that claimed his family.

He had come away from his home and his family with a few clothes and not much more. As his mother prepared him for his departure, as she prepared herself for the fact that she would likely never see him again, she took up thread and canvas. She made a wallet for his passport so that her reckless, bounding son would not lose the paper that would see him into safety. She produced an envelope to see Meyer into the envelope of the New World. Meyer made it. The wallet worked.

10 Culture and culture at the Royal Ontario Museum

An Anthropological Approach to a Marketing Problem

Introduction

The boy beside me is probably 8 years old. He is standing in front of a panel at the exhibit *Sharks! Fact and Fantasy.* This panel is meant to sum up a theme of the show: that sharks have more to fear from humans than humans do from them. At the top of the panel is a question, "What is one of the greatest dangers to sharks?" Below, there's a hinged flap. The visitor is meant to lift the flap and look into a mirror it conceals. Behold, that most dangerous species, Homo sapiens.

But things aren't going well. The boy keeps looking at the question and lifting the flap. He looks puzzled. I feel I should intercede.

"Can you read the question?"

"Yes," he says, and dutifully reads the question aloud: "What is one of the greatest dangers to sharks?"

He gives me a skeptical look, and asks, reluctantly, "Mirrors?"

I recall this episode not for the usual reasons: to demonstrate that museum professionals are sometimes too clever for their own good or that good intentions cannot protect us from the demon of miscommunication. I recall it to suggest there may be an invisible rift on the museum floor, that museums and visitors may be parting company.

The problem, I will suggest, is a cultural one. The museum constructs itself according to one set of cultural assumptions. Visitors, increasingly, come to the museum bearing another. The result, not infrequently, is mutual incomprehension. Too often, visitors gaze on museum creations thoughtfully, carefully, patiently . . . and miss the point entirely. More and more often, they do not come at all.

There are now, to put the matter plainly, two models at work in the museum world. There is the "traditional" museum culture which holds many curators, designers, and administrators in its gravitational thrall. I will call this the *preferment* model. And there is a consumer model that is being smuggled into the museum by its visitors in the form of old and new expectations. I will call this the *transformation* model.

Anthropological Research on the Museum Floor

This essay reports anthropological research conducted at the Royal Ontario Museum (ROM) by the author over three years, 1993–1995. During this period, I was on staff at the ROM as director of the Institute of Contemporary Culture. Several qualitative methods were used including depth, walk-about, and intercept interviews (McCracken 1988d). Interviews were conducted in respondents' homes and in the following permanent galleries and special exhibits of the ROM: *Ancient Egypt, Nubia, Canadiana, East Asia, European, Indigenous Peoples, Mammals, Birds, Dinosaurs, Evolution, Reptiles,* and "From the Collections" galleries as well as the Beny Gallery of the Institute of Contemporary Culture, the *Bat Cave,* the *Hardwood Forest,* the *Ming Tomb,* the *Heritage Gallery of Canada's Peoples,* and *Mankind Discovering,* the ROM's introductory exhibit.

Interviews were conducted with habitual, frequent, occasional visitors and with those who did not visit at all. Two groups of respondents were deliberately excluded: tourists (a captive audience for the ROM) and children on school tours (captives of another kind). Some interviews, especially the in-home ones, were relatively long in duration (e.g., two hours). Others, especially the "intercepts," were short (e.g., ten minutes). In total, sixty interviews were conducted with some seventy-five respondents over some twenty-four hours of contact.

The purpose of the research was a traditional anthropological one. It was to listen to visitors at length and in depth. It was to invite them to talk about the museum and its exhibits at their own pace, in their own way, in their own language. It was to watch them inside the museum as they experienced its entrance hall, signage, exhibit space, exhibit content, and other visitors. It was, finally, to see whether the cultural categories and assumptions according to which the visitor sees and experiences the museum could be inferred and laid bare. In sum, this study was designed to undertake research until, to adapt a phrase from the historians, the investigator could "hear the respondent thinking." It was to discover the visitor's point of view.

Glimpsing the museum from the visitor's point of view can be strange, even irritating. As we shall see, the visitor often cannot see what the museum believes to be obvious, insists on what the museum believes to be irrelevant, conjoins what the museum believes to be distinct, distinguishes what the museum believes to be indistinguishable, and otherwise so reconfigures the field of assumptions according to which the museum is constituted that we can only be astonished. We wander *their* museum in search of something familiar and occasionally we are rewarded with common terrain. More often, we find ourselves in a world that is sometimes vertiginously strange. It might as well be another world. It might as well be another planet. As in any anthropological study, a word of caution is in order. Some of what follows will strike some readers as peculiar. Your patience is requested.

Five Ethnographic Sketches

Here are five sketches from the ethnographer's notebook. They are carefully chosen and designed to make the analysis to follow appear irresistibly sensible.

Robby and His Dad

When I "intercept" Robby and his dad, they are engaged in close conversation about medieval Islamic armor. (All names used in this essay are fictional.) As it turns out, Robby has a school project on Marco Polo, so he's on the lookout for useful data and photographs. Robby comes to the ROM several times a year. His favorite exhibits are Dinosaurs and the Bat Cave. His favorite temporary exhibit was the recent *Sharks!* exhibit. He is a passionate, attentive visitor. He speaks with practiced scorn for his 4-year-old brother, who "just walks through" exhibits without really looking at them. A clear case of pearls before swine. The ROM is one of the great pleasures in Robby's life.

GM: How does the ROM feel compared to other places you go?
Robby: It's kinda like [brief pause] it's really interesting because you can see things for real instead of just pictures on TV. It makes a lot of more sense [*sic*].
GM: It makes the things you are studying at school more clear?
Robby: Yeah, I understand them a lot more if I saw what it really looks like instead of just pictures [*sic*].

Robby's father regards the ROM as a kind of annex to his son's education at school and home. And he agrees with Robby. The important thing about the ROM is that it makes knowledge tangible.

Dad: Robert is talking about his Marco Polo project at school. Well, we went upstairs and *saw* a bolt of silk and *saw* gems and spices: the kinds of things that were the essence of the trade. But he can see them physically and it helps him understand what he's reading. [Emphasis in original.]

Robby's world is blessed with a hundred distractions—movies from Disney, special effects from Industrial Light and Magic, and video games from

Xbox—not to mention the usual enthusiasms of an 8-year-old—playing soccer, watching basketball, eating cereal, riding bikes, reading comic books, arguing with his sister, building forts, wrestling with the family dog. That the ROM should be visible in a life so crowded with stimulation is remarkable. That it should have powers of enchantment is extraordinary. But Robby is unambiguous.

GM: You like discovering new things at the museum?
Robby: *Yes.* [Nods emphatically.]
GM: You do.
Robby: Yeah, because sometimes we miss exhibits and we promise we'll [breaks off] when we go back and see something we didn't see before and it gets [breaks off] and then [lowers voice to excited whisper] ooo, maybe there's something *more.*

All children should feel about museums the way Robby feels about the ROM.

Linda

I did two interviews with Linda: one in her home and one walkabout interview at the ROM. In both cases, Linda's 10-year-old daughter, Jenny, joined us. For the walkabout, we met in the entrance hall. I asked Linda and Jenny to walk through the museum as if I were not with them. This is an obvious and awkward fiction. It is impossible for respondents to forget they are being accompanied and scrutinized. They are, after all, being followed by a man with a camera who keeps asking, "So what are you thinking now?" But the fiction is a useful one. This is a useful way of understanding the visitors' experience on the floor (Ericsson and Simon 1980).

Linda decides to begin her trip by asking a staff member at the front desk what is new at the museum. As it happens, the staff member is a student from the nearby university and she suggests the best thing at the museum is the results of her professor's recent investigations now on display on the Mediterranean World floor. Linda is captured by this and decides to take her advice. Off we go.

As we leave the entrance hall, we approach an exhibit called *Mankind Discovering.* This was the museum's introductory exhibit. It summarized the process of discovery by which museum objects are collected and analyzed. It took the form of a large contained walkway in the shape of a U. The visitor entered the U at one end and exited at the other. I watch to see if Linda will stop to investigate. She does not.

In transit, Linda describes her general expectation of the museum world.

Linda: This place is so packed with potential things to learn that . . . it makes you come away thinking "I have *so* much to learn." Usually I come away with something that's interesting. One time I was here they had interesting costumes from all over the world. And I went home and started *sewing*. I don't think it was a conscious thing but . . . usually you come away with a little project or something you want to learn something more about. [Emphasis in original.]

We make our way to Mediterranean World, but by the time we get there Linda has forgotten her objective. She is now in the mode often exhibited by museum visitors, a kind of "forward-floating" motion. The visitor moves as if goal-oriented but demonstrates by facial expression and a constant scanning of the environment that they have not fixed on a destination. They are simultaneously purposeful and directionless.

We find our way eventually to the Egyptian gallery and here things begin to go subtly wrong. This is manifest, first of all, in Linda's gait. She slows virtually to a stop. She is no longer floating but stalled. She's found an exhibit, but she cannot find a place to *begin*. I ask her what she's thinking. She says, "It's a little overwhelming, a *lot* overwhelming." There is too much information, too much reading. But, she says, she'll "endure" it. After all, she points out, she's with her daughter.

And the difficulty then compounds itself. Linda says it's hard to understand what's being said in some of the text panels. (The problem is not reading the card but in grasping fully what it means.) So when Linda's daughter asks for explanation, Linda is uncertain of her answer ("I hope I'm covering it"). Sometimes she will ask for the assistance of museum personnel but this has problems of its own ("I feel like an idiot because it [the knowledge] is there but somehow it doesn't make sense to me.").

And things get worse. Linda is now beginning to hydroplane across the surface of the exhibit as uncertainty and avoidance interact. The more she meets with resistance in the exhibit, the more tempted she is to keep moving. The more she keeps moving, the more she feels she is failing her child's and her own expectations. Difficulty begets movement, movement begets self-repudiation. Linda is now caught in a self-perpetuating cycle of regret.

At the museum entrance Linda told me the museum often made her feel "small." The museum can be a daunting place, she said, a test that discovers her inadequacies. This gallery, I now gather, is exactly what she means. The Egyptian gallery feels diminishing. The early promise of the museum ("this place is so packed with potential things to learn") is beginning to evaporate. The possibility of learning (and the visitor's *ability* to learn) has been thrown into question. Linda is beginning to feel bad about herself. More exactly, the museum has succeeded in making Linda feel bad about herself.

The gloominess of these reflections is dispelled soon enough. Linda discovers the Tomb of Kitines in the Egyptian gallery. She is enchanted. She and Jenny walk through the doorway several times. Linda is much less nervous about "miscommunicating" the significance of the exhibit to her daughter. Engagement is reestablished. We're on our way again. Mother and daughter stop briefly to consider the study of ancient Egyptian clothing. Jenny points out that the male costume looks like her brother's karate outfit.

We make our way out of the Egyptian gallery and down to the second floor, which houses the "Life Sciences" collections of the museum. As we enter this gallery, Linda and her daughter begin to walk with new energy and enthusiasm.

GM: Linda, it feels like she [Jenny] is picking up the pace a little bit.
Linda: I am, too.
GM: Are you?
Linda: This is more my speed. It's more comfortable.
GM: Why?
Linda: I don't know. It feels more real!

Once again we are confronted by an embarrassment of riches. But this time the exhibit offers engagement as surely as the Egyptian gallery resisted it. We proceed to the Bat Cave and then to the Hardwood Forest. Linda has no difficulty finding a place to begin here. She answers her daughter's questions with great confidence. She is no longer hydroplaning. She has one or two criticisms of the exhibits. She doubts the value of all the Latin ("completely unnecessary for the average Joe"). Her daughter does a wordless point, which indicates, normally, the presence of something alarming. (More on this gesture below.) But in fact, mother and daughter are now more curious and relaxed. As Linda points out, everyone in these galleries seems more relaxed.

Barbara

It turns out Barbara hasn't been to the ROM in over twenty years. I am alarmed to hear this. She is exactly the kind of person the museum should reach with ease. She is a high-ranking executive at a large financial institution, well educated, accomplished, smart, and curious. I can hear myself thinking, "If the museum can't make contact with this woman, God help them with the rest of the world." In point of fact, nothing the museum has done in the last twenty years has gotten her attention with the exception of a show about contemporary teens, but even this failed to bring her in.

We begin our walkabout in the entrance hall of the exhibit, and the first thing that captures her attention is the totem (i.e., crest) pole in the stone stairwell. She remembers this from childhood visits. It evokes a sense of mystery, the art of Emily Carr, the "coolness of the forest." She looks to see if the Egyptian mummy is still here (it isn't). She remembers *that* as dry and frightening: "little fingers going [shudders] . . . a little hand comes sneaking out."

The totem pole and the mummy mark for Barbara the two extremes of the ROM. You are greeted by the "promise of the Pacific Northwest and the next thing you know everything is bleached bones in the sand." What could be "cool, moist, lush" ends up being "desert-like, dry, sandy." Barbara's prevailing sense of the museum is precisely this, that there is something desiccating about the institution. The image shows even in her description of museum visits: "My impression is that you get tired very quickly. It's something about the air, your eyes start blinking."

We move to *Mankind Discovering,* the U-shaped exhibit at the start of the museum. Barbara sees it and stops. "I see the entrance and I say 'I'm going to get stuck in a maze for 40 minutes.' " And now she is stalled and not sure where to go. I ask her why she is hesitating and she says, "I hope that I don't end up somewhere backing out apologizing. There's that hushed church-like feel. You might interrupt the service."

There are many reasons Barbara has not been here in twenty years. The ROM strikes her, to use her language, as dry, moldering, sleepy, old-fashioned, academic, and out of touch with contemporary realities. But most important, she sees it as an institution that takes an essentially patronizing attitude toward its visitors.

Barbara: There's a didacticism that I reject: "You don't know this, you should learn this." You think, "Ah, I'm an adult and don't *need* to learn this."

For Barbara, the ROM always seems to give off the impression that it knows better than she does. Barbara must play the supplicant, the ROM the grandee.

The Guys

On one of my intercept interviews, I encounter three young men who have just seen the museum and are about to leave. They are in their late twenties. Two are home from graduate school for the holidays. They tell me they haven't been to the ROM in many years. Their visit to the ROM seemed like a good way of filling time. ("We have the whole week to kill.")

As we talk I begin to see that the guys have a special attitude toward the ROM. They see the museum as an *amusement*. As it turns out, they have come in an ironic frame of mind, to mock and ridicule. They see the ROM as a kind of Larry "Bud" Melman (the character once featured on David Letterman): gauche, earnest, utterly unhip—and hopelessly unaware that any of this is so. The museum is, to use the once-fashionable term of affection/derision, "cheesy."

One guy: We are much better for having come to the museum. [Much laughter.]

The guys tell me they were surprised. Some of the museum was actually quite engaging. They particularly liked the "historical rooms" and the European armor as well as the Bat Cave and the Bird Room. And there were exhibits that were gratifyingly bad. Their hunt for irony was rewarded. The museum gave them some high Melmanian moments. One exhibit invited them to push a button. "We were expecting thunder or something, and a light goes on." [Much laughter.] But others parts of the museum were embarrassing. Exhibit technology seemed limited, particularly in the dinosaur exhibit. "It hasn't changed since I was 8."

There was lots of potential in the museum as a whole ("it could be fantastic"), but the guys agreed that the ROM had fallen badly behind. Generally, the visit was "boring." The ROM was now trailing the Art Gallery of Ontario (AGO), a rival arts institution in Toronto. The AGO, said the guys, is constantly changing. It's in touch with the world. These are the kind of guys constantly on the lookout for the opposite sex and I asked them: "So did you meet any girls?" One of them looked at me with surprise and said, "It would never occur to me to meet a girl at the ROM."

Nancy

Nancy is a frequent visitor. She comes to the ROM with her several children and husband. I ask her to use our walkabout to reconstruct a family visit. The family always begins, she tells me, in the same place.

Nancy: The kids love the mosaic [on the ceiling of the entrance hall], and we go to the second balcony [to see it] every time we come. We do the same things every time we come.

The second stop is the totem pole in the staircase. For this family, the pole is not an anthropological artifact so much as it is an imaginative resource. Nancy appreciates that it is an object from another culture with its own history and significance, but she wants her kids to interact with it in other ways as well.

Nancy: We make up stories. Is that a man or a child [in the totem pole]? We want to encourage them to use their imaginations. That's what this place is about: sparking creativity. [Breaks off.] The kids say the totem pole are ghosts [*sic*].

Nancy loves the drama of this suggestion ("You wonder whether the ghosts have been exorcised!") and she invites the family to treat all museum objects in this manner. She invites them to discover things that are "eerie," "gothic," and "a bit scary." This is for her much of the point of the visit.

I find myself telling Nancy the "story of the lost office." The director's office once stood at the top of a stairway, at the end of a bridge. Some years ago, the staircase was bricked in, the bridge cut off, and the office abandoned. I can't resist elaborating. "And, you know, Nancy, to this day, no one *really* knows why they did that." Nancy glimpses the dramatic possibilities immediately and together we speculate about an office draped in cobwebs and filled with hidden compartments and forgotten treasure. The story enters her museum lore immediately. This is one for the children.

The museum has a rich "oral tradition" filled with stories of curators' eccentricities and hidden staircases. Typically, this is treated as "insider's knowledge." Museum staff tell these stories when they do their own informal tours of the institution for friends and visitors. (The pragmatic function of this knowledge is to demonstrate the staff member's insider status and to endow the visitor with honorary status.) Sometimes this knowledge becomes an engaging part of the tour guide's tour. But generally the museum does not share its oral tradition with the public. This may well be a deliberately exclusionary act. It is, in any case, a pity. Stories from the "oral tradition" can be a useful "adhesive" binding the visitor and what is otherwise a distant, forbidding institution. Sharing these stories with the visitor has the effect of giving the museum human scale. It also has the effect of elevating the visitor, giving them insider status. Sharing the oral tradition is a good way to right the asymmetry of the museum-visitor relationship.

Interestingly, Nancy has no interest in interactive exhibits. As far as she's concerned, the museum is plenty interactive as it is. She has no sense of the museum as "dusty and musty." When she first joined the museum she found it a little "stuffy." (In a grand accent, she says, "People used to say they had 'been to the museum.'") But more and more, she finds it attended by families with different (or no) status motives.

Nancy's kids are particularly awed by the sense of scale they find at the museum. They are impressed by the sheer size of objects. They like to stand beside them and look up. They like their parents to stand beside them and look small.

Nancy has very clear educational objectives. The first is to let the kids see that they are part of a larger evolutionary project. She takes them to the dinosaur galleries.

Nancy: My son has enough understanding that you can say, "Once we were all fish, and then we got feet."

The second is to let them see that they are part of a single planet and a single biological system. ("I'm trying to communicate how small and fragile the planet is.") She is also trying to show them they are part of a single species.

Nancy: We [humans] are all one species. We all look like that [skull] underneath our skin. I'm communicating the common denominator and celebrating our differences.

What is striking about this exercise is how personal Nancy tries to make it. When she talks about the evolutionary project, she is not talking in a general way. She is showing the connection that links our species to every other species ("Once *we* were all fish. . . ."). What also impresses is her intellectual flexibility. She has no difficulty seeing the general in the particular. And she has no difficulty telling a story of hierarchically nested samenesses and differences in a single breath. More than one museum fails to organize its complexity with anything like this deftness.

If this sounds child oriented, it is. Nancy says that what she sees at the museum is largely determined by the presence of her children. ("Our epitaph will read 'we have to come back without the kids.'") For her own purposes, what really captures her are artifacts from other cultures.

Nancy: [At the museum] I can travel to other cultures. I'm fascinated with history, things that were made with human hands. The more primitive the better.

Analysis

What can we make of these data? Nancy doesn't much resemble Robby and his dad. Barbara doesn't resemble Linda. The guys don't resemble anyone else at all. On the face of it, five ethnographic sketches offer five "species" of museum life, the diversity of which appears to overwhelm the possibility of analysis. Analytically, we are met by the same diversity. These data are sufficiently rich to allow us to approach them from any one of several points of view: class, gender, age, parenting, design, content, the expressive properties of objects, and several other theories besides.

In this section I wish to subsume this diversity in a single account. This is not only because the point of an anthropological analysis is, or used to be, accounts that are embracing and holistic. It is because I believe that the problems of the contemporary museum are unitary in nature. Truly, the museum is tempted to solve them on an ad hoc basis. I believe that something more comprehensive and thoroughgoing is possible and necessary. I want to propose that we think about the interaction between the ROM and its visitors as the collision of two cultural models.

The Museum's Preferment Model

An idea wanders the museum. It is not an *official* presence. It is not a formal philosophy. It is rarely acknowledged in explicit terms. I have searched museum publications in vain for a formal statement (Anonymous 1921). This ideology never appears in print.

But it is very much part of the museum. It can be glimpsed wandering the museum most mornings and in the late afternoon. It especially likes to sit in the cafeteria when curators grouse over coffee about the present state of their institution. It also likes to insinuate itself into management and board meetings, where it can make itself the voice of reason or, more often, the shadow assumption on which deliberations turn. It even likes to follow museum visitors around the galleries. As we shall see, it can be, in this last capacity, truly haunting.

As befits a museum ghost, it is discreet. It never demands assent. It merely suggests itself as the course of common sense. Even this may be too strong, for usually it does not *suggest* itself at all. It works reflexively. It is simply there, unobserved, often unobservable. It works opportunistically, slipping into consciousness as the notion of last resort. And it never overstays its visit. Like any good ghost, it makes itself known and then makes itself scarce.

This idea descends from an ancient and honorable idea: "Through most of the nineteenth century, an international museum culture remained firmly committed to the idea that the first responsibility of a public art museum is to enlighten and improve its visitors morally, socially, and politically" (Duncan 1995, 16; cf. Greene 1993, 60; Passmore 1970). This is an idea with a mission: to transform visitors, to imbue them with qualities they did not have before. In every case, moral, social, and political, the transformation moves the visitor through social space. This is always seen to be, felt to be, an *upward* movement.

I suggest we call this the *preferment* model. The *Oxford English Dictionary* defines preferment as "the advancement or promotion in condition, status or position in life." Sixteenth-century England used the term for all kinds of advancement: through age grades, occupations, offices, or ranks in the hierarchy (Gainsford 1616, 62 verso). As it turns out, the transformations of the contemporary museum have a diversity, a breadth of their own. *Preferment* has useful range.

I believe that there are five variations in the preferment system. Museums transform by improving, civilizing, inspiring, instructing, and/or advancing their visitors. It is not unusual for these variations to commingle in the day-to-day existence of the museum. When Lamont describes her respondents as "view[ing] high culture as a civilizing experience that elevates both the soul and the mind, as if it had purifying virtues," it is possible to hear the civilizing, inspiring, and instructing variations all at once (Lamont 1972, 110). But it serves us to keep the variations separate, for they are, I believe, different ideas that spring from different impulses. More to the point, a finer analysis of the culture of the museum depends upon careful differentiation. I will endeavor to treat each variation individually below.

The *improvement* variation on this ideology is not easy to pin down. It is captured in a vague way by the supposition that museum visits leave the individual better for having come. This is not, or not only, a matter of knowing more. It is a matter of being different, improved. Some of this comes from the influential notion of culture articulated by Matthew Arnold. For Arnold, culture was about improvement in its most hyperbolic state: "Culture is . . . properly described . . . as having its origin in the love of perfection; it is *a study of perfection*" (Arnold 1993, 59; cf. Collini 1993, ix; Levine 1988, 223). According to this scheme, the public responsibility of the institution and the visitor is particular: "The great thing, it will be observed, is to find our *best* self, and to seek to affirm nothing but that" (Arnold 1993, 100).

Some part of the improvement variation comes from (and plays into) our culture's passion for "self-improvement" (Long 1987). This enthusiasm was, in one sense, the private counterpart to a public concern for *progress* that inspired Western societies in the nineteenth and early twentieth centuries. Both notions held that individuals should work ceaselessly to make themselves better (Cawelti 1965; Huber 1971; Pole 1980). Along with churches, universities, encyclopedias, night schools, the University of Chicago's Great Books series, and the Good Book, museums were and remain key sites for this transformation. As great "arks," they are supposed to represent all knowledge and accomplishment. They record cultural progress. They contribute to cultural progress. They are institutional acts of exhortation (Rydell 1984, 154–183).

The *civilizing* variation of the preferment ideology is also vague and understudied. Here the transformation is not merely a matter of perfection. It implies some notion of advancement from one stage to a more sophisticated one. (The pursuit of perfection has found a fish ladder, as it were.) Advancement moves upward through a hierarchy of classes, cultures, or civilizations. Individuals are seen to grow more civilized as they shift their focus and their allegiance upward.

We may press Arnold into service once more. There is no doubt that his seminal ideas on culture contributed to the construction of the museum's mission. But he is only one of several architects. We may credit nineteenth-century Christianity, Britain's colonial enterprise, and evolutionary theory in Canada, England, and America as well (Burrow 1966; Comaroff and Comaroff 1991; Cook 1985, 172; Twitchell 1983). Duncan captures some of this ideology in her wonderful book *Civilizing Rituals.* Unfortunately, she appears to conflate it with the spiritual variation of the preferment model. As a result, we do not yet have an unambiguously illuminating treatment of this aspect of museum life.

The *spiritual* variation refers to the museum as a place in which epiphanies occur. This is relatively well studied. Spiritual illumination is, after all, the kind of thing to which some intellectuals and scholars are prone. In this case, the museum is sometimes a surrogate for religious institutions, a place for the pursuit of a "secular religiosity."

> The main purpose of a collection of works of art was therefore seen to be
> the awakening of a spirit of reverence and devotion. Museums were temples
> and their directors and assistants priests. In an age when the power and ap-
> peal of ecclesiastical religion had faded, art was destined to take its place.
> (Hudson 1987, 46)

For many, museums became the surrogate for organized religion. Why else invest so heavily in space of cathedral scale and proportion? Why else insist on a reverential attitude from the visitor toward the art? ("Shhhh. No talking!") And as long as the religious idiom held, the transforming power of the museum was clear. The individual would be swept upward, elevated, purified by culture just as they had been by religion.

The connection between museums and a secular version of religiosity turns on the eighteenth- and nineteenth-century notion of the sublime. Rosenblum argued explicitly that the sublime was the most probable occasion of an intellectual's sense of reverence (Rosenblum 1975). Something less explicit but not less marked may be observed in Burke and Kant, the most influential writers on the topic (Burke 1958; Kant 1952). In the almost formulaic words of one observer, "The moment of the sublime was a transport of the spirit" (in Price 1986, 31).

But eventually the religious idiom fell away. The modernist approach to culture insisted on it. We came to think of museums as places in which illumination could be perfectly spiritual without being the least bit religious. The new regime held that cultural institutions could create an aesthetic, moral, emotional, and intellectual ascent that did not depend on (or result in) piety. We discovered that culture without religion can still prefer the individual— and that museums were an excellent place for this transformation to occur.

The *instructional* variation is relatively well understood. In this case, the individual is transformed by his/her interaction with the great bodies of knowledge represented by the cultural institution. This is not just a question of knowing more but of advancing in the larger order of things because of knowing more.

That advancement comes from knowledge, not from birth, was one of the most important principles of the humanists and the culture they helped construct (Caspari 1968). The museum's role in this upward transformation through knowledge has been well described by Hooper-Greenhill and will not further concern us here (Hooper-Greenhill 1992).

The variation I want to concentrate on is that of *social advancement*. According to this notion, the museum elevates the individual in social status. Of the five transformations of which the preferment system is capable, this is the most robust and the most active in the present museum world—robust but not quite material. It is, as I have noted above, a ghostly presence more acted upon than acknowledged. The social-advancement variation says that the museum can prefer individuals in social space, moving them from one standing to the next.

It is not hard to see why the museum should have status to confer. Like many museums, the Royal Ontario Museum has sought relationships with the highest-ranking members of its status communities. In the case of the ROM, this meant cultivating an association with the British royal family. (Rumor has it that the ROM adopted the word "Royal" in its name without royal charter.) Virtually half of the 1921 board of the museum held knighthoods. In the present day, it means appointing the governor general of Canada and the lieutenant governor of Ontario as "Honorary Patrons."

There is a Western notion that royal families are "founts" of status (Marston 1973; Zagorin 1971). This status can be distributed to and deployed by individuals and institutions who rise and fall as a result. This idea is in disrepute in parts of Canadian society but is still potent for some. For these people, the ROM is a status intermediary. It draws status from the apical superordinate. It then becomes a superordinate in its own right, conferring this status upon subordinates of its own. Status is important "cultural capital" in the ROM's economy (Bourdieu 1984; cf. Hall 1992, 263; Halle 1993, 196–200).

Museums also have had long, intricate relationships with local families of high standing. These families supply precious resources: social authority, cultural capital, and political influence. They have offered their children as curators, their spouses as volunteers, and their matriarchs and patriarchs as board members, patrons, and donors. They have made the museum a repository of material culture (e.g., china, furniture, art, and silver) that has helped define their status in the community (Warner, Low, Lunt, and Srole 1963, 107).

The relationship is not asymmetrical. Status flows *to* these families just as it flows *from* them. In the crudest case, the museum will trade social standing for infusions of cash. In effect, it launders wealth so that a "new" family may become (or begin to become) an "old" family. Normally, the exchange is more complicated and more delicate. Museum and family seek a balance in the exchange. There are many currencies in the exchange: money, events, names and naming, objects, prestige, standing, and influence of several varieties. What is given and what is gotten are calculated with some care. The bargainers seek a rough sense of parity (when an exquisite one is not possible). Inevitably, there are asymmetries. Some families rank so high they must necessarily *give* more status to the museum than they get. Others rank sufficiently low they must always *get* status more than they give. All of this requires careful calculation about what is owed to whom and someone on staff capable of making such calculations. In a robust status community, the museum is simultaneously a participant in, an arbiter for, a contributor to, and a beneficiary of the process by which status is reckoned and apportioned. (I appreciate that this "exchange" model of the relationship between families and the museum does not always square with the family's point of view. Many families see their contributions to the museum as "free gifts" offered in the classic tradition of *liberality* and not because of the consequences that may follow from the act of giving [Kelso 1929].)

Since Veblen, we have acknowledged the particular relationship between status and material culture (Veblen [1912] 1952). One of the calculations of status in our society says, crudely, "If I have art/culture, I must have money, and if I have money, I must have status." Like everything that follows from Veblen's "indexical" theory of status symbolism, this is too crude to be useful. A more satisfactory formula: if I have art/culture, I must have taste, and if I have taste, I must have status. This is a little better but still too crude. It suggests that taste is "digital" (something you have or you don't) when plainly it is "analogue" (something you have by degrees). The best calculation is perhaps this: if I have art/culture, I must have discernment, and if I have discernment, I must have status.

In this formula, objects become a demonstration of and a warrant for the individual's status. But only some objects will serve in this capacity. They must be scarce, expensive, and, in the traditional model, *fine.* For fineness in the object can be detected only by those who are discerning. And discernment exists only in those who are special, the select few who have this discernment by dint of training or, according to the ideology of some ancient families, birth. In a sense, the fineness of the object speaks to the fineness in the individual. The individual must have fineness to know fineness. Thus does the fineness of the object in some sense prove the fitness of individuals for high standing. They possess discernment and an essential fineness and therefore deserve their status. (A concern for fineness is not shared by everyone of high standing. To use the distinction suggested by Aldrich [1998, 79], it holds more interest for the "patrician" set than the "aristocratic" one. An interesting variation can be found among the French upper-middle and upper classes [Lamont 1992, 10, 88–128].)

The individual who collects fine objects rarely works alone. Often they solicit the aid and counsel of the curator who as a connoisseur has cultivated the ability to identify fineness. The curator can serve variously as instructor, confidant, and/or guarantor in the individual's collecting activity. The collector's access to the fineness of the object (and its status meaning) is now mediated by the curator. And the curator will often have established his or her own link between fineness and status according to which the extraordinary abilities of the connoisseur stand as a demonstration of social, intellectual, and/or academic standing.

I am not suggesting that connoisseurship reduces to a status-getting and -giving exercise. As the work of Hoving (1981, 20–24), Kramer (1995), and Montgomery (1982) make plain, the exercise is a distinguished intellectual tradition. And when joined to collector enthusiasm in this way, it becomes an extraordinary museological resource. The curator begins to build a relationship that will someday result, it is hoped, in donations to the museum. More to the point, when the curator gives advice to a collector, he or she is helping to select the very objects that will someday, it is hoped, enter the collection. Collector-curator-connoisseur relationships represent a strategic museum option and a vital intellectual tradition (Teather 1990, 28–29).

There is a reciprocity here too. The curator is giving *and* getting status associations. So is the collector. Potentially, very complicated transformational "chains" are possible. In one such chain, status goes full circle: the museum gets status from the curator as the curator gets status from the collector as the collector gets status from the object as the object gets status from the museum. But this is too simple structurally because it does not allow for different kinds and degrees of status. We must reckon any particular exchange according to the relative standing of the parties, objects, and institutions involved. Once again, some parties, objects, and institutions are always relatively more status-giving than status-getting while others are more status-getting than status-giving. It must also be observed that there are different kinds of status at work (e.g., academic versus social, achieved versus ascribed) that are variously valued by the exchanging parties. Once more, the calculation is a complicated one. But the larger point is clear. When these exchanges are performed felicitously, a status transformation takes place, as a result of which collectors and curators have more status than they did before the exchange.

There is another source of status on which the museum can draw. It is perceived to be a "house of knowledge" that offers definitive treatment of several bodies of academic knowledge. In this case, the museum is drawing not so much on the authority established by the university world and scholarship as on the social status that has been assigned to them. In the popular view, this world is austere, solemn, indifferent, admirably arcane, and astonishingly "brainy." Two particular types of scholars give additional "luster." The reputation of the curator-connoisseur establishes the museum as a place of sophistication, exotic travel, and high status. The reputation of the archaeologist establishes the museum as a place of adventure, exotic travel, and high romance. (Bernard Berenson established a defining idea of the connoisseur. The fictional Indiana Jones character created by Steven Spielberg establishes, perhaps, the defining popular idea of the archaeologist.) In this case, prestige comes not from knowing things but from sharing the prestige of those who do.

The museum's status comes from another source as well. It comes from the ability to make itself exclusive. Since Marx, we have formally acknowledged this aspect of status. The classic text is brief: "I wouldn't want to belong to any club that would have me as a member." A more formal statement may be found in Pierre Bourdieu, Alain Darbel, and Dominique Schnapper (1990; cf. Weil 1995). In this case, the museum increases its status by refusing or discouraging the participation of certain parties. This was once a matter of policy (Ames 1992; Cameron 1971). More and more, it has a de facto character. Consider the volunteers who sit in the lobby of the Metropolitan Museum of New York. Their purpose is to garner new memberships and they are, from one point of view, unmistakably attractive and welcoming. But they are, from another perspective, so perfectly dressed, coiffed, and composed, so evidently creatures of high status, that the average museum visitor must feel a little awed, if not entirely intimidated, by their presence. Membership sign-up, putatively open to all, begins to feel, in these circumstances, like a process of social scrutiny. A question haunts the interaction, "Am I really good enough to join this institution?" Many aspects of the museum can have this effect. The exterior and the lobbies of many museums are designed to impress and, perhaps, to intimidate. Every gala opening with its striped awnings and succession of limousines has this effect. By intention or habit, the public face of the institution can be a haughty one. Exclusivity fashioned in these ways creates status for the institution, and this is one of the resources on which it runs.

And it is here that the preferment model begins to show its darker side. For the preferment model often takes on an elitist quality. It persuades members of the museum community that they are entitled to treat the museum as a "magic circle" of privilege and to use their association with the museum as an opportunity for status aggrandizement. It gives them a warrant to "pull up the drawbridge" and exclude anyone with the wrong status credentials.

Sometimes this is a deliberate act of exclusion. More often, it is an invisible act. In this second guise, the preferment model has a ghostly quality. It is a shadow idea, one that insinuates itself into consciousness and decision making out of reach of conscious awareness. It works to shape attitudes toward the museum and its visitors, encouraging the participation of some and the exclusion of others. It works to create a "climate of opinion" in which certain ideas will flourish and others will not survive.

To the extent that museum staff may style themselves as intellectuals, it is clear that their inclination to insist on a vertical world represents a relatively old habit.

> In the early twentieth century, intellectuals based their reassertion of cultural supremacy upon a traditional and enormously influential view of human nature that was itself hierarchical. This hierarchy was described in language that drew upon a wide spectrum of analogous dichotomies. To express it in simplified, generic form, human nature involved an ongoing conflict between the lower instincts—emotions, drives, material needs— and the higher faculties—reason, spirit, imagination, among others. . . . These intellectuals believed that low, vulgar, common culture played upon the baser instincts, whereas superior culture emanated, in its creation and appreciation, from the higher, more subtle, complex, and integrative faculties. (LeMahieu 1988, 106; cf. Carey 1992, 85; Leavis 1930, 3, 26)

Recently, the food-service company at the Royal Ontario Museum created an outdoor cafe at the front of the building. Some curators were horrified that the museum should "lower" itself with this creation of a "beer garden." Others had no objection to the idea of a cafe but felt the execution of the idea was unfortunate. They felt that the cafe's fence was "wrong." The fence is large, wooden, white, and constructed from two-by-fours. It was criticized as "a little too country and western." "It looks," said one curator, "like we're preparing to hold a rodeo." So thoroughgoing is this tendency to pass judgment, there is a shorthand for it. "How very unROM," staff members will mutter sotto voce as they stroll past something new. No more needs to be said. In this status community, like all good status communities, the code is so clear and so shared that detailed criticism can be dispatched in just three words. The preferment system is not dead. It is not even feeling poorly. It is, for an apparition, remarkably robust.

I believe this phrase ("how very unROM") rings in museological heads again and again over the course of the day. Museum staff may hear it when contemplating hiring someone. ("Not quite ROM.") They may hear it when considering a visiting exhibit. ("But does it really fit in with what we do?") They may hear it when considering a marketing partner. ("I wonder, though, are they really ROM?") This is not the only voice that may be heard. And when it is heard, it does not always prevail. But I believe that this voice is powerfully influential. It is, I think, present in virtually all museum deliberations and more persuasive there than is sometimes acknowledged.

Recently a museum curator was asked what he wanted visitors to experience. "Awe," he said without hesitation. This is an unexceptional objective, one that springs readily to curatorial lips. Under finer scrutiny, perhaps it is not so unexceptional after all. Awe presupposes an asymmetry between the visitor and the museum. Visitors who experience awe must find themselves rendered small and the museum rendered big. Awe is an act of deference.

"Nonsense," the curator will say. "In the face of the majesty of museums, its objects and traditions, I experience awe as much as anyone." But the curator's awe is not the visitor's awe. After all, the curator is, priest-like, a participant in the world that the visitor is meant to venerate. The curator may be subordinate to the museum, but he or she is *super*ordinate to the visitor. When curators insist on awe as an objective, they engage, perhaps without meaning to, in an act of professional aggrandizement. They are playing out the imperatives of the preferment system.

This is a summary treatment of the preferment system. In this system, the museum is constantly seeking out the precious resource of status on the one hand and variously distributing and apportioning it on the other. As a result, the museum may present itself as a transformational institution, one that is capable of endowing visitors with status. According to the preferment model of this ideology, the museum is seen to advance people in social space so that they possess higher social standing than before.

There is no question that some visitors are deliberate and enthusiastic players in the preferment system and that they can and do avail themselves of the status it makes available. They are keen to leave the ROM publication *Rotunda* on their coffee tables. This is no accident. As Edward Shils (1970), an authority on the North American status system, put it, "A title or emblem conferred by the major deference-bearing institutions of a society is an entitlement to deference" (429). They are pleased to let slip at cocktail parties how much they enjoyed the recent ROM exhibit. In sum, ROM members and visitors sometimes "cash in" on the status-bearing properties of the institution. They evoke their status as elevated social creatures. There is no doubt that Kelly is right to suggest that they sometimes treasure the fact of having been to the museum more than the experience of actually being there (Kelly 1984).

But not always. There are instances in which visitors are not enamored of, or participants in, the preferment system. As the preceding ethnographic data show, visitors are often daunted by the status-bearing qualities of the institution. We may recall Nancy, who said she found the museum "stuffy" at first. It is, she told us, a place she associates, and not kindly, with pretensions of grandeur.

Another respondent, one not detailed in the ethnographic data given above, was still more forthcoming. Anne is another "natural" for the museum: smart, educated, interested in the world. But she has not come to the museum in many years. I asked her why.

> [It's as if] you are supposed to come in all in awe [of the museum], like you don't know enough. I'm a university graduate, not a stupid person, but I feel that way going through [an exhibit]. [Pause.] Maybe it's a sense of . . . holier than thou.

But the effects of the preferment system are even more evident in the case of Linda. When she begins to hydroplane in the Egyptian gallery, it is precisely because she has found herself judged and found wanting.

Thus have the transformational powers of the museum been pressed into service, with disastrous consequences. Instead of engaging Linda in a process of preferment, it engaged her in a process of diminishment. Instead of advancing her in social space, it demoted her in social space. ("I feel so little!") The preferment model haunts this visitor just as much as it does museum staff. But in this case, the haunting is dramatically more troubling. It proves destructive of Linda's sense of self-esteem and it prevents her from participating in the museum.

Barbara's reaction is more telling still. She tells us that she rejects the "didacticism" of the institution and the sense that the museum knows more and better than she. She is taking aim at the authority and the superordination of the institution. And she particularly refuses the asymmetry of the relationship: the presumption that the ROM is the grand font of knowledge and status to which she comes as a supplicant, an empty vessel eager to be filled. What she is doing here is refusing some of the basic terms of the preferment model. She does not acknowledge the institution's authority or her own need to be promoted in the social and intellectual worlds.

The natives are restless. Nancy, Anne, and Barbara all voice skepticism for the preferment model. Linda is prepared to let herself be judged by the model, but it is not a happy interaction. It does not help create engagement or build a relationship. The men in the sample take another point of view. Robby and the guys treat the preferment model as an irrelevance. Plainly, all of this spells trouble. The model that has done so much to shape the institution is now looked upon with suspicion. It is active and influential in the culture of the museum, but it is increasingly irksome or irrelevant in the culture of the visitor.

There is an "insider's" temptation here to declare these museum visitors Philistines. It is to say, as Matthew Arnold might have done, that these individuals have *refused* to participate in an elevating relationship with the ROM and that they have done so out of motives that bring discredit to us all. It is to say that by refusing the museum model, they have refused culture and the very possibility of preferment. And we hear these sentiments with some frequency. Some museum staff are quick to paint visitors as poor unfortunates who are too craven or deluded by popular culture to benefit from what the ROM has to offer. Thus does the institution defend itself.

But the data must give us pause. There is nothing obviously "vulgar" about these respondents. They appear to be at the center of the "market" the museum has the capacity to reach with greatest ease. Educated, sophisticated, and curious, these are the people who should have the greatest "native" sympathy for what the museum does. The data will not support the traditional "Philistine" rebuttal with which museums dismiss their critics.

The problem is not Culture but culture. These respondents do not refuse the museum because they are not sufficiently sophisticated. They refuse it because they come to the museum with ideas of their own.

The Consumer Model: Transformation in a New Key

There was a time when Western societies were in the thrall of the preferment model. Virtually everyone took pride in where they stood in the social hierarchy, and they devoted time and income to objects and activities that would promote them in this hierarchy (Bushman 1992). Consumption, as we now say, was aspirational. Individuals hoped for upward mobility. Consumers engaged in conspicuous consumption with precisely this goal in mind. Clothing, home furnishing, educational decisions, career choices—all of these pursued an improvement of the individual's social standing. The preferment model was the single most powerful "compass" at work in the social world.

But we have seen the preferment model under steady attack and in steady decline. The social and cultural forces responsible are many and various (McCracken 1997, 79–89). Democratizing forces at work in Western culture from the early modern period, and in the New World from its founding, continue apace (de Tocqueville 1966; LeMahieu 1988). What was not already in train was advanced by the cultural revolutions that took place in youth culture in the 1960s and the 1990s (Coupland 1991; Gitlin 1987; Linklater 1991; Pray 1997). The rise and relative triumph of Hollywood, television, and popular music made their own signal contributions. It is too soon to say that the preferment model is over. It is too soon to say that it has been reduced to the status of a minority preoccupation. But it may be observed that it has been joined by increasingly robust alternatives.

One of the most striking of these was the rise of a consumer society—an extraordinary departure from the preferment model (Carson, Hoffman, and Albert 1994; McKendrick, Brewer, and Plumb 1982; Williams 1982). This new social form reversed the asymmetry of the relationship. Now it was the consumer, not the institution, who was seen to be the arbiter of what counted. In the consumer society, institutions were suddenly eager to accommodate themselves to the wishes of the individual. In the place of high-handed presumption came an entirely different attitude.

The consumer society has changed the expectations visitors have of the museum. Some visitors still come looking for the status transformation of the preferment model, as the example of Linda makes clear. But many more come looking for transformations of another kind. The new visitor comes looking, as we shall see, for experiences that do not pull them upward in the hierarchy but outward into a world of experience. They come looking for engagements not with status mobility but with a kind of existential mobility. Visitors come looking for new experiences, emotions, and participations. These experiences are still transforming, but they are transforming in new modalities according to different cultural logics.

Totemism in the Modern Museum

Nancy's children believe the totem poles at the ROM to be "eerie," "gothic," "a bit scary," and probably "haunted." This is not because Nancy does not know or care that the poles are the work of another culture. She understands this, and she wants her children to understand it. But Nancy and her family have succeeded in "discovering" another meaning in the totem poles. These poles engage because they *alarm*.

Barbara sees this quality of alarm in the mummies. They are, she says, "all dry and whispery." When she sees a ROM mummy, it is hard not to imagine "a little hand [that] comes sneaking out." She sees this quality in the Bat Cave. Here, too, there is the "slightly eeky possibility of bats in your hair." Barbara shudders at the thought.

Anne finds this quality in other aspects of the museum:

I'm not enamored with bugs. [But] the kids like it. [They say,] "Oh, gross me
out!" They like that sense. They get queasy [and ask,] "Do [we] have
those in Toronto, in the backyard?" It's like going to a horror show. . . .
It's a fascination as well as a fear. It's like scary stories.

Alarm is not without didactic value. I asked an 11-year-old male to tell me
about mummies. He did so with gusto and admiration.

They are people who died, but just the kings and stuff. They would bury the
dog alive. They would take out its brain. They would put it in jars. They
would put garlic in their intestines. It was pretty weird. It was neat, but
you would think "Why did they do it?" and you'd want to find out.

Thus speak the visitors. What are they telling us? They are saying that some
part of the pleasure and engagement of the museum experience comes from
a sensation of alarm. They expect to be frightened. Within certain limits, in
certain ways, they want to be frightened. This is not thrill-seeking. Visitors
do not seek alarm for its own sake. They do not come to the museum for the
same reasons they ride a roller coaster. These visitors come to the museum to
take possession of its gothic quality and use it for their own purposes.

Mother [reading text]: "Shark attacks are very rare."
Daughter: What does "rare" mean?
Mother: They don't happen very often.
Daughter [relief laced with disappointment]: They don't?

The topics of fear and alarm, as I will attempt to show in what follows, are
not unknown to the museum experience. But this low and, from a preferment
point of view, unbecoming motive has been much treated in the literature.
See David Halle for a fleeting reference to working-class and upper-class reactions to "primitive art" (Halle 1993, 148, 150). Halle notes that "the willingness of residents to display masks that they nevertheless found ugly is in-
triguing. Here the attraction of masks appears to lie in their unaesthetic
rather than in their aesthetic qualities. This underlines the need to seek out
the symbolic meaning that the objects must possess" (150). For our purposes,
this point needs to be made a little differently. The attraction of sharks appears to lie in their transformational rather than their educational meaning.
But the conclusion is the same: what counts are their symbolic meanings, not
their biodiversity/educational ones.

The exhibit *Sharks! Fact and Fantasy* had a purpose: to debunk the myths
surrounding sharks, to demonstrate they are not the ruthless, bloodthirsty
creatures of legend and lore. Frequently this noble message found its way
home. But just as often visitors supplied a message of their own. They did not

come to see gentle, misunderstood creatures of the deep. They came looking for creatures who were frankly, unmistakably, usefully alarming.

There was evidence of this everywhere. The children were especially demonstrative. The very little ones (ages 2 and 3) were openly terrified. Several parents were called upon to remove their kids from the exhibit. One of them told me, "She was really frightened and it took awhile to calm her down. I think she was frightened because it was dark." One little boy about 5 kept running up to fiberglass sharks with a look of some panic while he repeated the phrase "Silly! You're silly!" He was addressing the fiberglass.

Many children did a wordless point. In this event, children will often race up to the artifact ahead of their parents. They point at the artifact and move their gaze back and forth between artifact and parents. They say nothing, but there is something urgent, almost beseeching about the gesture. The pointing hand appears to say, "This needs an explanation. Please attend to this now." Parents respond in reassuring tones. "That's a big fish, isn't it, Hank? It's a [here they scan the exhibit text for identification] a bottlenose shark!" And with this the child, who now looks rather less terrified, stops pointing and races on.

Older children are somewhat more explicit about what is happening in the exhibit. I asked one 11-year-old boy what he liked about sharks, and he told me, "They are very large and they have sharp teeth." Again, there was a combination of admiration and fear in this. Apparently, these two qualities travel in pairs.

This is alarm with a purpose. In point of fact, this is alarm with many purposes. All of these turn on our culture's version of totemism. In the case of traditional societies of the kind examined by Levi-Strauss, totemism is a cultural creation that posits a relationship between a natural system and a cultural one. In the case of Australian aboriginals, two "systems of difference" are made to correspond so that a species of animals may stand for a moiety or group. The totemism of the contemporary Western worlds is different in virtually every particular, but it remains a process by which the meanings assigned to nature are used to give definition to the individual or the group (Drummond 1996; Levi-Strauss 1963; Sapir and Crocker 1977; Tambiah 1969). In the case of *Sharks! Fact and Fantasy*, there was a great deal of "transformation" activity.

Consider the child who calls the shark "silly." On the face of it, this appears to be a particularly inappropriate way to express his anxiety. (In Silverstein's term [1976], the *pragmatic* usefulness of "silly" is precisely that it allows superordinate parties to express their disapproval of subordinate parties.) But it was clear what the little boy intended. He was in a state of alarm. He was in the presence of something large and threatening, and several things were unclear. Did this "creature" have agency or was it "just" a model? If it had agency, was it malevolent? Was it within or beyond control? What definitions and rules applied to it? Did *any* definitions or rules apply to it? This fiberglass "creature" swamped the little boy's sense of scale, his sense of safety, and his sense of order.

To protect himself, the little boy did what his mother always does in these circumstances. He summoned the controlling powers of language. More particularly, he summoned the very word his mother uses when her little boy goes out of control. Every time he plays the "wild thing" (to use Sendak's famous term), she calls him "silly" (Bettleheim 1976; Sendak 1963). She says, "Don't be silly." In the company of these fiberglass sharks, he knows what to do. "Silly! You're silly!"

This transformation activity has a certain hubris to it. The little boy pays himself an enormous, an outrageous, compliment when he suggests that there is a resemblance between himself and a shark. But this is, perhaps, the nature of childhood. When this little boy breaks the rules and becomes a "wild thing," he feels himself the very agent of chaos. And his parents confirm this for him. Why else would they work so hard to bring him under control again? Why would they seek to constrain him with acts of punishment and language?

In this transformation moment, a little boy felt the current of alarm that runs through this exhibit and responded to it totemically: by claiming a similarity between himself and the shark, by seeking to control the shark as his parents seek to control him. I was to see transformation acts of this kind happen again and again at the *Sharks! Fact and Fantasy* exhibit.

Teenage boys, for instance, engaged in unmistakable totemism. It is worth observing that it is exceedingly difficult to persuade teenage boys to visit a museum. One of the remarkable things about the *Sharks!* exhibit was precisely that they came in such numbers and with so little prompting. More to the point, the show drew the most inaccessible group within the category, the ones who normally regard museum attendance as a declaration of effeteness. In other words, *Sharks!* brought in a gender (male), age (young), and self-definition ("cool") that are almost impossible to attract.

You only had to watch and talk to this group for a short time to see why they were there. They came in groups. They would enter the exhibit, exclaim at the size of the models, and grin nervously and somehow, if you will forgive a mixed metaphor, "wolfishly." Significantly, they wished to know the gender of the models they were looking at. "Males, obviously!" one of them snorted. They felt the fear these animals engendered and there was a certain pleasure in the sheer intensity of the sensation. ("Man, what a rush!" as one of them put it.)

But they also treated the fear as a challenge and withheld themselves from it. None of these young men showed their fear beyond the first exclamation. There were no further expressions of alarm and certainly no wordless points. Plainly this took some work. I saw blankness that bespoke suppression. The expression they allowed themselves was a wolfish grinning as if to say, "We know what this fear is and it does not bother us." They had moved on to the second order of business. Having expressed admiration, they were now mastering the fear. The point of the exhibit was to feel the fear and then to master it. To this extent, the exhibit was a test, one of the many that these young men seek out and use to "prove" their gender credentials.

But this transformation moment was not done. There was a third stage. Once they had felt and mastered the fear occasioned by the exhibit, they were now free to claim it as their own. Another cultural logic appears to be at work here. If you can feel and master the fear of the shark, you come to absorb some of its qualities. You are now *fearful* in the other sense of the term. In a manner of speaking, you have been deputized by these sharks. Their qualities are now (for certain purposes, for a certain period) your own. At some level, the *Sharks!* exhibit served these young men as an Anthrax concert or Schwarzenegger movie might have done. It played out and let them claim certain qualities essential to the way they defined their gender.

Teen girls used the alarm quite differently. They too felt the power of the fiberglass models ("These are *scary.*"). But unlike the boys with whom they had sometimes come, they did not feel any obligation to conceal or control this alarm. As they traveled through the exhibit in groups, teen girls would freely express the emotion of alarm as they confronted each new provocation in the exhibit. This became a collective response. They would draw closer together. They would cling to one another. They acted as if to protect one another from the imminent danger. Shared vulnerability created shared emotion, and this created solidarity. The purpose of this alarm was to intensify connections in the group.

The difference between teen girls and boys came out vividly in one particular interview. I talked to a boy and a girl around 16. They had come to the exhibit together. The girl volunteered that she was frightened by the show: "Well, I think [the sharks] are pretty scary." I asked her boyfriend if he was frightened and he replied, "Yeah, sorta," which he appeared to regret immediately. Had he said too much? Had he controlled too little? Would he be allowed to identify with sharks having so "openly" admitted his fear of them?

When I asked what they were looking forward to in the rest of the exhibit, the girl was forthcoming. She expected to continue to be alarmed and to cling to her boyfriend for support. (Plainly, in this "dating" context, fear has particular pragmatic uses. But it also plays out the "fear calls for solidarity" logic of her gender and her age.) "What about you?" I asked the boy and he replied with gusto and too quickly: "More fear, I hope!" Plainly this was compensatory. Having admitted to fear, he was now telling me he could "take" it. Unfortunately, his eagerness broke the first rule of "man to man" talk in our culture: never overdo it. He spotted his error immediately and ducked his head in shame. Transformational self-definition is easy for teens to get wrong and the punishment (often self-inflicted) is cruel.

I will end these remarks on the transformational uses of the *Sharks!* exhibit for teenagers by observing the fashion choice of one particularly dangerous-looking young man. He came to the exhibit wearing a greasy battered hat emblazoned with the logo of his hockey team, the San Jose Sharks.

Some readers may prefer to explain the *Sharks!* exhibit behavior under discussion in psychological terms: as a simple matter of people "liking to be afraid." This is, as many psychological accounts are, reductive and unilluminating. It gives us no way to understand the nature of the fear (this theory cannot tell the difference between fear occasioned by the *Sharks!* exhibit, a horror movie, and a fairground ride). More significant, this account gives us no way of penetrating (or, for museum purposes, managing) what people do with their fear. Once we have identified the emotion and the motive, the work of explanation (and illumination) are over and we are poorer, not richer, for it.

The totemism of the *Sharks!* exhibit was not quite lost on its creators. In fact, they sought to play upon it. The exhibit was crowded with suggestions of similarities between culture and the natural system. When the exhibit talked about what sharks eat, it used several human themes, including a "Seafood Market," the term "marine cuisine," and the phrases "I can't believe I ate the whole thing" and "Blue Plate Special for the mighty Megamouth!" When the exhibit talked about the nocturnal character of sharks, it used the heading "I Love the Night Life." The visitor was invited repeatedly to glimpse similarities between the world of humans and the world of sharks and invited to transfer properties from one to the other.

It is clear enough what was intended. The exhibit organizers had established a clear and consistent theme: sharks are not really so dangerous. What better way to cleanse sharks of their terrifying properties than to argue that they are, finally, not so very different from you and me? Little did they know that all their metaphors actually ran in the wrong direction. Exhibit visitors were greeted with the argument that "sharks are just like us," when what they wanted to hear was the opposite: "We are just like sharks." Our visitors were there to take on sharkness. And the sharkness they were looking for was not "gentle creature of the deep" but shark as pagan terror. No wonder, then, that the 8-year-old had trouble with the mirror beneath the flap. Everything else ran against expectation. Why shouldn't this?

But this is not the only place the exhibit team failed to grasp the real cultural logic of the exhibit. The person chosen to supply the voice-over for parts of the show was Merlin Olsen. No doubt he seemed a good choice. He has an authoritative voice and he is a celebrity of very considerable standing in the United States. Someone on the design team may even have said, "The guy is perfect. He was a terrifying football player and now he's gentle and avuncular." Quite so. The transformation the exhibit sought for sharks had already taken place for Mr. Olsen.

But from a transformation point of view, Mr. Olsen was a most unfortunate choice. After all, he is, like the metaphors in the show, moving in the wrong direction. He began his public celebrity as a fierce and violent participant in America's most fierce and violent game. He was, as football players are supposed to be, a natural force on the edge of civilized life. And then the transformation: from bloodstained warrior to a thoroughly tame "color" commentator to an actor in family drama to a spokesman for a flower company. He is now a "bear of a man" in the most utterly benign sense of the term. This makes him one of the worst possible celebrities for *Sharks!*.

Exhibit designers clearly do not grasp the ineptness and unaptness of their metaphors and celebrities. And in fact they didn't need to. Visitors looked right through the good-natured "Blue Plate Special" stuff and right past Mr. Olsen's companionable chatter and got right at what they had come for: glimpses of themselves as shark-like and terrifying. It was as if the planners of this show couldn't do anything right but it didn't really matter because, really, they couldn't do anything wrong. When the audience comes with a transformation agenda this powerful, we could shout the poetry of Emily Dickinson at them and they would still absorb "sharkness" and come away sated.

I do not think that the transformation aspect of this exhibit escaped just the originators of *Sharks!*. When ROM staff met to discuss the show and to wonder at the sheer number of people it had brought through our doors, discussion ranged far and wide. Several explanations were given, but no one talked of alarm or totemism. I listened for a while and then piped up "Don't you think the show had a certain gothic quality? Don't you think people were a little, you know, frightened?" Many people turned to look at me as if I had taken leave of my senses. "Frightened?" said the appalled and astonished looks, "Get a hold of yourself, man, this is a *Museum*" (cf. Weiss, Weinstein, and Dykes 1988, 19).

I am persuaded that visitors came to the *Sharks!* exhibit with transformation intentions. And I am persuaded that these intentions spring from what is, relatively speaking, an ancient culture that visitors have been smuggling into museums for many decades—a standing expectation that they can come to the museum and be (among other things) constructively, totemically, usefully alarmed.

Generally, museums do not see this. They are so wedded to Enlightenment readings of their mission or the preferment model that they cannot see it. There is a temptation to dismiss the alarm-seeker as a thrill-seeker. The problem, finally, is a cultural one. Museums are, in a manner of speaking, "blinded by science." More exactly, they are blinded by culture. The alarm-seeker must be a Philistine. Those who visit without *museum* cultural expectations must come without any culture at all.

Models in Collision

There was a time when visitors were prepared, indeed obliged, to accept exhibits at face value. The exhibit would, in a sense, propose (and then help craft) a relationship between the visitor and the museum. In most cases, the museum played the knowing, privileged, superordinate party, the one that set the terms of engagement. It was for the visitor to accept these terms, embrace the exhibit, and, quietly, consent to the relationship into which the museum had bid them enter. Visitors were unmistakably the subordinate party.

But this contract is now in question. When visitors look at an opening, welcoming exhibit of the museum and refuse to enter it, they are sending a message. They are saying they have their own ideas about what is and what is not an attractive, habitable exhibit. More than that, they are saying they have their own ideas about what is and is not an acceptable, desirable relationship. They are saying, in effect, "I will not come as a supplicant. You do not know better."

This is no small change in attitude. It is something closer to a wholesale revolt. Consider the new attitude toward the exhibit "path." Most exhibits are given a path so that the museum can be certain that the visitor will see the right things in the right order at the right pace. Some visitors now resist this path as if it were an imposition. Anne said she hated "exhibits that force you to go from A to B to C." Respondents said they feel they are being "funneled," "channeled," even "controlled." And many respondents in the *Sharks!* exhibit said how much they liked the fact that there was no single way to move through the gallery. The exhibit path, once an unexceptional aspect of the museum experience, has begun to feel to some visitors like a tyranny. As one respondent put it: "There's a didacticism that I reject: 'You don't know this, you should learn this.' You think 'Ah, I'm an adult. I don't *need* to learn this.'"

Most striking, visitors are saying that they believe they can be left to their own resources, that they wish to create their own exhibits out of the "raw" materials made available to them by an exhibit. They refuse the imposition of a narrative order. This is not because they dislike narrative. (Their enthusiasm for this convention has survived everything, including the postmodernists' insistence that narrative is dead.) It is because they resent the imposition of someone else's order. There is something patronizing about this order, about the tone that says, "Let us explain this for you. Let us help you understand" (McCracken 1995).

The cultural shift happening at the museum should not surprise us. It is happening (or has happened) throughout the rest of our culture. All the great institutions—medicine, universities, religion, high culture—are, each for its own reasons, falling silent as the intellectual authorities they once were. Where they have not, individuals have seized the initiative and challenged this authority. The immense popularity of New Age arts and self-help therapies may be read as a conspiracy to reject the once-ironclad authority of science in general and medicine in particular (McCracken 1997, 60–61).

It's also worth remembering that the "low" cultures (Hollywood movies, television, radio, magazines, newspapers) distinguish themselves from "high" cultures precisely by their willingness to cater to popular taste. The object of these enterprises is to read "consumer" expectations and conform to them. This means, at the very least, that the consumer is increasingly accustomed to being treated as the "arbiter" of his or her own choices. Most of contemporary culture now routinely treats the individual as an equal, if not a superordinate (Bushman 1994; Levitt 1960). It is perhaps not very surprising that visitors bridle when, wittingly or not, the museum insists they are subordinates.

I think there is reason to believe that this consumercentric model may be undergoing a shift of its own. As the contemporary world becomes more dynamic and transformational, consumers find themselves living in a fluid, unpredictable world. They are less and less in possession of "the facts" and more and more prepared to take what we might call "navigational coordinates" from the products, services, and communications made available by the private and public sectors (McCracken 1997, 2001).

If this surmise is correct, we are leaving a world in which the consumer is king and entering one in which the consumer is once more prepared to look to corporations, governments, or cultural institutions for advice and counsel. This is *not* a return to the old preferment model. The consumer is not prepared to return to deference or any kind of asymmetrical relationship. And this is *not* a movement away from consumer sensitivity. Anything put before the consumer must be crafted to meet existing needs, wants, and expectations. But we may be witnessing the possibility of a new relationship between the organization and the consumer. In this new model, the private- or public-sector enterprise is no longer concerned merely with playing back what the consumer appears to want. We are now also concerned with playing out where the consumer is going in a world that is increasingly liquid with possibility and dynamism. This is a new "added value."

Three Visitors, One Typology

Let us take three respondents and use their experiences of the museum as the foundation for a typology of consumer segments.

Let's begin with Linda. Here is a woman who accepts the old terms of the relationship. She is quite prepared to come to the ROM as a supplicant. She believes that she does not know enough. She believes the ROM can teach her more. She believes that it can, to return to our preferment model, advance her in the larger scheme of things. In this case, the old asymmetrical model prevails.

But it does not work. As we have seen, Linda's visit to the ROM was an exercise in self-doubt. She found the exhibits difficult. As we noted, difficulty created a kind of hydroplaning in the exhibit space and this created self-repudiation. Linda might have said, "It's not my fault." She might have refused the superordinate status of the institution before which she was now wanting. Instead, she gave herself over to a self-perpetuating cycle of regret.

In Linda's case, the visitor accepts the traditional asymmetrical model and lets herself be damned by it. The outcome is obvious. She can come to the museum and suffer the consequences that follow from her self esteem. Or she can stay away. That's what she does. She would like to come to the museum more often. She really feels she ought to be a frequent visitor. But the emotional and social punishment that visits impose on her are too large a price to pay. Many of the individuals talk willingly about how they "ought" to go to the museum but never do. One wonders how many of them feel as Linda does.

And what about Barbara? She has no doubt about the nature of the structural relationship with the museum. As far as she is concerned, the museum may *not* play the superordinate party. It may *not* stand on its dignity. It may no longer assume a posture of "knowing better" or "knowing more." Certainly she will no longer play the subordinate party. She will not play the supplicant. She will no longer assume a status of one who "knows worse" or "knows less." Barbara's solution is obvious. She avoids the museum. She never goes there. In an egalitarian society, there is something galling about an institution that insists on being asymmetrical. One wonders how many of the people who never come to the museum feel as she does. They would no more come here than they would to a particularly seedy bar on the wrong side of town. Both presuppose social relationships that do not apply to their lives.

And what about Nancy? A different model appears to apply here. Nancy loves to come to the museum. She loves to bring her children. As it turns out, Nancy has found her own solution. She has simply dispensed with the asymmetrical model. By force of personality or native inventiveness, she has found a way through the traditional terms of reference imposed by the museum. She has done so by reinventing her relationship with the museum.

Nancy would laugh at the idea that there is a path through an exhibit. This is not to say that she doesn't follow it from time to time. But she does not regard it as obligatory. Nancy does not read labels religiously. She is happy to have them but amused to think that anyone would regard them as an obligation. Nancy never has the sense that she should really do one more gallery before leaving. She would be amused to think that the invention of ghost stories for the totem poles would be frowned on by curators. It is impossible to imagine Nancy suffering the self-doubt that so paralyzed Linda. In sum, Nancy feels no sense of duty to the rules of the institution or to the rules of its discourse.

It's not much of an exaggeration to say that Nancy has taken a kind of "ownership" of the ROM. But we might go a step farther and suggest that she has actually established an "authorship" as well. Nancy feels free to invent her own exhibits and routines at the museum. (Museum staff do not record the ceiling of the entrance hall as an exhibit, but Nancy has made it one for her children.) Nancy takes possession of the gothic qualities of the place and weaves them into marvelous stories for her children. Nancy is inventing the museum for her own purposes. Nancy is so little daunted by the once-majestic authority of the institution that she has effectively supplanted it. She has engaged in an ethnomuseology. She is now her own curator. (She even lets her children play the curator: "I let them make up stories.")

Nancy has reinvented the institution by refusing asymmetry. For her the museum is nothing more (and nothing less) than a bundle of educational, imaginative, and social opportunities. She feels free to choose the ones she likes and to ignore the ones she doesn't. In fact, Nancy feels herself entirely at liberty at the museum. Everything is optional. There is no burden of "shoulds" or "oughts." It is hard to know whether Nancy has made herself the equal of the museum. It is just possible she has made herself its superordinate. There is something distinctly aristocratic about the aplomb with which she picks and chooses her way through what it has to offer. Plainly, she never pays for her admission in the coin of deference. Plainly, she believes that we need her much more than she needs us (Silverman 1995).

Three visitors give us three very different glimpses of the museum. Linda sees the ROM according to the old asymmetrical model—only to find herself damned by it. Barbara has moved away from this model; indeed, she has repudiated it. In the process, she has repudiated the museum world. Until things change, she won't be back. Nancy has rejected the old model as well. In its place, she has created a new model that refuses asymmetry and appropriates the powers of the museologist for herself and her family.

Conclusion

The museum's self-definition and self-presentation continue to turn on the preferment model of museology. Captives of this ghostly notion, the museum creates exhibits that often stand a great distance from the cultural matters that concern its visitors. The result is inevitable. Visitors stare steadily at exhibits and leave unmoved or diminished. "Cretins!" "Philistines!" the museum declares them. "They have no culture. It's not our problem. It's not our fault. It's those visitors . . . those ungrateful, bad-mannered wretches."

The mask comes off. The museum expects visitors to defer before its accomplishments. It is, after all, the institution's right. The museum is the font of knowledge and status. Consumers are the subordinate party who come for advancement. If they fail to appreciate what the museum believes they need to know, well, that is their choice . . . and their problem. After all, the museum tried. It did its little bit of noblesse oblige and if consumers don't like it, well, *tant pis*. Thus does the museum confirm its prejudice and its marginality.

But the fact that our visitors do not embrace *museum* culture does not mean they embrace no culture at all. Or, to put this in the language of the title of this essay, the fact that visitors do not embrace Culture does not mean that they are without culture. We need to understand that visitors have taken leave of the cultural assumptions of museums and moved on to very different ones. More simply, they have moved away from the preferment model. Not just moved away, in point of fact, they have declared it diminishing, wounding, and estranging. In the place of this model, they have invented models of their own. They may even consider the possibility that the museum be restored to its status as a cultural arbiter. But the preferment model is dead. To insist on it, even unofficially, is to compromise the institution's ability to play any kind of compelling role in the twenty-first century, to cripple the museum beyond hope of recovery. The preferment model may serve museum staff for private status purposes. It cannot serve them for public ones.

What does the public have most to fear from museums? Museum maker, lift that flap.

Figure 10.1. "Get an Afterlife." Used with permission of the Royal Ontario Museum © ROM.

APPENDIX A:
Advertising Campaign for the Royal Ontario Museum

(Advertisements courtesy of Roche Macaulay & Partners, Toronto, and Royal Ontario Museum; permission to reproduce gratefully acknowledged.)

If the Royal Ontario Museum remains the captive of a preferment model, some of its marketing has moved on. The print advertisements discussed here were created by Roche Macaulay & Partners (then Geoffrey B. Roche and Partners) for the Royal Ontario Museum in 1994–1995. They appeared in Toronto subways, in illuminated bus shelters, on billboards, and on large banners on the exterior of the museum.

The first of these (not pictured) shows a suit of armor and the text "Dragon Food. In A Tin." This ad has a characteristic Roche Macaulay cunning. It begins with a symbol of the ROM, its armor. (The ROM once ushered visitors almost immediately into an armor hall, and a long-standing association was formed.) Something interesting then happens. This distinguished, precious status symbol is mocked. It becomes mere tin. The occupant, in the heraldic, chivalric tradition a heroic character driven by purity of intention and noble

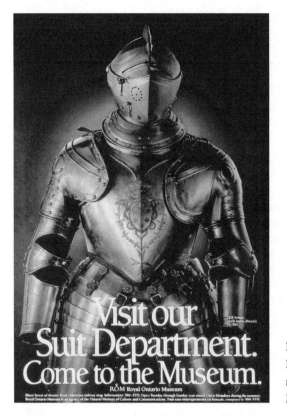

Figure 10.2. "Visit our Suit Department." Used with permission of the Royal Ontario Museum © ROM.

birth, becomes mere food. (Tuna?) The mythical dragon is credited as real—and hungry. St. George returns to us as fast food.

From a marketing point of view, the outcome is felicitous. The museum gets down off its high horse. It diminishes itself with a self-deprecating humor—a Canadian pastime. It admits to the existence of dragons and demonstrates a certain whimsy. All this appears in a larger package that says "think about something familiar in a new way." In sum, this ad helps move the museum from the *preferment* model to the *consumer* one in a single, elegant repositioning gesture. It transforms an institution known to be stuffy, self-important, and status conscious into a place capable of wit, imagination, and departure. Crucial for strategic purposes, it does this with sufficient intelligence and style to allow the museum to preserve its claim to seriousness, elevated status, and its amour propre.

The second advertisement (not pictured) shows an Egyptian mummy with the text "The Body Is 2/3 Water. Come See The Other 1/3." Once more Roche Macaulay begins with a ROM treasure, one of its signature objects. Having satisfied this most urgent marketing objective (lead with your strength), it then seizes an opportunity for deeper engagement. The ad speaks directly to the anxiety visitors often feel, and, more important, *like* to feel, in the museum. ("A body without water! Yuk!") To this extent, it speaks directly to the "gothic" strategy discussed in this essay. (Mummies are, after all, dead bodies surrounded by the terrible mystery of the ages, the imputation of grave-robbing, the possibility of curses.)

But the ad does not stop there. It uses fear and anxiety to begin the process of education. ("Really? Two-thirds water! How did they manage that?") Without this third step, the museum fails its particular agenda. Fear without edification ends up looking like emotion-mongering and, in the language of the usual curatorial complaint, "mere entertainment" when something more instructive is called for.

There is a subtle strategic daring at the bottom of this ad—and this is the ad's last act. Mummies have a double significance, as Barbara, a respondent for this study, pointed out. They are a symbol of the most romantic aspects of the museum heritage—and they are the ROM brand. But they are also a symbol of the "desiccation" that the ROM is seen to perform on much of what it touches. Museum visitors claim frequently that the ROM takes fascinating subjects and makes them dull. And Barbara pointed out (bless respondents who actually begin the analysis), the mummy also evokes the "desert dryness" of the institution, of things that have had two-thirds of their interest removed. The mummy stands for the best and worst of the ROM and the visitor's frequent ambivalence.

Roche Macaulay goes right after this discomfort. It says, in effect: "No, wait, this museum is interesting in just the way you think it's interesting. We know why you find the mummy moving and we embrace this just as much as we do the Egyptologist's version."

The 1980s restored values challenged by the 1960s. It did so with phrases like "Get a life." This potent little slogan said: "Put '60s values behind you, get on with your life."

By the mid-1990s, when this ad appeared (see fig. 10.1), '80s values were themselves beginning to wane. This ad seized the moment. It said: "Put the things of the '80s behind you, consider things beyond materialism and individualism." What doubled the effect of the ad was that it also evoked the New Age shift taking place in North American culture.

Part Six
Advertising

Strategy:

This section offers an anthropological treatment of advertising. The essay offers a glimpse of the advertising industry. The article offers a more academic treatment of this approach, showing, in particular, how the anthropological approach to advertising differs from the information-processing point of view.

11 Taking Madison Avenue by Storm

Yesterday (March 25, 2004), I was standing in the lobby of Ogilvy Worldwide in New York City waiting to get through security. In front of me are three fresh-scrubbed guys with new clothes, new haircuts, new shoes. They are looking around them with awe and anticipation.

I engage one of them, a tall Asian kid with spiky hair, in conversation and he tells me they are from the Miami School of Design. They are here to see what life looks like in the Big Leagues. I can see them thinking "and some day I will stride through this lobby like I own the place . . . maybe." They are very nervous. Clearly, it's time for the old-timer to give a pep talk.

"Hey, you'll wow them with your ideas," I say.

One of the kids actually hangs his head and says with heartfelt sincerity, "I don't have any ideas."

"No, no, no," I can hear myself thinking, "this is not the way you take Madison Avenue by storm."

Peppier talk is called for.

"The ideas are already here, like electricity. It's the strangest thing. You get into the boardroom, you start talking, and the ideas flow. The trick is to step into the moment. It's like improv. Don't censor. Just talk. The ideas are there in the heavens waiting for a chance to get into the room. You have to let them know that they can channel through you."

He looks at me with surprise and relief.

"It's a kind of groupmind thing," I say. "Eventually, you are thinking out of one another's heads."

The kids look at me with hope and skepticism. I am old enough to know what I am talking about. On the other hand, maybe I'm too old to know what I'm talking about.

And then I say, "It's as much fun as you can have with your clothes on."

And they laugh at this. Obviously, I'm a nut.

They get signed in and as they move toward the elevators, I say, "Knock 'em dead."

One of them turns and laughs and waves.

12 Advertising

Meaning versus Information

> Why do consumers read or view advertising? Well, they must expect some
> benefit. Perhaps they receive some information.
>
> —Shugan 1982, 118

Abstract

This essay examines two models that have been used in the study of
advertising: the information-based model and the meaning-based model. It
argues that the information-based model has two theoretical insufficiencies.

Introduction

The prevailing paradigm in consumer research conceives of the consumer as someone who is information centered, someone constantly seeking
out and manipulating information in order to make choices between consumer goods and services. Much of the model-building rehearsed in consumer behavior texts is designed precisely to give a systematic account of this
information and the manner in which it reaches, and is then manipulated by,
the consumer. Much of the research reported in the field uses this paradigm
to identify the important questions and data. For some in the field of consumer research, an information-based model on the consumer has become
the foundation of inquiry.

Plainly this model has served us well and plainly it will continue to do so.
This model has achieved such preeminence, however, that it is easy for us to
forget that it is only one of several alternatives with which we can make sense
of consumer behavior and undertake consumer research. The purpose of this
essay is to consider one of these alternatives.

The meaning-based model recited here treats the consumer as someone
who is meaning centered. It asks what happens to our vision of the consumer
and, more particularly, to our vision of advertising when we adopt this rather
different perspective. It is hoped this meaning-based model will prove an illuminating and useful addition to the theoretical armory now at the disposal
of the scholar engaged in consumer research.

A useful way of thinking about this discussion is provided by T. S. Kuhn's concept of competing scientific paradigms (1962). I do not wish to evoke the whole of this model, but it is useful to observe that the information-based and the meaning-based approaches are in some respects very like competing paradigms. They begin from different assumptions, they work toward different conclusions, they capture different kinds of data. These are fundamental differences, not a simple division of academic labor. These two paradigms construe the world quite differently.

The Kuhnian perspective, interestingly, has a polemical value for both paradigms. It encourages us to see that the following criticism of the information-processing model is bound to accuse it falsely. My criticism will resort to assumptions, techniques, and data that the information-based model is not designed to accommodate. Virtually all of my criticisms can be met with the countercriticism: "But our model was never designed to do what you say it does not do." In the words of Kuhn, much of my criticism will "read through" the information paradigm and therefore fail to come to grips with its proclaimed purposes and projects. I grant this readily.

But the Kuhnian approach can also be used to support the cause of criticism. It tells us that prevailing paradigms are well advised to take account of the seditious mutterings of the kind that are made against it here. It is, after all, from just such mutterings that new paradigms rise to overturn the old order. Kuhn's perspective suggests that it is, when possible, better to accommodate mutterings than to exile them.

A Meaning-Based Model of Consumption

Let me briefly characterize the meaning-based model and then outline the approach it takes to advertising. This model says that the consumer is an individual in a cultural context engaged in a cultural project. Both the context and the project are culturally constituted. The context consists of the culturally specified ideas of person, object, activity, time, and space in which the culture consists. I have dealt with this elsewhere in some detail and will not elaborate it here (McCracken 1986a).

The project is an ongoing enterprise by which the individual conceives of self, family, status, nation, and world. This project consists in the selection of key notions from a range of alternatives and the more-or-less thorough and harmonious enactment, refinement, and integration of these notions in a single life (Hirschman 1986; McCracken 1986b, 1986c). In this scheme, the self and a life are "always in production, in process" (Bruner 1984a, 3). What Bakhtin (1981, 270) says of language applies equally well to the self:

A unitary language is not something given but is always in essence pos-
ited—and in every moment of its linguistic life it is opposed to the realities
of heteroglossia. But at the same time it makes its real essence felt as a force
for overcoming this heteroglossia, imposing specific limits to it, guarantee-
ing a certain mutual understanding and crystallizing into a real, although
still relative, unity.

The project is a continual one in two senses. It is, first of all, intensely processual, so that its objective, the construction of a life, is realized not with a
single operation or a series of operations but through the act itself. The project does not have a beginning and an end; it is fulfilled as it is undertaken.
Second, the project is constantly changing as the individual is driven to
change by circumstance, preference, and the life cycle. New projects become
necessary as the individual ages, as some projects prove impractical, as some
of them are completed, and as the world around the individual changes. All
of these factors call for new projects. It is, for both of these reasons, perpetual.

The model of consumption that follows from this perspective says that the
world of goods is a cultural construction and that culture is constantly being
played out in goods. The ideational and material aspects of the world are intimately linked in ways that we understand and in ways that we are only beginning to understand. Cultural meanings, those in goods and those outside
of them, make up the cultural context of consumption.

Consumer goods are also essential to the project by which our lives are constructed. Consumer goods, in their anticipation, choice, purchase, and possession, are an important source of the meanings with which we construct
our lives. They are also an important instrument by which we capture, experiment with, and organize the meanings with which we construct our lives.

Advertising in the Meaning-Based Model

Advertising plays an interesting role in the context and the projects of
consumption. As I have suggested elsewhere, advertising is one of the ways
we get into goods (McCracken 1986a). It is the conduit through which meanings are constantly transferred from the culturally constituted world to the
consumer good. Ads are what Lotman and Uspensky (1978, 213) would call
a "diecasting mechanism." Lotman and Uspensky devised this term for language and its "transformation of the 'open' world of realia into a 'closed'
world of names" (213). But it applies equally well to advertising, especially in
a culture like our own that is constantly opening up the world of sensation
and signification to novel elements and configurations. Advertising helps capture these old and new cultural meanings and invest them in consumer goods

where they become accessible to the consumer. A process of constant experimentation takes place in which meanings are suggested and revised, combined and recombined. Advertising puts at the disposal of modern culture an area of play, experimentation, and innovation with which to fashion new cultural meanings and reorganize and reassign old ones. It is where culture does its diecasting.

In a more mundane manner, advertising serves as a kind of dictionary constantly keeping us apprised of new consumer signifieds and signifiers. We cannot read the cultural context without this source of instruction. In this capacity, advertising makes an important contribution to the context of consumption.

But let us now consider the contribution advertising makes to the consumer's project. Martin Silverman (1971) speaks of the intense interest that the Banagan people of the Pacific paid to the newspapers and magazines in a time of astonishing dislocation and stress. He wondered what they were looking for there and concluded finally that they were looking for some thinkable, actionable vision of themselves. Modern consumers, untouched by crisis but subject nevertheless to change, examine advertisements for a similar reason. They are searching out meaning there.

Consumers are looking for something they can use in their construction of new versions of the self, the family, a community. They are seeking not meaning with a capital "M," the existential notion of the term. They are looking for small meanings, concepts of what it is to be a man or a woman, concepts of what it is to be middle aged, concepts of what it is to be a parent, concepts of what a child is and what a child is becoming, concepts of what it is to be a member of a community and a country. These are the projects that preoccupy us on a continual basis. These are our preoccupations in a time and place that has given the individual liberties in matters of self-definition. What were once liberties are now a necessity. We are both free and forced to exercise them. One of our sources of instruction and experimentation here is the advertisement. When the consumer looks at ads, he or she is looking for symbolic resources, new ideas and better concrete versions of old ideas with which to advance their project. Meaning moves from culture to us through goods.

A Meaning-Based Critique of the Information-Based Model

This notion of the consumer, of consumption, and of advertising, is not new to us. Versions of this concept have been floating around in anthropology and consumer research for more than a decade (cf. Belk 1982;

Hirschman and Holbrook 1981; Holman 1980; Sherry 1991; Williamson 1978). But we have not yet fully contemplated the implications of this model for the information-based concept of advertising. We have yet to take these ideas into the lion's den. This essay suggests only a first pass in this effort, a quick dash across the arena, as it were. More detailed criticism may be forthcoming from braver souls.

From the meaning-based point of view, the information-processing model's treatment of advertisement is unsatisfactory because it does not give a satisfactory account of the principle components of the meaning-based approach described here. This model is prepared to come to terms with neither the cultural context of consumption nor the cultural project in which the consumer is engaged. The remainder of this essay will detail these problems with the model and specify the theoretical implications and origins of their difficulties.

Context

The information-processing approach ignores the cultural context of consumption. It provides no way of observing that the individual who is processing information is embedded in a highly structured and meaningfully constituted environment. It gives no way of permitting us to see that the individual is the recipient not just of information but also of meaning. As a member of a culture, the individual sees his or her world through an interpretive frame. This frame is culturally constituted. It is fashioned according to the specifications of the culture. The world he or she perceives is itself culturally constituted according to the specifications of culture. Everything that is perceived by the individual is therefore doubly mediated by culture. Culture constitutes both the world and the means by which it is apprehended.

The information-processing model divorces the individual from this cultural context. It fails to see that the individual is embedded in a meaningfully constituted world that has been divided up and organized by the beliefs of a culture. And it fails to see that the individual cannot apprehend this world except through a lens that is also the work of culture.

The existing models of decision processing sometimes have boxes marked "social influences" and arrows that connect these boxes to boxes marked "belief," "attitudes," "memory" and so on, but the relationship is rarely specified in a manner that captures the cultural meanings according to which consumption is organized. The absence of this specification means that the model must restrict itself to the "stuff" that takes place within the individual's head. But the model gives no way of including the collective meanings and conventions on which the individual draws and on which he or she operates.

For this paradigm, the individual does not live in a culturally constituted world. This criticism of an essentially psychological model for the study of social behavior has been made convincingly within the field itself (Harre and Secord 1972).

These limitations of the model make the full treatment of advertising difficult. When individuals regard advertisements or any other form of stimuli, they are looking at material that has been culturally constituted and they are interpreting it according to cultural conventions. These conventions specify perceptual acts at the simplest level and at the highest, like rhetorical rules. This highly coded, regulated material is unintelligible unless the consumer bears the interpretive frame that culture puts at his or her disposal.

Still more problematically, the model cannot show how the individual mind participates in the meaning-manufacture process of which advertising consists. Advertisements are deliberate attempts to put meaning into goods. This process depends on the observer of the ad, for it is this observer who is the final agent of the process of transference (Fournier 1998). In this understanding of advertising, the individual's mind is not merely drawing information from the ad, which it will then store in memory and variously grade and manipulate at the moment of decision. It is participating in the assignation of meaning to consumer goods.

When the information-based model takes no account of the cultural context, it reproduces one of the cardinal sins of the field of psychology. As Shweder (1984) put it, one of the chief "research heuristics" for the psychological sciences is that "what's really real is inside the skin; the individual person is the sole unit of analysis" (3). This narrow focus excludes from consideration the collective and the supraindividual, and it makes the individual the locus of all that need be taken into account to understand social behavior. The information-processing model commits itself to something very like methodological individualism (Lukes 1968, 1973b). It makes the individual the only locus of meaning and significance and supposes that within the teeming neurons of an individual brain one can discover and capture all the essential ingredients and logics of the decision-making process. Durkheim argued long ago that social facts cannot be accounted for by individual ones (Lukes 1973a, 20).

All of this is to say that the information-processing model restricts analytic attention to the individual. It eliminates from consideration the cultural context from which the individual draws his or her information, the cultural context which supplies the process by which this information is apprehended and manipulated, and the cultural context in which the individual enters into the advertising process to help manufacture certain kinds of consumer knowledge and signification. There is evidence that the field of psychology is now preparing to take account of the role of culture and shared information in information-processing, but the completion of this undertaking is apparently some way off (Harre and Secord 1972; Murphy and Medin 1985).

Project

The information-processing approach also ignores the cultural projects of consumption. It provides no way of understanding how the individual who is processing information is engaged in several formal and informal projects of the construction of self and world. It gives no way of permitting us to see that the individual is not just the recipient of meaning but is also active in its construction. As a member of a culture, the individual is engaged in fashioning ideas of self, family, and nation. These cultural activities are used to "perform" or "enact" these ideas and give them legitimacy, substance, credibility.

One of the chief ways in which both the individuals and collectivities of this culture perform and enact their ideas of self and world is through their consumer goods. Consumer goods, charged with cultural significance, serve as dramatic props and meaning sources. They supply ideas of gender, class, age, and lifestyle to individuals and help them make these ideas a tangible reality.

The information-processing model makes no provision for these cultural processes. This model assumes that what the individual wishes to draw from consumer goods are "benefits." The individual's "project," from this point of view, is to survey the marketplace until he or she is able to determine which product will best "satisfy" his or her "needs." This formulation makes no provision for the creative manipulation of this meaning in the construction of notions of self and world. I do not wish to dispute that consumers seek information in the pursuit of interest and benefits. But to suggest that this is all that is taking place is to very substantially underspecify the project in which the consumer is engaged.

The information-processing model tends instead to see the individual as a rational individual who is maximizing interest through the pursuit of calculable benefits. In this model, the individual is not constructing a concept and a reality of his or her world. He or she is seen instead to be calculating the surest way to satisfy needs.

This aspect of the theory also has certain disadvantages in the study of the nature of advertisements. First of all, and most obviously, it makes ever-so-slightly mysterious the fact that so much of advertising consists not of lists of information and descriptions of product benefits but of evocative images and text that appears to supply no obvious basis for rational product choice.

From a strict "benefits" point of view, it is not clear why advertisements should employ images of a leafy neighborhood or the deck of a sun-drenched sailboat. How do we get these things into the model? What happens to them once they are in the model? Can the model comprehend them in the literal and figurative sense? Are these "benefits," can they be calculated, does the individual take these symbols to be information for product choice? This is where the paradigm finds itself in the presence of endless amounts of anomalous data. I would say in opposition that individuals are constantly examining advertisements for material they can use in their construction projects. Certainly they "try to find some information" here, but it is also true that this is one of their key sources of meaning.

Here too it would appear that the information-processing model is reproducing one of the cardinal sins of one of its founding disciplines. This time the offender is not psychology but economics. What we see being smuggled into the paradigm when it makes benefits the objective of information processing and product choice is the "economic man" notion of human conduct. Both Sahlins (1976) and Douglas and Isherwood (1978) have complained about this tendency of the social sciences to attribute a marketplace rationality to social actors. Sahlins has gone so far as to suggest that even our marketplace behavior springs from concerns both more complicated and more cultural. Hirschman (1977) notes that the notion of "interest" is a historically created and limited one and that there was once a time when the term referred to the "totality of human aspirations" (32). The ideas that consumer research has borrowed from economics contain certain limitations that are reproduced in theoretical elaborations even as late and as distant as the information-processing model. The issue is not to dispense with the notion of rationality but to broaden it.

Conclusion

As Marshall Sahlins (1976) puts it, "Every theory makes a bargain with reality." Every theory trades certain kinds of knowledge at the expense of other kinds of knowledge. Or, to put this more forcefully, every piece of knowledge comes at the cost of a certain kind of blindness. This essay has observed that the information-processing model cannot contend with the cultural context and project of consumption. It must be noted, however, that the meaning-based model has its own insufficiencies. It cannot contend with certain aspects of the individual's response to the stimuli of advertising. It cannot pretend to do everything that the information-based model does for us and more besides. This would be an especially fraudulent advertising claim.

The point I wish to make here is only that there are crucial aspects of the consumption and advertising process that are not satisfactorily treated by the information-based model. Moreover, there would appear to be something in the very nature of the model that prohibits it from incorporating this material. If this is so, no mere tinkering with the model will save it from its insufficiencies. Now, if it is also true that the meaning-based model cannot serve as a replacement, what is required is a ground-up construction of new models. The virtue of this undertaking, aside from the new insight it would give us into consumption, is that it would help make the field of consumer research the producer of its own models. We have been traditionally the clients of other fields, heir to their models, and, as I have tried to suggest here, heir sometimes to the limitations of these models. The integration of information-based and meaning-based models is a project that can take place within the consumer research tradition. It is one of the projects by which we can begin to make ourselves the center of our own theory development.

Part Seven
Marketing

Strategy:

This section is devoted to the idea that products, services, and brands take some of their value from the meaning-management performed by marketing professionals.

This section opens with an essay that looks at value as it comes downstream from the marketing system and finds its way into the life of a little girl.

The article for this section offers a systematic view of how marketing creates value through the meaning-management process.

13 Sarah Zupko, Meet Mrs. Woolworth

Commerce has a way of making capital colorless. Here's a corrective. (All names and figures are sheer guesswork and offered for illustrative purposes only. With apologies to Frank Capra.)

Sarah Zupko is a little girl in Red Deer, Alberta. Her dad took her into town today. It's January 4, 1948. Her dad stops at Woolworth's for a coffee at the counter. He falls into conversation with his friends, other farmers, there: crops, water tables, combines, silage, almanacs, Indian summers, and spring.

Sarah is pretty sure she couldn't care less. She wanders through the aisles and comes eventually to rest in front of an illuminated glass case. There under glass is a watch, its perfect little numerals marching around the dial, delicate hands now still, and a metal band of cunning silver; a bracelet really. It is $9.60.

Sarah visits the case and the watch on every visit into town, and magically, on her ninth birthday, in late March, the watch is hers. The birthday party, thunderous with farm children and festivity, falls silent. The watch is hers.

The rest is economics. The Woolworth's store in Red Deer keeps half of the $9.60 and the Chicago distributor keeps half of what's left. By the time Mr. and Mrs. Zupko's $9.60 finds its way into the Woolworth's fortune, it has become around 33 cents.

Value has migrated from a glass case to a large vault. But it does not stay there.

The Woolworths are building a summer home, and 7 cents is spent to help hire men to clear the land that runs down to the point. The value Mr. Zupko extracted as winter wheat from prairie soil will actually now return to the ground as Mrs. Hudson, wife of one of the laborers, spends part of it to buy the seed for her summer garden. A dime will go to help pay for Mr. Woolworth's dues at the Century Club, and part of this will be spent on that beeswax that is used to give club chairs and tables the glow they give off in the light of the fire that burns all day in the library. Another dime will go to the grand tour the eldest Woolworth daughter will take to Europe that year, a trip from which she will return with a taste for poetry and men who are a little bit dangerous. A few cents will even go to help pay for the clasp that holds the necklace that Mrs. Woolworth wears to the social event of the season, where it will be eclipsed by the still-more-magnificent jewelry worn by that jumped-up Mrs. Chetwin, a creature who has finally pushed Mrs. Woolworth from her accustomed place of splendor.

The Woolworth family is a little like the mouth of the Fraser River, the place from which the tiny purchases made upstream by little girls in obscure places come rushing into the world, released from transit and their colorless state as mere capital into labor, summer homes, spring vegetables, beeswax, grand tours, poetry, necklaces, and social failure.

We've said nothing of the upward flow, about the value created by Woolworth's working its way into a glass case and a watch . . . and from there into parental solicitude and a little girl's sense of herself. That's for the article to follow. The watch that played the conduit for this flow upward and downward now sits in an antique store in Winnipeg, Manitoba, once more in a glass case, waiting for another chance to turn commerce into culture.

14 Meaning-Management

An Anthropological Approach to the Creation of Value

As a practical and intellectual enterprise, marketing turns, to some extent, on the question of value. Value is the basis of price. It is the font of profit. The firm is designed to create and capture value. This concept of marketing is widely accepted. It serves as a powerful foundation for our understanding of what marketing is, the identification of the problems marketing must solve to serve the business community, and the intellectual agenda that directs the academic's interest.

But do we have an exhaustive definition of value? This essay will argue that we do not. Some value comes from cultural meaning. Marketing, it will argue, generates value partly because it generates meaning. One of the things the marketing manager is managing is meaning. Meanings are party to the marketing process at several points. This aspect of value, I will argue, has no systematic part in most marketing calculations. It makes a cameo appearance when we talk about brands and advertising, but it is more foundational than this. The purpose of this essay is to suggest how meaning as value might be made a more systematic part of the marketing model.

The *practice* of marketing long ago came to terms with the role of meaning. Every manager is a de facto meaning-manager. Unofficially and implicitly, firms operate with the battle-weary understanding that well-constructed, well-managed meanings add value, create consumers, sell products, advance careers, generate profit, and raise stock prices even as they have come to see that badly constructed, badly managed meanings confuse the consumer, diminish brands, damage careers, generate losses, and help pull stock prices down. The real problem, often, is the academic models. I believe that they fail to give us a formal and exhaustive understanding of the role of meaning.

One of the ways to approach this problem is to think about culture as a fifth C. I understand that this is a common rhetorical ploy for someone who is trying to claim a piece of the intellectual terrain that is marketing theory. Call it a new C or another P and we're halfway to glory. But I believe that meaning plays sufficiently important a role that this proposal is not far fetched. But let me be clear. I am not proposing we add a fifth C, merely that we think about marketing theory for a moment this way.

I adapt John Deighton and Bob Dolan's model, adding culture at the top of the cascade as one of the fonts of value, as in figure 14.1. Placing culture

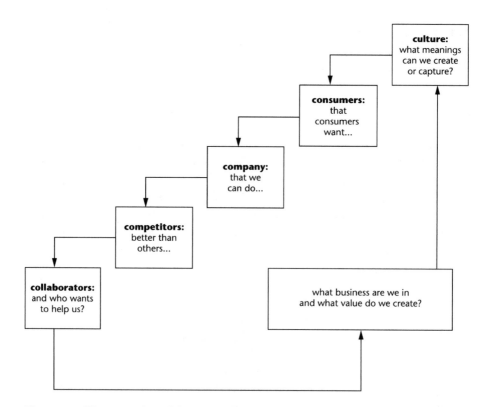

Figure 14.1. The 5 Cs, adapted from a model created by John Deighton and Robert Dolan and circulated at the Harvard Business School. Used with permission of the Harvard Business School.

here helps to show where meaning comes from and its role in the traditional interrelationship of customers, company, competitors, and collaborators. It helps show how the firm can manage meaning to create customers, profit, and its place in the world.

This model says that every product and service is made up of its physical properties, functional features, and cultural meanings. Figure 14.2 suggests the kind and the range of meanings that any consumer good or service can draw upon. Typically, a well-constructed and well-managed brand will claim meanings from most, sometimes all, of these domains.

Each of the perimeter boxes represents a cultural domain. And each domain has its own characteristics, categories, structure, and logic. Gender, to take one example, may be seen as a continuum: relatively male to relatively female. Products charged with gender are well known. They include Marlboro cigarettes and Chanel perfume. It could be argued that clothing brands

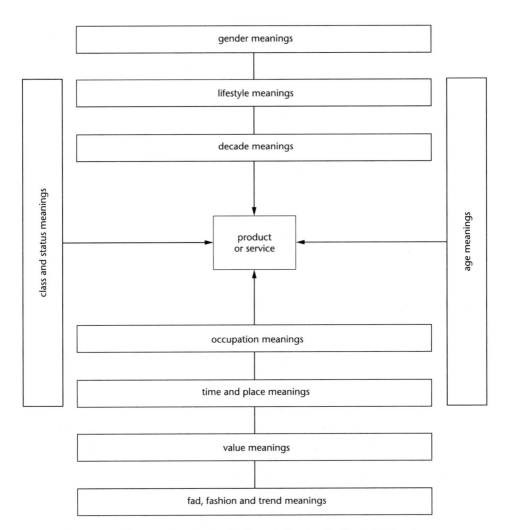

Figure 14.2. Meaning Sources for Product or Service, by Grant McCracken

can be (and have been) mapped across the full range and that almost every possible type of maleness can be mapped across the full range, as can almost every type of femaleness. But it would be wrong to oversimplify. Each domain of meaning is crowded with multiple versions, conflicting logics, and has been shaped and reshaped by social developments and historical events (e.g., feminism). Still, there is relative clarity to the cultural domains and the meanings they contain.

These meanings come from somewhere. They come from culture, as figure 14.3 suggests. And they are captured for the product or service through de-

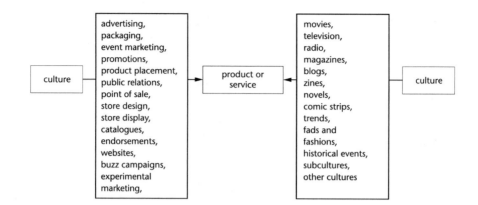

| culture | | advertising,
packaging,
event marketing,
promotions,
product placement,
public relations,
point of sale,
store design,
store display,
catalogues,
endorsements,
websites,
buzz campaigns,
experimental
marketing, | product or
service | movies,
television,
radio,
magazines,
blogs,
zines,
novels,
comic strips,
trends,
fads and
fashions,
historical events,
subcultures,
other cultures | culture |

Figure 14.3. Meaning Sources and Delivery Devices, by Grant McCracken

livery vehicles, some of which fall within the marketing envelope (column A) and some of which fall without (column B). One of the objectives of good marketing is to maximize the delivery devices the firm controls (column A) and capture the outcomes of the ones it doesn't (column B).

And meanings go somewhere. They end up in the life of the consumer. In this case, the product has delivered value because it has delivered meaning. This is, in part, why the consumer is buying the product or service—to obtain the meaning contained in it.

The consumer has access to many meaning sources beyond the ones provided by marketing. But the ones provided by marketing are vital to the self-invention or self-completion of the individual. This is one of the reasons that meanings add value. We do not have the full inventory of cultural meanings and delivery devices that would allow us to deal with this question in detail, but it is possible that there are some kinds or degrees of cultural meanings that are available to the individual only as a consumer. And it is, survey or no, manifestly clear that certain meanings that most people treat as essential to full participation in the contemporary world come from this source.

Consumers could find other sources of this meaning, and sometimes they do. But this "outsourcing" comes at a cost. At the least, this is a self-imposed marginality. Without the meanings made available by the marketing system, the individual is, for some social and cultural reasons, incomplete or at least pallid.

Meaning-Management and the Marketing Model

The meaning-management model suggests a way to supplement the intellectual and practical agenda established by Robert Dolan's *Schematic of*

Marketing Process (1998). We may assess each of the pieces of Dolan's schematic and observe the way meaning enters in.

Company

Strictly speaking, any brand can be charged with any meaning. This is a measure of the range of possibility open to the marketer. But strategically, it's clear that each product category and brand has a heritage, a body of meanings that have come to surround the brand over time. An inventory of this heritage will show that some meanings are richer and more accessible for the brand than others. It *is* possible to begin with a clean slate, but it is more strategic to take advantage of the meanings already in place.

Several questions are germane. What cultural meanings exist in the category? Plainly, the automobile industry has been making and managing cultural meanings quite different from those of packaged goods.

What, then, are the meanings in the brand? We know that brands are complicated bundles of meaning partly because they have been picking up meaning through the efforts of several generations of managers. What is this set of possibilities? What are the special claims or properties that the brand has in the world of meaning (e.g., logos, spokespeople, long-standing sponsorships)? This stage of analysis determines what meanings the company does well and what meanings are most easily within its grasp.

Macallan, the single malt scotch whisky, rose from obscurity to the status of a leading brand by crossing the tone of fly-fishing (a sport of robust but thoughtful masculinity) and the "fit and finish" of *New Yorker* editorial copy. The outcome was a kind of "patrician Marlboro man." The cunning of the strategy was that it allowed the new scotch drinker to engage in the connoisseurship implicit in the single malt revolution without having to worry about being seen as self-conscious, effete, or affected. In this particularly skillful piece of meaning-management, Macallan found a way to capture the cultural meaning that would capture market share.

Competitors

What meanings do competitors control? What ground have they staked out? What are their strengths and vulnerabilities? What are their historical inclinations and reflexes? In what direction does their corporate culture take them? In what direction do their strategic inclinations take them? This stage of the analysis asks what meanings competitors control and what meanings are within their reach. The strategic question then becomes which of these meanings can be devalued, which can be won away, and which can be eclipsed by the creation of a more powerful package of brand meanings.

It is clear that competitors shape one another by their competition over meaning. Often they end up creating their own little competitive universe of meanings. The cola wars have created a study in the competitive struggle over meaning-management. The Coca-Cola Company, with an early advantage and decades of careful marketing, controlled the meanings of the mainstream: exuberance, excitement, sociality, centrality. Pepsi-Cola, as a relative newcomer, had no choice but to claim meanings that were more marginal, risk taking, dynamic. As it happened, these meanings spoke to a new and vital marketing segment—young people. By making itself cooler, hipper, more youthful, and more current, Pepsi could capture vital meanings and market shares.

Coca-Cola was caught in the middle. If it went after Pepsi's strategy and segment, it put its mainstream franchise at risk. If it left the margin to Pepsi, it risked being repositioned as clumsy, clueless, and old-fashioned. The meaning-management calculation of the moment said that it came down to this choice. Coca-Cola endured Pepsi, and for a time it gave away the segment in question. More recently, meaning-management strategies have changed. Coca-Cola now manages meanings in such a way that it can protect the massive middle of the market *and* address what we used to call the Pepsi generation.

This means that there are multiple product lines, advertising campaigns, and meaning-management strategies. One segment is vaguely aware of the messages Coca-Cola sends to other segments, but this segment tunes in only on the one meant for it. Here too competitive advantage comes through better, more delicate, more cunning meaning-management.

Collaborators

Who can help us make meanings? Sometimes firms establish alliances. These are collaborators who can supply meanings that the brand has not successfully generated for itself. Here, too, what is called for is a fine reckoning of who controls which meanings and whether and how these meanings can serve the interests of the brand.

We may take as our case in point here the possible relationship between Harley-Davidson and Jack Daniels. Current marketing practice might well mandate this as a useful collaborative relationship. After all, there appears to be a connection here. From a cultural point of view, the motorcycle and the bourbon occupy the same cultural terrain. But is this good grounds for collaboration? A meaning-management point of view suggests that a brand does not want relationships with brands that manufacture the *same* (or virtually the same) cultural meaning. What is sought is a relationship that gives the Harley-Davidson new and useful meanings and markets.

Customers

Meaning-management demands very particular questions here. Who is the customer? What meanings do they habitually use? Where do they find these meanings? How are their meaning needs changing as changes take place in their life stage, family structure, self-definition, and lifestyle? Typically, we have resorted to ethnographic methods to determine these needs, but a more systematic approach to the role of meanings in value opens up the possibility of methods that are more precise and more quantitative. Plainly this stage of strategy is foundational. Without a precise understanding of the meanings customers care about, the rest of the meaning-management process must be compromised.

Levi Strauss & Co. had a particular cultural meaning thrust upon them. In the 1950s, their jeans became a symbol of the rebel without a cause. Jack Kerouac, James Dean, and Marlon Brando became inadvertent brand champions. The 1960s were kinder still. Levi's became the choice of a counterculture and hippies, yippies, and the SDS alike. This claim to cool served the company handsomely. A Levi Strauss vice president calls it "a crucial corporate equity worth billions of dollars." This makes it all the more surprising that Levi Strauss lost track of cool. With the rise of alternative, hip-hop, skater, and other trends, young people moved toward baggy jeans, a trend Levi Strauss believed to be a passing fancy. They now see they were wrong. In the words of a new member of the management team, "Loose jeans is not a fad; it's a paradigm shift" (Espen 1999, 54). Losing track of cool proved costly. Sales of $7.1 billion in 1996 fell to $6 billion for 1998 and the company was obliged to lay off nearly 6,000 employees. Meaning-mismanagement is expensive.

We are accustomed to the volatility of youth markets. But it applies equally well, I believe, to more "mature" markets. We have seen new consumer interest in four-wheel drive (4WD) vehicles. For some players in the automobile industry, this trend looked relatively transparent. Consumers wanted a car capable of going off road for camping trips and fishing expeditions. But it quickly became apparent that something else was at work. As we now know, most customers will never use 4WD capability, they will never take their vehicles off road, and, most interesting, they will continue to regard 4WD as a desirable attribute and a sensible purchase.

This was bad news for the manufacturers who simply added 4WD to existing models. For it was not 4WD, as 4WD, that the consumer wanted. Something else was at work. Consumers were responding to the "mean streets" of America with a concern that luxury automobiles might be an invitation for abuse. They were suddenly in the market for status markers that were robust, for elegance that was well armored. Along came a second trend. Consumers were less interested in "badges of status" and more interested in the possibility of new and adventurous experiences (Pine and Gilmore 1999). The consumer sought 4WD not because it allowed him or her to go off road but because the size and functionality of such a vehicle gave both the vehicle and the owner a new resourcefulness and formidableness.

Jim Schroer, Ford vice president in charge of global marketing, captured this nicely in his planning for the Lincoln Navigator.

> If we were thinking only in terms of demographics, we would have developed another car for the older people who drive the Lincoln Town Car. But if I really understand this brand, Lincoln, then where can I take it? To a minivan? To a truck? What would a Lincoln minivan look like? You define a brand by its intangible psychological essence, not by its demographics. (Goldberger 1999, 33)

Does the appeal of the Lincoln Navigator lie in its "intangible psychological essence"? It should be possible to establish a more precise reading of what the consumer wanted from a sports utility vehicle (Fournier 1996).

Marketing Segmentation

Meaning-management says, What does a market look like when segmented by meaning needs? How does each segment map onto the general culture? How do all the segments "map" relative to one another? This is often what is going on in marketing practice. The object for a meaning-management point of view is to see whether these de facto strategies can be tested, strengthened, and made more systematic and more sophisticated. Too often marketing segmentation that attempts to capture "markets by meanings" ends up with an ad hoc scheme that takes no account of the cultural parameters in place.

Selection of Target Markets

Meaning-management makes target selection a more precise and strategic undertaking. It lets the firm ask, "Which segment most cares about the meaning we manufacture and how do we deliver it?" Assuming that every segment is constantly in motion, discarding old meanings and seeking new ones, the question then becomes, "Where is our segment going and how can we be there to meet it?" This is both an academic question and a managerial one. We do not now have the models or measures to understand how meanings change or consumers move. Nor do we have the early warning devices or response strategies that would serve managers when they do so.

Marketing segmentation is sometimes meaning segmentation. This is sometimes the surest way to escape marketing myopia. It is the surest route to capturing the consumer's point of view. But segmenting demographically often tears through the cultural map. It splits where we should lump and lumps where we should split. Psychographic and lifestyle segmentation can have the same limitation. People may look like "young moderns" or "affluent empty nesters" from the outside, but this is almost certainly not the way they see themselves. This outsider's perspective seals the observer away from understanding the cultural meanings the customer cares about and the segments they establish in the marketplace.

Product and Service Positioning

What is needed here are meaning maps that show where company and competitive products are positioned. These are essential, and creating them is one of the developmental tasks of a meaning-as-value approach to marketing. Certainly something like this is generated by perceptual maps, but sometimes these are artificial constructs unrooted in the culture that supplies the options. Industry practice does often position products and services in terms of meaning, but again often these maps do not capture the culture from which meaning comes.

Marketing Mix

All the pieces of the marketing mix are meaning-makers. All of them are vehicles by which meanings are "delivered" from the general culture to the product or service.

Product and Service

The product and service is a bundle of physical properties, functions, and meanings. We are quite good at thinking about the first two aspects of the product and service and somewhat less good about the third. But Kotler is clear on this point. "Broadly defined, products include physical objects, services, persons, places, organizations, [and] ideas." His "three levels of the product" model locates meanings at the center of the model, in the core product (Kotler and Armstrong 1999, 238–239; Levitt 1986, 74). A meaning-

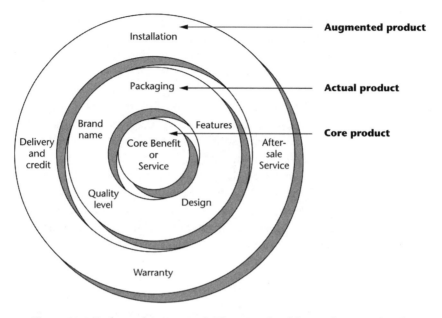

Figure 14.4. Kotler and Armstrong's Three Levels of the Product. Used with permission of the authors.

management approach calls for an exhaustive, accurate, strategically useful account of the meanings here.

We are sometimes encouraged to think about these meanings as the "personality" of the brand, but it is not clear that this is always an illuminating or useful metaphor. The meanings of the product or service are not always the characteristics of an individual personality. They are often neither consistent nor integrated. It is not clear, in fact, that the consumer thinks of the brand as a personality or person from whom meanings are being borrowed. Brands are more like bundles or, in the metaphor of the moment, "buckets" of meaning, aggregations more than associations. Rarely do they meet even the minimum conditions of personality or personhood in our culture. It's not clear we would want them to. The "personality" metaphor may create more confusion than clarity for the field of meaning-management.

But this observation begs the question. What kind of buckets does a product or a brand represent? What are the formal properties of these meanings? How do they intersect? How do they interact? We have had a clear view of this theoretical work since Sidney Levy's magisterial work appeared over forty years ago (Levy 1959). There is evidence of work in progress, but an immense amount of work remains to be done (Belk 1991; Kleine and Kernan 1991; Richins 1994a, 1994b).

A key area of research here is the possibility of a multiplicity of meaning. How can a product mean several things to several segments? As consumers become more diverse, this issue becomes more urgent. It is not unusual for meaning-managers to find themselves required to speak to several segments with a single product, communications campaign, or retail outlet. If the task of loading a product up with a single set of well-chosen and -designed meanings has proven difficult, the management of several distinctly different meanings within a single product must test us to the limit.

This task is not unprecedented. The Gap appears to be enjoying very considerable success talking to segments as diverse as baby boomers on the one hand and Gens X and Y on the other. Hollywood routinely makes movies that honor the age-old theatrical principle of many things for many people. The automobile industry dallied with a disastrous policy of dispatching this task by removing everything from a new design that threatened to offend any segment. This led to the unhappy decade of the 1970s, when cars became hard to distinguish from each other. This demonstrates, I think, that the solution to a diverse market of conflicting expectations cannot be fainthearted risk management. Blandness is no place of safety. Indeed, as markets splinter, it is more dangerous than it has ever been before.

Another question of interest here: How do meanings migrate and what can be done when they do? We know, for instance, that Black & Decker watched with alarm as the introduction of power tools for the home market had the effect of diminishing the credibility of Black & Decker products in the professional tradesmen class. Only its launch of a new brand, DeWalt, could restore this crucial meaning. When meaning migration of this kind can happen to a brand with the power of Black & Decker, no brand is immune. The second point to make here is that the meaning migration was provoked by the most ordinary marketing practice—brand extension. Dolan shows that Black & Decker's response to this problem was an exemplary instance of meaning-management. But he also makes plain that Black & Decker solved the problem on a "one off," ad hoc basis without the aid of a meaning-management system that might have given them early warning and the opportunity to manage the problem before it became a crisis (Dolan 1995a, 1995b, 1995c, 1998).

But it is not just crisis that encourages better meaning-management. Success demands it as well. HBO has done an impressive job of establishing a distinctive brand in the world of television and cable. Programming such as *Oz, The Chris Rock Show, The Sopranos, Sex and the City,* and *The Larry Sanders Show* all gave the brand a new edginess, a new power, and a new problem. HBO has captured an important, youthful, influential, and prosperous segment of viewers. But they have also managed to corral meanings that make them alarming to other segments and the cable providers HBO must rely on to find its way to market. The meaning-management task is delicate: to maintain and maximize the "alternative" position they have accomplished while placating more-conventional players.

Place/Channels

When Quaker purchased Snapple in 1994, they did so out of sound marketing motives (Deighton 1999). For one thing, Snapple was strong in the cold channel (i.e., street vendors, delicatessens, restaurants, recreation areas, etc.), where Quaker's Gatorade was weak. Gatorade, it turned out, was strong in the warm channel (i.e., supermarkets), were Snapple was weak. It looked like a useful match. From a channel-management point of view, Quaker's purchase of Snapple made a compelling argument.

From a meaning-management point of view, the matter was less straightforward. Snapple has done an extremely good job of capturing the constellation of cultural meanings of the 1990s sometimes referred to as the "alternative" movement (not to be confused with, but not unrelated to, the "New Age" category). This was done through the cunning deployment of rich meaning sources that included deliberately maladroit advertising (with spokesmodel Ivan Lendl mispronouncing the name of the brand and the studied populist amateurism of spokesmodel Wendy Kaufman) as well as endorsements from Howard Stern and Rush Limbaugh. For a moment, Snapple made itself the beverage choice of Gen X and the meanings of the brand were clear. They were odd, counterintuitive, unglamorous, and perfectly in tune with a decade that began with the release of Nirvana's anthem "Smells Like Teen Spirit" in 1991. Snapple managed to capture "cheesy," a beloved and potent notion for the decade and its generation. On the strength of this adroit piece of meaning-management, Snapple managed to grow the brand from $80 million in sales in 1989 to $516 million in sales in 1993.

Snapple has worked hard to use the cold channel. First of all, the channel was disaggregated, a network of family-owned distributors servicing convenience chains, pizza chains, and mom-and-pop stores. This was Snapple country: out of the way, marginal, alternative—and it may be right to think that the cold channel helped to make some of the meanings that the brand achieved. It was also, and more important, the very place that a Snapple choice was likely to be made. The consumer was out, eating, talking, circulating, and inclined to make the fashionable choice. The cold channel was precisely the place the consumer was likely to choose Snapple because that was precisely the place already charged with alternative meanings and the very place the consumer was likely to want to display these meanings.

Would Snapple meanings work in the warm channel? The first question: How well would alternative meanings of the brand survive in the overlit, mainstream, scrubbed, and utterly unhip circumstances of the supermarket? The second: Does anyone make a "fashion choice" in a supermarket? Do consumers buy cool in bulk? Do consumers stock up when purchasing the latest thing? When Quaker resolved to buy Snapple because they believed they could move it "to the next level" and sell it in the warm channel, a crucial marketing calculation appears to have been missing. It is not clear that anyone got a very clear fix on the meanings of the product and asked whether and how these could be made to work in the channel under consideration.

Place and channels make meanings, whatever else they do. We have seen retail convulsed by the struggle to nourish (or failure to nourish) the meaning-making aspects of the place of sale. The history of retail can be told as the story of experimentation in which various meaning-making strategies are played out. Here, too, we have no systematic account. But it is precisely here, I would argue, that retail may respond to and defend itself against the challenge of e-commerce in the short term even as it decides how it might participate in this revolution in the long term.

Channels add meaning and they take them away. Even well-managed brands are irreparably damaged by the buying environment. Cole Haan advertising and catalogues deliver cultural meanings, but when Cole Haan products appear in a Clark's chain store, much of this meaning evaporates. Clairol is not well served by the clutter and confusion of a CVS. Microsoft meanings are obscured by the "stack it high, sell it cheap" inclinations of a Staples. Sometimes retail is where brand meanings go to die. Or, in the more judicious language of Buchanan, Simmons, and Bickart, "[R]etailers are able to negate the equity of an established brand through their display decisions" (Buchanan, Simmons, and Bickart 1999, 353).

This is perhaps one of the reasons that department stores were obliged to give way to brand boutiques. Ralph Lauren could guarantee meaning delivery only when it controlled the in-store environment. And this is perhaps why catalogues have done so well. It is sometimes possible to supply and control meanings better between the pages of a well-designed catalogue than in the usual retail outlet. To take one example, IKEA does a much better job of meaning-management in the catalogue than on the floor. This is, I think, one of the things that holds out promise for Internet commerce. With the arrival of broadband, especially, it should be easier to manage meanings on line than off.

Starbucks, Pottery Barn, Eddie Bauer, Sunglass Hut, Putumayo, and Old Navy have started to focus on music with the introduction of their own compilation CDs. To create the right in-store experience, it is necessary to choose this music very carefully. This is an enormous opportunity to add value by adding meaning. Music may be the single most important device for delivering meaning to the retail environment and the retail environment's ability to deliver meaning to the brand. Once more, we don't know in any precise way how it makes meanings or how these meanings interact with those created by other retail elements. But these retailers have struck upon a second opportunity. They are selling their music on a CD that consumers can take with them. This is an important opportunity to manage meanings right "into the life" of the consumer (Farber 1999).

The moment of consumption is the last occasion for meaning-management: this is where the consumer is "opening up" the product and "getting at" its meanings. Recent research demonstrates that the rituals and strategies with which consumers take possession of the meanings of products and services is crucial (Wallendorf and Arnould 1991). We are beginning to suspect that the consumer is not the passive recipient of the meanings of objects but an active player in the process of their making (Fournier 1998).

Here, too, research is indicated. We do not have a clear idea how retail makes meanings. What role does music play? What are the interactions between store design, decoration, patron, and music? In a perfect world, every brand would control its point of sale, as Ralph Lauren does. The question is: How does it protect and enable meanings when this is not possible? Are consumers "constructing" or "finishing" the meanings that come to them through the marketing system? How would a meaning-management strategy assign tasks to the several players in the system?

Promotion

Too often this is thought of as a matter of telling the consumer about a product. Or it is thought about as a matter of persuasion, a process of coaxing the consumer into a decision he or she might not otherwise make. A value-as-meaning approach rejects both of these interpretations. It says that promotion is often the most important part of the process by which the firm can manufacture the meanings the product must have for the target market selected and the product and service positioning that has been fixed upon. Well-made meanings give competitive advantage. Extremely well-made meanings, especially in a marketplace of relatively unsophisticated meaning-managers, ensure success. It will be noted that in the meaning-management approach, promotion ends up much farther upstream in the marketing process.

Advertising is the preeminent meaning maker. Of all the devices at the manager's disposal, this is the best known and the most effective. The Gap reached out and captured a naturally occurring meaning, the explosive popularity of the swing phenomenon. Others are obliged to make their meanings as Marlboro has done over many decades of dedicated meaning manufacture. The Marlboro man, pernicious as he now seems to us as the "hero" of a dangerous practice, is an exquisitely accomplished piece of meaning-management. The figure represents freedom, individualism, tranquility, resourcefulness. A naturally occurring gender meaning is at work here, but it is clear that in creating this brand icon, Marlboro shaped as much as it borrowed. And in this category meaning is everything. In blind testing, consumers are hard pressed to tell the difference between one brand and another. What brings them to Marlboro are the meanings supplied by the brand (Lohof 1969).

How does advertising make meaning? This is a question on which there is some considerable research. We are clearer on the role of images and language. It is now possible to show how advertising makes meaning in a very detailed way. Of all the pieces of the meaning-management research agenda, this is the place where the most progress has been made (Kover 1995; McCracken 1987b; McQuarrie and Mick 1996, 1992; Mick and Buhl 1992; Mick, Burroughs, Hetzel, and Brannen 2004; Scott 1994).

Advertising is an endangered species these days. One of the champions of one-to-one marketing, Regis McKenna, has taken it to task. Advertising, he claims, has a "dirty little secret: it serves no useful purpose. In today's market, advertising simply misses the fundamental point of marketing—adaptability, flexibility, and responsiveness" (McKenna 1991, 75). This is wrong. Advertising remains an extraordinary device for the meaning-manager. But not an irreplaceable one. It may well be that e-commerce finds ways to use the Internet to make meanings and to make them better. Advertising has been high handed on the one hand and intellectually irresponsible on the other. It doesn't really have a place to hide.

Catalogues are another very powerful meaning maker. Catalogues use images and text to give meanings to products that would otherwise be quite ordinary. The IKEA enterprise is a good example. Taken individually, IKEA products are distinguished by a little Scandinavian design and not much else. It is only after they are observed in the magnificently controlled and constituted pages of the IKEA catalogue that they begin take on IKEAness and their special and quite substantial appeal. Great catalogues make meanings so powerfully that it is not unusual to hear consumers say that they "want to live in the catalogue." Meanings have been so perfectly and appealingly constituted there that the objects are not just charged by association but become mementos of the consumers' visits.

Another example of meaning-management through catalogues was the so-called "Owner's Manual" of the J. Peterman Company. John Peterman had a very clear idea of the meanings he wanted for his products—"unique, authentic, romantic, journey, wondrous, and excellent"—and he came up with several catalogue innovations that proved adept at evoking and investing these meanings. But he claims now, after the collapse of his company in the late 1990s, that he was not entirely clear about how to manage meanings. He notes, for instance, that it was wrong to sell a "heart of the ocean" *Titanic* necklace. It was appealing in its own right and it sold well. But Peterman now notes, "It was not authentic; it was tied too completely to the movie. . . . It was a costly success in terms of our brand's integrity" (Peterman 1999, 62).

Peterman also regrets his attempts to leverage his association with the Jerry Seinfeld show. He created an "Elaine Benes" suit. "It was one of those little decisions that was slightly off point of our brand. . . . The problem was that it was a tick in the wrong direction. It may have been an excellent suit, but it did not embody any of the other elements. It was not romantic or wondrous. It represented no sort of journey. And it was not authentic; it was tied to a TV show that was entirely fictional."

Both of these appear to us to be a marketing no-brainer. Most of us would have said, "You've got a Seinfeld connection? You can think of a way to tie into the most popular movie of all time? Make it happen." But Peterman is right; these were bad ideas for the J. Peterman Company, and good meaning-management will tell us so. The meanings that the firm stood for, the ones it created for its products and its consumers, were about an Edwardian era, about romance, journey, wonder, and authenticity. Seinfeld was about none of these. And *Titanic* was about *Titanic* before it was about these meanings. It had shanghaied these meanings for its own purpose. And once they were resident there they could not be leveraged for Peterman purposes.

Peterman says, "We were adding items because we felt that the more items we offered, the more opportunity people would have to buy. . . . But the more is better theory didn't work for us in practice. The more items we offered, whether through the catalog or through the stores, the less special—the less 'Peterman'—each new item became." It is now clear to Peterman that the meaning-management imperatives of his enterprise should have prevented him from following a very commonplace marketing strategy, the expanded product offering. He sees that now. In the absence of a more robust sense of meaning-management, any one of us, and I include myself, could have made this mistake.

Pricing

This brings us to the nub of the issue. What are meanings worth? How should we calculate their value? According to this discussion, it does look as if the meanings of the product are some part of the value of the product. It is possible to calculate most precisely the costs of producing these meanings. It would serve us if we could calculate what has been accomplished.

That pricing is a meaning-management issue is made clear by Dolan and Simon in their discussion of "price image." Dolan and Simon demonstrate that the low price of Black & Decker brand household products so damaged brand image that only a change in brand name could put the matter right. Conversely, Hartmann Luggage manages this issue by using the price of the premium product variant to define and give value to the line. As they put it, "The high price for the top item presents an image and facilitates an educational process which brings the right image to the whole line" (Dolan and Simon 1996).

In the case of Tweeter, a retailer of higher-end audio and video equipment, a series of good management choices created a damaging price image (Gourville and Wu 1997). High-end products, small upscale stores, superior customer service, limited advertising—all of these were sound decisions for one or another marketing purpose. But together they sent the message that Tweeter was "expensive." This was even the unintended implication of the weekly advertisements in which Tweeter slugged it out for market share. When consumers compared the prices of middle-range equipment suppliers with those from the higher-end Tweeter, they came away with the impression that Tweeter charged more for the same products. Even the most obvious and necessary marketing undertaking needs to be examined for its meaning-making implications.

One of the challenges here is to find a way to think about how to value the meanings of the brand. Every product is a de facto experiment in this field, and some of them might give us pause. To take an extreme example, there are product categories in which meanings would appear to account for a great deal of the value of the product. The introduction of quartz technology had obvious consequences for the luxury watch industry. A $15 quartz timepiece could now keep time *more accurately* than mechanical watches priced at thousands of dollars. Adding $100 worth of materials and styling made the visually perceptible differences between the quartz and the mechanical watch begin to disappear to all but the trained eye. With the addition of luxury materials, the real differences between the mid-range watch and the high-range one became still harder to detect. We might argue that a good deal of the price of the Patek Philippe comes from the meanings of the brand and (here's where it gets tricky) perhaps even from the pricing of the brand. On the one hand, this is a simple question: How does meaning-management enable Patek Philippe to capture so much otherwise unwarranted value? On the other, it gives rise to another question: Do some strategies for capturing value (i.e., pricing) also serve as strategies for making it?

Bibliography

Adams, Marie Jeanne. 1973. "Structural Aspects of a Village Art." *American Anthropologist* 75 (February): 265–279.

Adorno, Theodor. 1991. *The Culture Industry: Selected Essays on Mass Culture.* New York: Routledge.

Agrest, Diana, and Mario Gandelsonas. 1977. "Semiotics and the Limits of Architecture." In *A Profusion of Signs,* ed. Thomas Sebeok, 90–120. Bloomington: Indiana University Press.

Aldrich, Nelson W., Jr. 1988. *Old Money: The Mythology of America's Upper Class.* New York: Vintage.

Altman, Irwin, and Carol M. Werner, eds. 1985. *Home Environments.* New York: Plenum Press.

Altman, Irwin, Amos Rapoport, and Joachim F. Wohlwill, eds. 1980. *Environment and Culture.* New York: Plenum Press.

Ames, Kenneth L. 1982. "Meaning in Artifacts: Hall Furnishings in Victorian America." In *Material Culture Studies in America,* ed. Thomas J. Schlereth, 206–221. Nashville, Tenn.: The American Association for State and Local History.

Ames, Michael M. 1992. *Cannibal Tours and Glass Boxes.* Vancouver: University of British Columbia Press.

Anonymous. 1921. *Guide to the Galleries of the Royal Ontario Museum.* Toronto: University of Toronto Press.

Anonymous. 1941. "Veronica Lake's Hair: It Is a Cinema Property of World Influence." *Life Magazine* 2, no. 21: 58–61.

Anonymous. 1954a. Advertisement: "Studebaker: The Thrifty '54 Studebakers Are the Only Really Modern Cars in America." *Life* 36, no. 11: inside front cover.

Anonymous. 1954b. "Sales Acceleration Leaves Detroit Auto Men Breathless." *Advertising Age* 25, no. 1: 3, 46.

Anonymous. 1954c. "National Pastime, Looking over Cars." *Life* 36, no. 5: 16–17.

Anonymous. 1954d. Advertisement: "Let Lincoln Show You What Modern Driving Means." *Life* 36, no. 16: 94–95.

Anonymous. 1954e. Advertisement: "Lincoln Shows How New Your Car Should Be." *Life* 36, no. 9: 42–43.

Anonymous. 1954f. Advertisement: "Notice how many more people are arriving in Lincolns?" *Life* 36, no. 22: 42–43.

Anonymous. 1954g. Advertisement: "Kaiser: Power-on-demand." *Life* 36, no. 22: 101.

Anonymous. 1954h. Advertisement: "Oldsmobile 'Dream Car.'" *Life* 36, no. 8: 42–43.

Anonymous. 1954i. Advertisement: "Cadillac: Where a Man Is Seen at His Best." *Life* 36, no. 18: 130–131.

Anonymous. 1954j. Advertisement: "Cadillac: Worth Its Price in PRESTIGE." *Life* 36, no. 11: 6–7.

Anonymous. 1954k. Advertisement: "Dodge: Elegance in Action." *Life* 36, no. 3: inside front cover.

Anonymous. 1954l. Advertisement: "Buick: Even the Swing of the Doors Is New." *Life* 36, no. 19: 13.

Anonymous. 1954m. Advertisement: "Buick: You're Fashion First—With the Last Word in Cars." *Life* 36, no. 14: 154.

Anonymous. 1954n. Advertisement: "Chrysler Corporation: Here's Wonderful Inside News for You." *Life* 36, no. 18: 46–47.

Anonymous. 1954o. Advertisement: "Fisher: High Fashion Note All over America This Year!" *Life* 36, no. 9: 6–7.

Anonymous. 1954p. Advertisement: "Plymouth: New '54 Plymouth: Under the Beauty Solid Value." *Life* 36, no. 7: 55.

Anonymous. 1954q. Advertisement: "This Year Buy a '54 Studebaker." *Life* 36, no. 2: 2.

Anonymous. 1954r. Advertisement: "Chrysler: What Kind of 'Hat' Does Your Horsepower Wear?" *Life* 36, no. 22: 34–35.

Anonymous. 1954s. Advertisement: "Presenting the Beautiful New Packards for '54." *Life* 36, no. 16: 18–19.

Anonymous. 1954t. Advertisement: "General Motors: Way, Way Ahead!" *Life* 36, no. 10: 100–101.

Anonymous. 1954u. Advertisement: "Fisher: Night Scene by '21." *Life* 36, no. 21: 64–65.

Anonymous. 1954v. Advertisement: "Announcing the Hudson Hornet Special." *Life* 36, no. 22: 110.

Anonymous. 1954w. Advertisement: "Extra Dividends at No Extra Cost in the '54 Ford." *Life* 36, no. 9: 114.

Anonymous. 1954x. Advertisement: "Chevrolet: Some Sensible Reasons Why It's Still More Fun to Own a Chevrolet." *Life* 36, no. 22: 49.

Anonymous. 1954y. Advertisement: "Two Fords are a dollar and sense proposition." *Life* 36, no. 22: 7.

Anonymous. 1954z. Advertisement: "Buick: High style—High power—High-air intake, too." *Life* 36, no. 7: 55.

Anonymous. 1954aa. Advertisement: "DeSoto Automatic." *Life* 36, no. 11: 88.

Anonymous. 1954bb. Advertisement: "Buick: From up front comes a still finer ride." *Life* 36, no. 16: 8–9.

Anonymous. 1954cc. Advertisement: "Pontiac: Something Big Has Happened to General Motors' Lowest Priced 8." *Life* 36, no. 8: 118–119.

Anonymous. 1954dd. Advertisement: " 'Car of the Future' styling comes true in five General Motors cars you can buy today." *Life* 36, no. 5: 22–23.

Anonymous. 1954ee. "Billions for Defense Build Wondrous Weapons." *Life* 36, no. 1: 12–19.

Anonymous. 1954ff. "Mass-Produced Car of the Future." *Life* 36, no. 1: 71.

Anonymous. 1954gg. "The New American Domesticated Male." *Life* 36, no. 1: 42–45.

Anonymous. 1954hh. Advertisement: "Buick: Here the stylists went all out." *Life* 36, no. 2: 46–47.

Anonymous. 1955a. "B&B Revives 'Craft' Motif in 1st Drive for Studebaker." *Advertising Age* 26, no. 48: 8.

Anonymous. 1955b. Advertisement: "Thrill of the Year Is Buick." *Maclean's Magazine* 68, no. 6: 37.

Anonymous. 1955c. Advertisement: "Studebaker: Craftsmanship with a Flair." *Time* 66, no. 22: 8.

Anonymous. 1955d. "Plymouth Hikes '56 Ad Budget 18%; Seeks to Garner 11½% of Market." *Advertising Age* 26, no. 41: 2, 114.

Anonymous. 1955e. "Autos: Step to the Rear." *Time* 66, no. 22: 82.

Anonymous. 1955f. "GM's Motorama to be Lavish Spectacle; Will Also Show Cars." *Advertising Age* 26, no. 2: 96.

Anonymous. 1955g. "General Motors Wages Record Ad and Promotion Drive for Powerama Show." *Advertising Age* 26, no. 36: 4, 68.

Anonymous. 1955h. "Ford's '55 Nine-Month Profits Top Those of Any Prior Full Year: Breech." *Advertising Age* 26, no. 45: 3.

Anonymous. 1955i. Advertisement: "Buick: Flashing new getaway from the very first inch." *Life* 36, no. 50: 5.

Anonymous. 1955j. "That Next Promotion Could Kill You." *Advertising Age* 26, no. 13: 16.

Anonymous. 1956a. Advertisement: "Buick: The Forward Look." *Time*, September 17, 17.

Anonymous. 1956b. Advertisement: "Buick: Flight into Anywhere." *Time*, July 16.

Anonymous. 1956c. Advertisement: "Pontiac: Moonlit Drive." *Time*, August 27, 32.

Anonymous. 1956d. Advertisement: "Oh-h-h-h! those '56 Oldsmobiles." *Time*, January 9, 40.

Anonymous. 1956e. "The U.S. Air Force: The Nation's Youngest Service Has Entered the Supersonic Age." *Time*, March 5, 42–51.

Anonymous. 1956f. Advertisement: "Buick: Now Dynaflow Goes Airplanes One Better." *Life* 37, no. 14: 4.

Anonymous. 1968. *Choosing Accessories for the Home*. Michigan State University Cooperation Extension Service Bulletin E-635.

Anonymous. 2002. Official Biography of Brig. Gen. Charles E. "Chuck" Yeager. Internet Site for Edwards Air Force Base. Available online: http://www.edwards.af.mil/history/docs_html/people/yeager_biography.html.

Anonymous. N.d.a. "Rocketman's Hood Ornaments and Automobilia." Website at http://www.ultranet.com/~rocketmn/rocketman.html. Accessed August 2002.

Anonymous. N.d.b. "Sales figures for the 1954 Buick." Available online: http://www.buicks.net.

Appaduari, Arjun, ed. 1986. *The Social Life of Things: Commodities in Cultural Perspective*. Cambridge: Cambridge University Press.

Ariely, Yehoshua. 1966. *The Future-Directed Character of the American Experience*. Jerusalem: Magnes Press, Hebrew University.

Arnold, Matthew. 1993. *Culture and Anarchy and Other Writings*. Ed. Stefan Collini. Cambridge: University of Cambridge Press.

Atkin, Charles, and Martin Block. 1983. "Effectiveness of Celebrity Endorsers." *Journal of Advertising Research* 23 (February/March): 57–61.

Austin, J. L. 1965. *How to Do Things with Words*. New York: Oxford University Press.

Baker, Michael J., and Gilbert A. Churchill. 1977. "The Impact of Physically Attractive Models on Advertising Evaluations." *Journal of Marketing Research* 14 (November): 538–555.

Bakhtin, Mikhail M. 1981. *The Dialogic Imagination: Four Essays by Mikhail M.*

Bakhtin. Translated by Caryl Emerson and Michael Holquist. Austin: University of Texas Press.

Banham, Reyner. 1970. *Theory and Design in the First Machine Age.* New York: Praeger.

Barber, Benjamin R. 1995. *Jihad vs. McWorld.* New York: Random House.

Baritz, Loren. 1990. *The Good Life: The Meaning of Success for the American Middle Class.* New York: HarperCollins.

Barnouw, Erik. 1978. *The Sponsor: Notes on a Modern Potentate.* New York: Oxford University Press.

Barry, David. 1988. *Street Dreams: American Car Culture from the Fifties to the Eighties.* London: Macdonald Orbis.

Barthes, Roland. 1973. *Mythologies.* London: Granada, Paladin.

Basham, Frances, Bob Ughetti, and Paul Rambali. 1984. *Car Culture.* New York: Plexus.

Batchelor, Ray. 1994. *Henry Ford: Mass Production, Modernism, and Design.* Manchester: Manchester University Press.

Baudrillard, Jean. 1983. "The Ecstasy of Communication." In *The Anti-Aesthetic: Essays on Postmodern Culture,* ed. Hall Foster, 126–134. Port Townsend, Wash.: Bay Press.

———. 1989. *America.* Translated by Chris Turner. London: Verso.

Baumeister, Roy F. 1986. *Identity: Cultural Change and the Struggle for Self.* New York: Oxford University Press.

Baumgartner, M. P. 1988. *The Moral Order of a Suburb.* New York: Oxford University Press.

Baxandall, Rosalyn, and Elizabeth Ewen. 2000. *Picture Windows: How the Suburbs Happened.* New York: Basic Books.

Bayley, Stephen. 1979. *In Good Shape: Style in Industrial Products, 1900 to 1960.* London: Design Council.

Belk, Russell W. 1982. "Acquiring, Possessing, and Collecting: Fundamental Processes in Consumer Behavior." In *Marketing Theory: Philosophy of Science Perspectives,* ed. Ronald F. Bush and Shelby Hunt, 185–190. Chicago: American Marketing Association.

———. 1984a. "Cultural and Historical Differences in Concepts of the Self and Their Effects of Attitudes toward Having and Giving." In *Advances in Consumer Research,* vol. 11, ed. Thomas C. Kinnear, 753–760. Provo, Utah: Association for Consumer Research.

———. 1984b. "Manifesto for a Consumer Behavior of Consumer Behavior." In *AMA Winter Educators' Conference: Scientific Method in Marketing,* ed. Paul F. Anderson and Michael J. Ryan, 163–167. Chicago: American Marketing Association.

———. 1985. "Materialism: Trait Aspects of Living in the Material World." *Journal of Consumer Behavior* 12, no. 3 (December): 265–280.

———. 1987a. "The Role of the Odyssey in Consumer Behavior and in Consumer Research." In *Advances in Consumer Research,* vol. 14, ed. Melanie Wallendorf and Paul Anderson, 357–361. Provo, Utah: Association for Consumer Research.

———. 1987b. "A Child's Christmas in America: Santa Claus as Deity, Consumption as Religion." *Journal of American Culture* 10, no. 1 (Spring): 87–100.

———. 1991. "The Ineluctable Mysteries of Possessions." *Journal of Social Behavior and Personality* 6, no. 6 (June): 17–55.

———. 1998. "Possessions and the Extended Self." *Journal of Consumer Research* 15, no. 2 (September): 139–168.

Bellow, Saul. 1987. "Foreword." In Allan Bloom, *The Closing of the American Mind,* 11–18. New York: Simon & Schuster.

Berger, John. 1972. *Ways of Seeing.* London: British Broadcasting Corporation.

Berger, Peter, and Thomas Luckmann. 1964. "Social Mobility and Personal Identity." *Archives Europeenne De Sociologies* 5: 331–343.

Berghoff, Bruce. 1995. *The GM Motorama. Dream Cars of the Fifties.* Detroit: Motorbooks International.

Berman, Marshall. 1980. *The Politics of Authenticity: Radical Individualism and the Emergence of Modern Society.* New York: Atheneum.

———. 1982. *All That Is Solid Melts into Air: The Experience of Modernity.* New York: Simon and Schuster.

Berstein, Basil. 1975. *Class, Codes, and Control.* New York: Schocken Books.

Bettelheim, Bruno. 1959. "Joey: A 'Mechanical Boy.'" *Scientific American* 200: 116–127.

———. 1976. *Uses of Enchantment: The Meaning and Importance of Fairy Tales.* New York: Alfred A. Knopf.

Blaszczyk, Regina Lee. 2000. *Imaging Consumers: Design and Innovation from Wedgwood to Corning.* Baltimore: Johns Hopkins University Press.

Bletter, Rosemarie Haag. 1985. "The World of Tomorrow: The Future with a Past." In *High Styles: Twentieth-Century American Design,* ed. Lisa Phillips and David A. Hanks, 84–127. New York: Whitney Museum of American Art.

Bloch, Peter H. 1982. "Involvement beyond the Purchase Process: Conceptual Issues and Empirical Investigation." In *Advances in Consumer Research,* vol. 9, ed. Andrew Mitchell, 413–417. Ann Arbor, Mich.: Association for Consumer Research.

Blumberg, Paul. 1974. "The Decline and Fall of the Status Symbol: Some Thoughts on Status in a Post Industrial Society." *Social Problems* 21, no. 4 (April): 480–498.

Bogosian, Eric. 1995. *Suburbia.* New York: Theatre Communications Group.

Bonnafous, Gilles. n.d. "Les concept cars de la General Motors: La Buick XP 300." Available online: http://www.motorlegend.com/dossiers/retrospective/gm_concept/gm25.php.

Boorstin, Daniel J. 1961. *The Image: A Guide to Pseudo-Events in America.* New York: Harper and Row Publishers.

———. 1974. "Advertising and American Civilization." In *Advertising and Society,* ed. Yale Brozen, 11–23. New York: New York University Press.

———. 1978. *The Republic of Technology: Reflections on Our Future Community.* New York: Harper & Row.

Borden, Neil H. 1950. *Advertising: Text and Cases.* Chicago: Richard D. Irwin.

Boschetti, Margaret. 1968. *Color Harmony for Interiors.* Michigan State University Cooperative Extension Service Bulletin no. 637.

Bourdieu, Pierre. 1984. *Distinction: A Social Critique of the Judgment of Taste.* Trans. Richard Nice. Cambridge, Mass.: Harvard University Press.

Bourdieu, Pierre, Alain Darbel, and Dominique Schnapper. 1990. *The Love of Art: European Art Museums and Their Public.* Trans. Caroline Beattie and Nick Merriman. Palo Alto, Calif.: Stanford University Press.

Bradbury, Malcolm, and James Walter McFarlane. 1991. "The Name and Nature of Modernism." In *Modernism: A Guide to European Literature 1890–1930,* ed. Malcolm Bradbury and James Walter McFarlane, 19–55. London: Penguin Books.

Brantlinger, Patrick. 1983. *Bread and Circuses: Theories of Mass Culture as Social Decay.* Ithaca, N.Y.: Cornell University Press.

Braudel, Fernand. 1973. *Capitalism and Material Life, 1400–1800*. Trans. Miriam Kocham. London: Weidenfeld and Nicolson.

Brean, Herbert. 1954. "'54 Car: 3 Years Old at Birth." *Life* 36, no. 3: 80–92.

Brenan, Charlotte W. 1939. *The Arrangement of Home Furnishings for Comfort, Convenience, and Beauty*. Cornell Bulletin for Homemakers no. 388.

Brewer, John, and Roy Porter, eds. 1993. *Consumption and the World of Goods*. London: Routledge.

Bronner, Simon J. 1983. "'Visible Proofs': Material Culture Study in American Folkloristics." *American Quarterly* 35, no. 3: 316–338.

Brooks, Tim, and Earle Marsh. 1992. *The Complete Directory to Prime Time Network TV Shows, 1946–Present*. New York: Ballantine.

Brown, Barbara B., and Carol M. Werner. 1985. "Social Cohesiveness: Territoriality and Holiday Decorations." *Environment and Behavior* 17, no. 5: 239–265.

Bruck, Jan, and John Docker. 1989. "Puritanic Rationalism: John Berger's Ways of Seeing and Media and Culture Studies." *Continuum: The Australian Journal of Media & Culture* 2, no. 2: 77–95.

Bruner, Edward M. 1984a. "Introduction: The Opening Up of Anthropology." In *Text, Play and Story: The Construction and Reconstruction of Self and Society*, ed. Edward Bruner, 1–16. Washington, D.C.: American Ethnological Society.

———, ed. 1984b. *Text, Play, and Story: The Construction and Reconstruction of Self and Society*. Washington, D.C.: American Ethnological Society.

Bruner, Edward M., and Phyllis Gorfain. 1984. "Dialogic Narration and the Paradoxes of Masada." In *Text, Play and Story: The Construction and Reconstruction of Self and Society*, ed. Edward M. Bruner, 56–79. Washington, D.C.: American Ethnological Society.

Buchanan, Lauranne, Carolyn J. Simmons, and Barbara A. Bickart. 1999. "Brand Equity Dilution: Retailer Display and Context Brand Effects." *Journal of Marketing Research* 36, no. 3 (August): 345–355.

Burke, Edmund. 1958. *A Philosophical Inquiry into the Origin of Our Ideas of the Sublime and Beautiful*. Edited by James T. Boulton. London: Routledge & Kegan Paul.

Burrow, J. W. 1966. *Evolution and Society: A Study in Victorian Social Theory*. Cambridge: Cambridge University Press.

Bush, Donald J. 1975. *The Streamlined Decade*. New York: G. Braziller.

Bushman, Richard L. 1992. *The Refinement of America: Persons, Houses, Cities*. New York: Alfred A. Knopf.

Calinescu, Matei. 1983. "From the One to the Many: Pluralism in Today's Thought." In *Innovation/Renovation: New Perspectives on the Humanities*, ed. Ihab Hassan and Sally Hassan, 263–288. Madison: University of Wisconsin Press.

———. 1987. *Five Faces of Modernity*. Durham, N.C.: Duke University Press.

Cameron, Duncan F. 1971. "The Museum, a Temple or the Forum." *Curator* 14, no. 1: 11–24.

Campbell, Colin. 1983. "Romanticism and the Consumer Ethic: Intimations of a Weber-Style Thesis." *Sociological Analysis* 44, no. 4: 279–295.

———. 1987. *The Romantic Ethic and the Spirit of Modern Consumerism*. Oxford: Basil Blackwell.

Caplovitz, David. 1967. *The Poor Pay More*. New York: Free Press.

Carey, John. 1992. *The Intellectuals and the Masses: Pride and Prejudice among the Literary Intelligentsia, 1880–1939*. London: Faber and Faber.

Carlisle, Susan G. 1982. "French Homes and French Character." *Landscape* 26, no. 3: 13–23.

Carrier, James G. 1992. "Occidentalism: The World Turned Upside-Down." *American Ethnologist* 19, no. 2 (May): 195–212.

Carrithers, Michael, Steven Collins, and Steven Lukes, eds. 1985. *The Category of the Person: Anthropology, Philosophy, History.* Cambridge: Cambridge University Press.

Carson, Cary, Ronald Hoffman, and Peter J. Albert, eds. 1994. *Of Consuming Interests: The Style of Life in the Eighteenth Century.* Charlottesville: University Press of Virginia.

Carswell, J. William, and David G. Saile, eds. 1986. *Purposes in Built Form and Culture Research.* Lawrence: University of Kansas, School of Architecture and Urban Design.

Casey, Roger N. 1997. *Textual Vehicles: The Automobile in American Literature.* New York: Garland Publishing.

Caspari, Fritz. 1968. *Humanism and the Social Order in Tudor England.* New York: Teachers College Press.

Cawelti, John G. 1965. *Apostles of the Self-Made Man: Changing Concepts of Success in America.* Chicago: University of Chicago Press.

Cawelti, John G., and Bruce A. Rosenberg. 1987. *The Spy Story.* Chicago: University of Chicago Press.

Cheal, David. 1988. "The Post Modern Origin of Ritual." *Journal for the Theory of Social Behavior* 18 (September): 269–290.

Cheever, John. 1969. *Bullet Park: A Novel.* New York: Knopf.

Chinoy, Ely. 1955. *Automobile Workers and the American Dream.* Garden City, N.Y.: Doubleday and Company.

Clark, Clifford E., Jr. 1976. "Domestic Architecture as an Index to Social History: The Romantic Revival and the Cult of Domesticity in America, 1840–1870." *Journal of Interdisciplinary History* 7, no. 1 (Summer): 33–56.

———. 1986. *The American Family Home, 1800–1960.* Chapel Hill: University of North Carolina Press.

Classen, Constance, David Howes, and Anthony Synnott. 1995. *Aroma: The Cultural History of Smell.* London: Routledge.

Clifton, James A. 1989. "Alternate Identities and Cultural Frontiers." In *Being and Becoming Indian: Biographical Studies of North American Frontiers,* ed. James A. Clifton, 1–38. Chicago: Dorsey Press.

Cohen, Lizabeth A. 1982. "Embellishing a Life of Labor: An Interpretation of the Material Culture of American Working-Class Homes, 1885–1915." In *Material Culture Studies in America,* ed. Thomas J. Schlereth, 289–305. Nashville: The American Association for State and Local History.

Cohn, Bernard. 1980. "History and Anthropology: The State of Play." *Comparative Studies in Society and History* 22, no. 2: 198–221.

———. 1987. *An Anthropologist among the Historians and Other Essays.* Delhi and New York: Oxford University Press.

Cohn, Jan. 1979. *The Palace or the Poorhouse: The American House as Cultural Symbol.* East Lansing: Michigan State University Press.

Coleman, Richard P., and Lee Rainwater. 1978. *Social Standing in America: New Dimensions of Class.* New York: Basic Books.

Collini, Stefan. 1993. "Introduction." In Matthew Arnold, *Culture and Anarchy and Other Writings.* Ed. Stefan Collini. Cambridge: Cambridge University Press.

Comaroff, Jean, and John Comaroff. 1991. *Of Revelation and Revolution: Christianity, Colonialism and Consciousness in South Africa.* Chicago: University of Chicago Press.

Cook, Ramsay. 1985. *The Regenerators: Social Criticism in Late Victorian England Canada.* Toronto: University of Toronto Press.

Cordwell, Justine, and Ronald A. Schwarz, eds. 1979. *Fabrics of Culture.* The Hague: Mouton.

Corn, Joseph J. 1983. *The Winged Gospel: America's Romance with Aviation, 1900–1950.* New York: Oxford University Press.

Coupland, Douglas. 1991. *Generation X: Tales for an Accelerated Culture.* New York: St. Martin's Press.

Cowen, Tyler. 1998. *In Praise of Commercial Culture.* Cambridge, Mass.: Harvard University Press.

Craig, Robert M. 1990. "Transportation Imagery and Streamlined Moderne Architecture: A Case for a Design Typology." In *Roadside America: The Automobile in Design and Culture,* ed. Jan Jennings, 15–28. Ames, Iowa: Press for the Society for Commercial Archaeology.

Creighton, Thomas H., and Katherine M. Ford. 1961. *Contemporary Houses Evaluated by Their Owners.* New York: Reinhold Publishing Corporation.

Csikszentmihalyi, Mihaly, and Eugene Rochberg-Halton. 1981. *The Meaning of Things: Domestic Symbols and the Self.* New York: Cambridge University Press.

Danct, Brenda. 1986. "Books, Butterflies, Botticellis: A Sociological Analysis of the 'Madness' of Collecting." Paper given at the 6th International Conference of Culture and Communication, Temple University, Philadelphia, October 9.

Davis, James A. 1956. "Status Symbols and the Measurement of Status Perception." *Sociometry* 19, no. 3 (September): 154–165.

———. 1958. "Cultural Factors in the Perception of Status Symbols." *The Midwest Sociologist* 21, no. 1 (December): 1–11.

de Tocqueville, Alexis. 1966. *Democracy in America.* Ed. J. P. Mayer. New York: Harper Collins.

Debevec, Kathleen, and Jerome B. Kernan. 1984. "More Evidence on the Effects of a Presenter's Physical Attractiveness: Some Cognitive, Affective and Behavioral Consequences." In *Advances in Consumer Research,* vol. 11, ed. Thomas C. Kinnear, 127–132. Provo, Utah: Association for Consumer Research.

Deighton, John. 1999. "Snapple." Harvard Business School Case Study N9-599-126, July 8: 1–17. Available online: www.hbs.edu/research/cases.html.

Demsetz, Harold. 1974. "Advertising in the Affluent Society." In *Advertising and Society,* ed. Yale Brozen, 67–77. New York: New York University Press.

Denby, David. 1996. "Buried Alive: Our Children and the Avalanche of Crud." *The New Yorker* 72, no. 19: 48–58.

Deshpande, Rohit. 1983. "Paradigms Lost: On Theory and Method in Research in Marketing." *Journal of Marketing* 47 (Fall): 101–110.

Dettelbach, Cynthia Golomb. 1976. *In the Driver's Seat: The Automobile in American Literature and Popular Culture.* Westport, Conn.: Greenwood Press.

Dholakia, Ruby Roy, and Brian Sternthal. 1977. "Highly Credible Sources: Persuasive

Facilitators or Persuasive Liabilities?" *Journal of Consumer Research* 3 (March): 223–232.

Dickstein, Morris. 1989. "From the Thirties to the Sixties: The New York World's Fair in Its Own Time." In *Remembering the Future: The New York World's Fair from 1939 to 1964*, ed. Rosemarie Haag Bletter, 21–43. New York: Rizzoli.

———. 1999. *Leopards in the Temple: The Transformation of American Fiction, 1945–1970*. Cambridge, Mass.: Harvard University Press.

Docker, John. 1994. *Postmodernism and Popular Culture: A Cultural History.* Cambridge: Cambridge University Press.

Dolan, Robert J. 1995a. "The Black & Decker Corp (A): Power Tools Division." Harvard Business School Case Study 5-590-057, June 20: 1–14. Available online: www.hbs.edu/research/cases.html.

———. 1995b. "The Black & Decker Corp (B): 'Operation Sudden Impact.'" Harvard Business School Case Study 5-590-060, June 20: 1–6. Available online: www.hbs.edu/research/cases.html.

———. 1995c. "The Black & Decker Corp (C): 'Operation Sudden Impact,' Results 1992–1994." Harvard Business School Case Study 5-590-061, March 30: 1–9. Available online: www.hbs.edu/research/cases.html.

———. 1998a. "The Black & Decker Corporation Series: Teaching Note." Harvard Business School Case Study 5-598-0106, February 12: 1–22. Available online: www.hbs.edu/research/cases.html.

———. 1998b. "Note On Marketing Strategy." Harvard Business School Case 9-598-061, July 28: 1–16. Available online: www.hbs.edu/research/cases.html.

Dolan, Robert J., and Hermann Simon. 1996. *Power Pricing: How Managing Price Transforms the Bottom Line.* New York: Free Press.

Doucet, Michael J., and John C. Weaver. 1985. "Material Culture and the North American House: The Era of the Common Man, 1870–1920." *The Journal of American History* 72, no. 3 (December): 560–587.

Douglas, Mary, and Baron Isherwood. 1978. *The World of Goods: Towards an Anthropology of Consumption.* New York: W. W. Norton & Company.

Downes, Larry, and Chunka Mui. 1998. *Unleashing the Killer App: Digital Strategies for Market Dominance.* Boston: Harvard Business School Press.

Drucker, Peter Ferdinand. 1954. *The Practice of Management.* New York: Harper.

Drummond, Lee. 1986. "The Story of Bond." In *Symbolizing America*, ed. Herve Varenne, 66–89. Lincoln: University of Nebraska Press.

———. 1996. *American Dreamtime: A Cultural Analysis of Popular Movies and Their Implications for a Science of Humanity.* Lanham, Md.: Littlefield Adams Books.

Duncan, Carol. 1995. *Civilizing Rituals: Inside Public Art Museums.* London: Routledge.

Duncan, James S., ed. 1981. *Housing and Identity: Cross-Cultural Perspectives.* London: Croom Helm.

Dundes, Alan. 1980. "Thinking Ahead: A Folkloristic Reflection of the Future Orientation in the American Worldview." In Alan Dundes, *Interpreting Folklore*, 69–85. Bloomington: Indiana University Press.

Eells, George, and Stanley Musgrove. 1982. *Mae West: A Biography.* New York: William Morrow and Company.

Eighmy, Jeffery L. 1981. "The Use of Material Culture in Diachronic Anthropology." In *Modern Material Culture: The Archaeology of Us*, ed. Richard A. Gould and Michael B. Schiffer, 31–50. New York: Academic Press.

Eliade, Mircea. 1954. *The Myth of the Eternal Return.* Trans. Willard R. Trask. New York: Pantheon Books.

Elias, Norbert. 1983. *The Court Society.* Trans. Edmund Jephcott. New York: Pantheon.

Elliott, Richard, and Kritsadarat Wattanasuwan. 1998. "Brands as Symbolic Resources for the Construction of Identity." *International Journal of Advertising* 17, no. 2: 131–144.

Ericsson, K. Anders, and Herbert A. Simon. 1980. "Verbal Reports as Data." *Psychological Review* 87, no. 3 (May): 215–251.

Erikson, Erik H. 1968. *Identity: Youth and Crisis.* New York: W. W. Norton.

Ewen, Stuart. 1976. *Captains of Consciousness: Advertising and the Social Roots of the Consumer Culture.* New York: McGraw-Hill.

———. 1988. *All Consuming Images: The Politics of Style in Contemporary Culture.* New York: Basic Books.

Faber, Ronald J., Thomas C. O'Guinnard, and Raymond Krych. 1987. "Compulsive Consumption." In *Advances in Consumer Research,* ed. Paul Anderson and Melanie Wallendorf, vol. 14, 132–135. Provo, Utah: Association for Consumer Research.

Farber, Jim. 1999. "Retail Spins." *Entertainment Weekly,* August 6: 61–62.

Felson, Marcus. 1976. "The Differentiation of Material Life Styles: 1925 to 1966." *Social Indicators Research* 3: 397–421.

Finn, David W. 1980. "The Validity of Using Consumer Input to Choose Advertising Spokesmen." In *Advances in Consumer Research,* vol. 7, ed. Jerry Olson, 776–779. Ann Arbor, Mich.: Association for Consumer Research.

Firat, A. Fuat. 1986. "A Macro Theory in Marketing: The Social Construction of Consumption Patterns." In *Philosophical and Radical Thought in Marketing,* ed. Richard P. Bagozzi, Nikhilesh Dholakia, and A. Fuat Firat. Lexington, Md.: Lexington Books.

Fisher, Franklin M., Zvi Griliches, and Carl Kaysen. 1962. "The Costs of Automobile Model Changes Since 1949." *The Journal of Political Economy* 70, no. 5 (October): 433–451.

Fitzgerald, Frances. 1987. *Cities on a Hill: A Journey through Contemporary American Cultures.* New York: Simon and Schuster.

Fleming, Ian. 1953. *Casino Royale.* New York: Macmillan.

Flink, James J. 1975. *The Car Culture.* Cambridge, Mass.: MIT Press.

Forty, Adrian. 1986. *Objects of Desire: Design and Society from Wedgwood to IBM.* New York: Pantheon.

Fournier, Susan. 1996. "Land Rover North America, Inc." Harvard Business School Case Study 9-596-036, August 30: 1–16. Available online: www.hbs.edu/research/cases.html.

———. 1998. "Consumers and Their Brands: Developing Relationship Theory in Consumer Research." *Journal of Consumer Research* 24 (March): 343–373.

Fox, Richard G. 1991. "For a Nearly New Cultural History." In *Recapturing Anthropology,* ed. Richard G. Fox, 93–113. Santa Fe, N.M.: School of American Research Press.

Fox, Richard Wightman, and T. J. Jackson Lears, eds. 1983. *The Culture of Consumption: Critical Essays in American History, 1880–1980.* New York: Pantheon Books.

Frank, Thomas. 1997. *The Conquest of Cool: Business Culture, Counterculture, and the Rise of Hip Consumerism.* Chicago: University of Chicago Press.

Freedman, Samuel G. 1999. "Suburbia Outgrows Its Image in the Arts." *The New York Times,* February 28: section 2, page 1.

Friedman, Hershey H., and Linda Friedman. 1979. "Endorser Effectiveness as a Function of Product Type." *Journal of Advertising Research* 19 (October): 63–71.

Friedman, Hershey H., Michael J. Santeramo, and Anthony Traina. 1978. "Correlates of Trustworthiness for Celebrities." *Journal of the Academy of Marketing Science* 6 (Fall): 291–299.

Friedman, Hershey H., Salvatore Termini, and Robert Washington. 1976. "The Effectiveness of Advertisements Utilizing Four Types of Endorsers." *Journal of Advertising* 5 (Summer): 22–24.

Friedman, Monroe. 1985. "The Changing Language of a Consumer Society: Brand Name Usage in Popular American Novels in the Postwar Era." *Journal of Consumer Research* 11, no. 4 (March): 927–938.

Fromm, Erich. 1994/1941. *Escape from Freedom*. New York: Owl Books.

Frum, David. 2000. *How We Got Here: The 70's, the Decade That Brought You Modern Life (for Better or Worse)*. New York: Basic Books.

Gabor, Andrea, Jeannye Thorton, and Daniel P. Wiener. 1978. "Star Turns That Can Turn Star-Crossed." *U.S. News and World Report,* December 7: 57.

Gainsford, Thomas. 1616. *The Rich Cabinet*. London: n.p.

Galbraith, John Kenneth. 1958. *The Affluent Society*. Boston: Houghton Mifflin.

———. 1964. *The Scotch*. Boston: Houghton Mifflin.

———. 1981. *A Life in Our Times: Memoirs*. Boston: Houghton Mifflin.

Gans, Herbert J. 1967. *The Levittowners: Ways of Life and Politics in a New Suburban Community*. New York: Vintage Books.

———. 1974. *Popular Culture and High Culture: An Analysis and Evaluation of Taste*. New York: Basic Books.

Gartman, David. 1995. *Auto-Opium: A Social History of American Automobile Design*. New York: Routledge.

Geertz, Clifford. 1980. *Negara: The Theatre State in Nineteenth-Century Bali*. Princeton, N.J.: Princeton University Press.

Giedion, Sigfried. 1948. *Mechanization Takes Command: A Contribution to Anonymous History*. New York: Oxford University Press.

Gitlin, Todd. 1987. *The Sixties: Years of Hope, Days of Rage*. New York: Bantam Books.

Giuliani, Maria Vittoria, Mirilia Bonnes, and Carol M. Werner, eds. 1987. *Home Interiors: A European Perspective* 19, no. 2 (March): 146–259.

Glassie, Henry. 1973. "Structure and Function, Folklore and the Artifact." *Semiotica* 7, no. 4: 313–351.

Glover, Jonathan. 1988. *I: The Philosophy and Psychology of Personal Identity*. London: Penguin.

Goffman, Erving. 1951. "Symbols of Class Status." *British Journal of Sociology* II, no. 4 (December): 294–304.

Goldberger, Paul. 1999. "Annals of Design: Detroit Tiger." *The New Yorker* LXXV, no. 18 (July 12, 1999): 28–33.

Gordon, Jean, and Jan McArthur. 1985. "American Women and Domestic Consumption, 1800–1920: Four Interpretive Themes." *Journal of American Culture* 8, no. 3: 35–46.

Gottdiener, M. 1985. "Hegemony and Mass Culture: A Semiotic Approach." *American Journal of Sociology* 90, no. 5: 979–1001.

Gourville, John, and George Wu. 1997. "Tweeter Etc." Harvard Business

School Case Study 9-597-028, April 18: 1–24. Available online: www.hbs.edu/research/cases.html.

Greenberg, Cara. 1984. *Mid-Century Modern: Furniture of the 1950's*. New York: Harmony Books.

Greene, Jack P. 1993. "Convergence: Development of an American Society, 1720–1780." In *Diversity and Unity in Early North America*, ed. Philip D. Morgan, 43–72. London: Routledge.

Greenhouse, Carol J. 1985. "Anthropology at Home: Whose Home?" *Human Organization* 44, no. 3 (Fall): 261–264.

Greyser, Stephen A. 1972. "Advertising: Attacks and Counters." *Harvard Business Review* 50: 22–28.

Gromno, Sigmund. 1984. "Compensatory Consumer Behavior: Theoretical Perspectives, Empirical Examples and Methodological Challenges." In *1984 AMA Winter Educators' Conference: Scientific Method in Marketing*, ed. Paul F. Anderson and Michael J. Ryan, 184–188. Chicago: American Marketing Association.

———. 1986. "Compensatory Consumer Behavior: Elements of a Critical Sociology of Consumption." Working Paper, Norwegian Fund for Market and Distribution Research, Oslo, Norway.

Guazzo, Stephan. 1586. *The Civile Conversation of M. Stephen Guazzo*. London: n.p.

Guiles, Fred Lawrence. 1984. *Legend: The Life and Death of Marilyn Monroe*. New Yorker: Stein and Day.

Guillory, Dan. 1983. "Star Wars Style and American Automobiles." In *The Automobile and American Culture*, ed. Laurence Goldstein and David Lanier Lewis, 383–393. Ann Arbor: University of Michigan Press.

Gulick, John. 1973. "Urban Anthropology." In *Handbook in Social and Cultural Anthropology*, ed. J. Honigmarm, 979–1029. Chicago: Rand McNally.

Habermas, Jurgen. 1983. "Modernity—An Incomplete Project." In *The Anti-Aesthetic: Essays on Postmodern Culture*, ed. Hal Foster, 3–15. Port Townsend, Wash.: Bay Press.

Hall, John R. 1992. "The Capital(s) of Culture: A Nonholistic Approach to Status Situations, Class, Gender and Ethnicity." In *Cultivating Differences: Symbolic Boundaries and the Making of Inequality*, ed. Michelle Lamont and Marcel Fournier, 257–285. Chicago: University of Chicago Press.

Halle, David. 1993. *Inside Culture: Art and Class in the American Home*. Chicago: University of Chicago Press.

Handlin, David P. 1979. *The American Home: Architecture and Society, 1815–1915*. Boston: Little, Brown, and Co.

Handlin, Oscar. 1992. "Comments on Mass and Popular Culture." In *Mass Media in Modern Society*, ed. Norman Jacobs, 105–112. New Brunswick, N.J.: Transaction Publishers.

Haraway, Donna. 1991. "A Cyborg Manifesto: Science, Technology, and Socialist-Feminism in the Late Twentieth Century." In Donna Haraway, *Simians, Cyborgs and Women: The Reinvention of Nature*, 149–181. New York: Routledge.

Harre, R., and P. F. Secord. 1972. *The Explanation of Social Behavior*. Oxford: Basis Blackwell.

Harris, Neil. 1978. "Museums, Merchandizing, and Popular Taste: The Struggle for Influence." In *Material Culture and the Study of American Life*, ed. Ian M. G. Quimby, 140–174. New York: W. W. Norton & Company.

———. 1981. "The Drama of Consumer Desire." In *Yankee Enterprise: The Rise of the American System of Manufacturers*, ed. Otto Mayr and Robert C. Post, 189–216. Washington, D.C.: Smithsonian Institution Press.

Haskell, Molly. 1974. *From Reverence to Rape: The Treatment of Women in the Movies.* Chicago: University of Chicago Press.

Hayden, Dolores. 1981. *The Grand Domestic Revolution: A History of Feminist Designs for American Homes, Neighborhoods and Cities.* Cambridge, Mass.: MIT Press.

Hebdige, Dick. 1982. "Towards a Cartography of Taste, 1935–1962." In *Popular Culture, Past and Present*, ed. Bernard Waites, Tony Bennett, and Graham Martin, 194–218. London: Croom Helm.

Henry, Jules. 1963. *Culture Against Man.* New York: Vintage.

Hillier, Bevis. 1983. *The Style of the Century, 1900–1980.* New York: Dutton.

Hine, Thomas. 1986. *Populuxe.* New York: Knopf.

Hirsch, Paul M. 1972. "Processing Fads and Fashions: An Organization-Set Analysis of Cultural Industry Systems." *American Journal of Sociology* 77, no. 4 (January): 639–659.

Hirschman, Albert O. 1977. *The Passions and the Interests: Political Arguments for Capitalism Before Its Triumph.* Princeton, N.J.: Princeton University Press.

———. 1982. *Shifting Involvements.* Princeton, N.J.: Princeton University Press.

Hirschman, Elizabeth C. 1981. "Comprehending Symbolic Consumption." In *Symbolic Consumer Behavior*, ed. Elizabeth Hirschman and Morris B. Holbrook, 4–6. Ann Arbor, Mich.: Association for Consumer Research.

———. 1985. "Scientific Style and the Conduct of Consumer Research." *Journal of Consumer Research* 12, no. 2 (September): 225–239.

———. 1986. "The Creation of Product Symbolism." In *Advances in Consumer Research*, ed. Richard J. Lutz, 327–331. Provo, Utah: Association for Consumer Research.

Hirschman, Elizabeth C., and Morris B. Holbrook. 1986. "Expanding the Ontology and Methodology of Research on the Consumption Experience." In *Perspectives on Methodology in Consumer Research*, ed. D. Brinberg and R. J. Lutz, 213–251. New York: Springer-Verlag.

Hirschman, Elizabeth C., and Morris Holbrook, eds. 1981. *Symbolic Consumer Behavior.* Ann Arbor, Mich.: Association for Consumer Research.

Hodder, Ian, ed. 1989. *The Meaning of Things: Material Culture and Symbolic Expression.* London: Unwin Hyman.

Holbrook, Morris B. 1987a. "Mirror, Mirror, on the Wall, What's Unfair in Reflections on Advertising." *Journal of Marketing* 51, no. 3 (July): 95–103.

———. 1987b. "From the Log of a Consumer Researcher." In *Advances in Consumer Research*, ed. Melanie Wallendorf and Paul Anderson, 365–369. Provo, Utah: Association for Consumer Research.

———. 1987c. "What Is Consumer Research?" *Journal of Consumer Research* 14, no. 1 (June): 128–132.

Holbrook, Morris B., and Elizabeth C. Hirschman. 1982. "The Experiential Aspects of Consumption: Consumer Fantasies, Feelings, and Fun." *Journal of Consumer Research* 9, no. 2 (September): 132–140.

Holdsworth, Deryck W. 1977. "House and Home in Vancouver: Images of West Coast Urbanism, 1886–1929." In *The Canadian City: Essays in Urban History*, ed.

Gilbert A. Stelter and Alan F. J. Artibise, 186–211. Toronto: McClelland and Stewart.

Holman, Rebecca. 1980. "Product Use as Communication: A Fresh Appraisal of a Venerable Topic." In *Review of Marketing,* ed. Ben M. Enis and Kenneth J. Roering, 250–272. Chicago: American Marketing Association.

Holt, Douglas B. 2002. "Why Do Brands Cause Trouble? A Dialectical Theory of Consumer Culture and Branding." *Journal of Consumer Research* 29 (June): 70–90.

Hooper-Greenhill, Eilean. 1992. *Museums and the Shaping of Knowledge.* London: Routledge.

Horn, Richard. 1985. *Fifties Style: Then and Now.* Harmondsworth: Penguin.

Horowitz, Daniel. 1985. *The Morality of Spending: Attitudes toward the Consumer Society in America, 1875–1940.* Baltimore: Johns Hopkins University Press.

Hoving, Thomas. 1981. *The King of the Confessors.* New York: Ballantine.

Hovland, Carl I., Irving L. Janis, and Harold H. Kelley. 1953. *Communication and Persuasion: Psychological Studies of Opinion Change.* New Haven, Conn.: Yale University Press.

Hovland, Carl I., and Walter Weiss. 1951–1952. "The Influence of Source Credibility on Communication Effectiveness." *Public Opinion Quarterly* 15 (Winter): 635–650.

Howe, Irving. 1970. "The Culture of Modernism." In *Decline of the New,* ed. Irving Howe, 3–33. New York: Harcourt, Brace and World.

Huber, Richard M. 1971. *The American Idea of Success.* New York: McGraw-Hill Book Company.

Hudson, Kenneth. 1987. *Museums of Influence.* Cambridge: University of Cambridge Press.

Huyssen, Andreas. 1995. *Twilight Memories: Marking Time in a Culture of Amnesia.* New York: Routledge.

Isaac, Rhys. 1988. "Ethnographic Method in History: An Action Approach." In *Material Life in America, 1600–1860,* ed. Robert Blair St. George, 39–61. Boston: Northeastern University Press.

Jackson, J. B. 1976. "The Domestication of the Garage." *Landscape* 20, no. 2 (Winter): 11–19.

Jackson, Lesley. 1991. *The New Look: Design in the Fifties.* London: Thames and Hudson.

Jameson, Frederic. 1983. "Postmodernism and Consumer Society." In *The Anti-Aesthetic: Essays on Postmodern Culture,* ed. Hal Foster, 112–125. Port Townsend, Wash.: Bay Press.

Jardine, Lisa. 1996. *Worldly Goods: A New History of the Renaissance.* London: Macmillan.

Jay, Martin. 1988. "Scopic Regimes of Modernity." In *Vision and Visuality,* ed. Hal Foster, 3–28. Seattle: Bay Press.

Jennings, Jan, ed. 1990. *Roadside America: The Automobile in Design and Culture.* Ames, Iowa: Press for the Society for Commercial Archaeology.

Jhally, Sut. 1987. *The Codes of Advertising: Fetishism and the Political Economy of Meaning in the Consumer Society.* New York: St. Martin's Press.

Jochnowitz, Eve. n.d. "Feasting on the Future: Food at the New York's World Fair." Available online: http//www.nyu.edu/classes/bkg/eve-wf.

Jodard, Paul. 1992. *Raymond Loewy.* London: Trefoil Publications.

Johnson, Nunnally, dir. 1956. *The Man in the Gray Flannel Suit.* Los Angeles: Twentieth Century Fox.

Jones, Steve. 1997. *Virtual Culture: Identity and Communication in Cybersociety.* Thousand Oaks, Calif.: Sage Publications.

Joseph, Benny W. 1982. "The Credibility of Physically Attractive Communications: A Review." *Journal of Advertising* 11 (July): 15–24.

Joseph, Nathan. 1986. *Uniform and Nonuniform: Communication through Clothing.* Westport, Conn.: Greenwood Press.

Kahle, Lynn R., and Pamela M. Homer. 1985. "Physical Attractiveness of the Celebrity Endorser: A Social Adaptation Perspective." *Journal of Consumer Research* 11 (March): 954–961.

Kaikati, Jack C. 1987. "Celebrity Advertising: A Review and Synthesis." *International Journal of Advertising* 6, no. 2: 93–103.

Kamen, Joseph M., Abdul C. Azhari, and Judith R. Kragh. 1975. "What a Spokesman Does for a Sponsor." *Journal of Advertising Research* 15 (April): 17–24.

Kant, Immanuel. 1952. *The Critique of Judgement.* Trans. James Creed Meredith. Oxford: Clarendon Press.

———. 1990. *Foundations of the Metaphysics of Morals and What Is Enlightenment?* New York: Macmillan.

Katz, Donald. 1992. *Home Fires.* New York: Harper Collins.

Kauffman, Stuart A. 1995. *At Home in the Universe: The Search for Laws of Self-Organization and Complexity.* New York: Oxford University Press.

Kavanaugh, James V. 1978. "The Artifact in American Culture." In *Material Culture and the Study of American Life,* ed. Ian M. G. Quimby, 65–74. New York: W. W. Norton.

Kelly, Barbara M. 1989. *Suburbia Re-Examined.* New York: Greenwood Press.

———. 1993. *Expanding the American Dream: Building and Rebuilding Levittown.* Albany: State University of New York Press.

Kelly, Robert F. 1984. "Museums as Status Symbols II: Attaining a State of 'Having Been.'" In *Advances in Non-Profit Marketing,* vol. 2, ed. Russell W. Belk. Greenwich, Conn.: JAI Press.

Kelso, Ruth. 1929. *The Doctrine of the English Gentleman in the Sixteenth Century with a Bibliographical List of Treatises on the Gentleman and Related Subjects Published in Europe to 1625.* Urbana: University of Illinois Press.

Klebha, Joanne M., and Lynette S. Unger. 1983. "The Impact of Negative and Positive Information on Source Credibility in a Field Setting." In *Advances in Consumer Research,* vol. 10, ed. Richard P. Bagozzi and Alice M. Tybout, 11–16. Ann Arbor, Mich.: Association for Consumer Research.

Klein, Naomi. 2000. *No Logo: Taking Aim at the Brand Bullies.* Toronto: A. A. Knopf.

Kleine, Robert E., III, and Jerome B. Kernan. 1991. "Contextual Influences on the Meanings Ascribed to Ordinary Consumption Objects." *Journal of Consumer Research* 18, no. 3 (December): 311–324.

Kleine, Susan Schultz, Robert E. Kleine, and Chris Allen. 1995. "How Is a Possession 'Me' or 'Not Me'? Characterizing Types and an Antecedent of Material Possession Attachment." *Journal of Consumer Research* 22 (December): 327–343.

Kluckhohn, Clyde, and Florence R. Kluckhohn. 1964. "American Culture: Generalized Orientations and Class Patterns." In *Conflicts of Power in Modern Culture,* ed. Lyman L. F. Bryson and R. M. MacIver, 106–128. New York: Cooper Square Publishers.

Kolbert, Elizabeth. 1995. "Americans Despair of Popular Culture." *The New York Times,* August 20: section 1, page 23.

Korosec-Serfaty, P., ed. 1976. *Appropriation of Space: Proceedings of the Third International Architectural Psychology Conference at the Louis Pasteur University, Strasbourg, June 21–25, 1976.* Strasbourg-Louvaine Na Neuve: CIACO.

Kotler, Philip, and Gary Armstrong. 1999. *Principles of Marketing.* 8th ed. Upper Saddle River, N.J.: Prentice Hall.

Kover, Arthur. 1995. "Copywriters' Implicit Theories of Communication: An Exploration." *Journal of Consumer Research* 21, no. 4 (March): 596–611.

Kramer, Hilton. 1995. "Studying the Arts and the Humanities: What Can Be Done?" In *Against the Grain: The New Criterion on Art and Intellect at the End of the Twentieth Century,* ed. Hilton Kramer and Roger Kimball, 74–81. Chicago: Ivan R. Dee.

Krampen, Martin. 1979. "Survey of Current Work on the Semiology of Objects." In *A Semiotic Landscape: Proceedings of the First Congress of the International Association for Semiotic Studies,* ed. Seymour Chatman et al., 158–168. The Hague: Mouton.

Kron, Joan. 1983. *Home-Psych: The Social Psychology of Home and Decoration.* New York: Clarkson N. Potter.

Krugman, Paul. 1998. "End Luxury Car Envy, Before It Destroys the World." *USA Today,* January 13: 13A.

Kubrick, Stanley, dir. 1968. *2001: A Space Odyssey.* Los Angeles, Calif.: Metro-Goldwyn-Mayer.

Kuhn, T. S. 1962. *The Structure of Scientific Revolutions.* Chicago: University of Chicago Press.

Kunstler, James Howard. 1994. *Geography of Nowhere.* New York: Free Press.

Kurzweil, Ray. 1999. *The Age of Spiritual Machines: When Computers Exceed Human Intelligence.* New York: Viking.

Kuspit, Donald B. 1993. *The Cult of the Avant-Garde Artist.* Cambridge: Cambridge University Press.

Laird, Pamela Walker. 1998. *Advertising Progress: American Business and the Rise of Consumer Marketing.* Baltimore, Md.: Johns Hopkins University Press.

Lakoff, George, and Mark Johnson. 1980. *Metaphors We Live By.* Chicago: University of Chicago Press.

Lamont, Michele. 1992. *Money, Morals and Manners: The Culture of the French and the American Upper-Middle Class.* Chicago: University of Chicago Press.

Lasch, Christopher. 1978. *The Culture of Narcissism: American Life in an Age of Diminishing Expectations.* New York: W. W. Norton & Company.

Laumann, Edward O., and James S. House. 1970. "Living Room Styles and Social Attributes: The Patterning of Material Artifacts in a Modern Urban Community." *Sociology and Social Research* 54, no. 3 (April): 321–342.

Lawrence, Roderick J. 1981. "The Social Classification of Domestic Space: A Cross-Cultural Case Study." *Anthropos* 76: 649–664.

———. 1982. "Domestic Space and Society: A Cross-Cultural Study." *Comparative Studies in Society and History* 24, no. 1: 104–130.

———. 1984. "Transition Spaces and Dwelling Design." *Journal of Architectural and Planning Research* 1: 261–271.

Le Wita, Beatrix. 1994. *French Bourgeois Culture.* New York: Cambridge University Press.

Leach, William R. 1984. "Transformations in a Culture of Consumption: Women and Department Stores, 1890–1925." *The Journal of American History* 71 (September): 319–342.

Lears, T. J. Jackson. 1981. *No Place of Grace: Antimodernism and the Transformation of American Culture 1880–1920.* New York: Pantheon.

Leavis, F. R. 1930. *Mass Civilisation and Minority Culture.* Cambridge: Minority Press.

Lechtman, Heather, and Robert S. Merrill, eds. 1977. *Material Culture: Styles, Organization, and Dynamics of Technology.* St. Paul: West Publishing Co.

Lee, Ang, dir. 1997. *The Ice Storm.* Los Angeles: Fox Searchlight Pictures.

LeMahieu, D. L. 1988. *A Culture for Democracy: Mass Communication and the Cultivated Mind in Britain between the Wars.* Oxford: Clarendon Press.

Levine, Lawrence W. 1988. *Highbrow/Lowbrow: The Emergence of Cultural Hierarchy in America.* Cambridge, Mass.: Harvard University Press.

Levinson, Barry, dir. 1987. *Tin Men.* Los Angeles: Touchstone Pictures.

Levinson, Barry. 1990. *Avalon; Tin Men; Diner: Three Screenplays.* New York: Atlantic Monthly Press.

Levi-Strauss, Claude. 1963. *Totemism.* Trans. Rodney Needham. Boston: Beacon Press.

———. 1966. *The Savage Mind.* Chicago: University of Chicago Press.

Levitt, Theodore. 1986. "Differentiation—of Anything." In *The Marketing Imagination,* ed. Theodore Levitt, 72–93. New York: Free Press.

Levy, Sidney J. 1959. "Symbols for Sale." *Harvard Business Review* 37, no. 4 (July/August): 117–124.

———. 1978. "Hunger and Work in a Civilized Tribe." *American Behavioral Scientist* 21, no. 4 (March/April): 557–570.

———. 1981. "Interpreting Consumer Mythology: A Structural Approach to Consumer Behavior." *Journal of Marketing* 45 (Summer): 49–61.

Levy, Sidney J., and Dennis Rook. 1999. *Brands, Consumers, Symbols, and Research.* Thousand Oaks, Calif.: Sage Publications.

Lewis, David, and Laurence Goldstein, eds. 1983. *The Automobile and American Culture.* Ann Arbor: University of Michigan Press.

Lewis, Judith. 2001. "Design Is Evil." *Wired Magazine* 9, no. 1 (January): 194.

Linklater, Richard, dir. 1991. *Slacker.* New York: Orion Classics.

———. 1996. *SubUrbia.* Beverly Hills: Castle Rock Entertainment.

Lipset, Seymour M., and Reinhard Bendix. 1959. *Social Mobility in Industrial Society.* Berkeley: University of California Press.

Livingstone, Sonia M. 1990. *Making Sense of Television: The Psychology of Audience Interpretation.* New York: Pergamon Press.

Loewy, Raymond. 1951. *Never Leave Well Enough Alone.* New York: Simon and Schuster.

———. 1955. "Jukebox on Wheels." *The Atlantic Monthly* 195, no. 4: 36–38.

———. 1979. *Industrial Design.* Woodstock, N.Y.: Overlook Press.

Lohof, Bruce A. 1969. "The Higher Meaning of Marlboro Cigarettes." *Journal of Popular Culture* 3, no. 3: 441–450.

Long, Elizabeth. 1985. *The American Dream and the Popular Novel.* London: Routledge & Kegan Paul.

———. 1987. "Reading Groups and the Postmodern Crisis of Cultural Authority." *Cultural Studies* 1, no. 3 (October): 306–327.

Lotman, Yu N., and B. A. Uspensky. 1978. "On the Semiotic Mechanism of Culture." *New Literary History* 9 (Winter): 211–232.

Lovejoy, Arthur O. 1950. *The Great Chain of Being: A Study of the History of an Idea.* Cambridge, Mass.: Harvard University Press.

Lukes, Steven. 1968. "Methodological Individualism Reconsidered." *British Journal of Sociology* 19 (June): 119–129.

———. 1973a. *Emile Durkheim: His Life and Work.* Harmondsworth: Penguin.

———. 1973b. *Individualism.* Oxford: Blackwell.

MacDonald, John D. 1964. *The Quick Red Fox.* New York: Ballantine.

Mailer, Norman. 1973. *Marilyn: A Biography.* New York: Grosset and Dunlap.

Major, John M. 1964. *Sir Thomas Elyot and Renaissance Humanism.* Lincoln: University of Nebraska Press.

Mander, Jerry. 1978. *Four Arguments for the Elimination of Television.* New York: Morrow Quill.

Marchand, Roland. 1985. *Advertising the American Dream: Making Way for Modernity, 1920–1940.* Berkeley: University of California Press.

Marcus, George E. 1985. "Spending: The Hunts, Silver, and Dynastic Families in America." *Archives Europeennes de Sociologie* 26, no. 2: 224–259.

Marcus, Greil. 1995. "The Deborah Chessler Story." In Greil Marcus, *The Dustbin of History,* 225–240. Cambridge, Mass.: Harvard University Press.

Marcuse, Herbert. 1964. *One-Dimensional Man.* Boston: Beacon Press.

Marias, Julian. 1972. *America in the Fifties and Sixties.* Trans. Blanche De Puy and Harold C. Raley. University Park: Pennsylvania State University Press.

Marling, Karal Ann. 1994. *As Seen on TV: The Visual Culture of Everyday Life in the 1950s.* Cambridge, Mass.: Harvard University Press.

Marsh, Peter E., and Peter Collett. 1986. *Driving Passion: The Psychology of the Car.* Boston: Faber and Faber.

Marshall, Christy. 1987. "It Seemed Like a Good Idea at the Time." *Forbes* (December 28): 98–99.

Marston, Jerrilyn Green. 1973. "Gentry Honor and Royalism in Early Stuart England." *The Journal of British Studies* 13, no. 1: 21–43.

Martineau, Pierre. 1954. "Snob Appeal Losing Ground." *Advertising Age* 25, no. 43: 12.

———. 1958. "Social Classes and Spending Behavior." *Journal of Marketing* (October): 121–130.

Marx, Leo. 1964. *The Machine in the Garden: Technology and the Pastoral Ideal in America.* New York: Oxford University Press.

May, Elaine Tyler. 1989. "Explosive Issues: Sex, Women, and the Bomb." In *Recasting America: Culture and Politics in the Age of Cold War,* ed. Lary May, 154–170. Chicago: University of Chicago Press.

Mayer, Martin. 1958. *Madison Avenue, U.S.A.* New York: Harper and Brothers.

Mayer, Robert. 1978. "Exploring Sociological Theories by Studying Consumers." *American Behavioral Scientist* 21 (March/April): 600–613.

McClelland, David K. 1961. *The Achieving Society.* New York: Nostrand.

McCoy, Esther. 1985. "The Rationalist Decade." In *High Styles in Twentieth-Century American Design,* ed. Lisa Phillips and David A. Hanks, 130–157. New York: Whitney Museum of American Art.

McCracken, Grant. 1982. "Rank and Two Aspects of Dress in Elizabethan England." *Culture* 2, no. 2: 53–62.

———. 1985. "Dress Colour at the Court of Elizabeth I: An Essay in Historical Anthropology." *Canadian Review of Sociology and Anthropology* 22, no. 4 (November): 515–533.

——. 1986a. "Culture and Consumption: A Theoretical Account of the Structure and Movement of the Cultural Meaning of Consumer Goods." *Journal of Consumer Research* 13, no. 1 (June): 71–84.

——. 1986b. "Upstairs/Downstairs: The Canadian Production." University of Guelph, Department of Consumer Studies, Working Paper no. 86-104.

——. 1986c. "Lois Roget: Curatorial Consumer." University of Guelph, Department of Consumer Studies, Working Paper no. 86-105.

——. 1986d. "Advertising: Meaning or Information?" In *Advances in Consumer Research,* vol. 14, ed. Paul Anderson and Melanie Wallendorf, 121–124. Provo, Utah: Association for Consumer Research.

——. 1987. "Culture and Consumption among the Elderly: Research Objectives for the Study of Person-Object Relations in an Aging Population." *Ageing and Society* 7, no. 2 (June): 203–224.

——. 1988a. *Culture and Consumption: New Approaches to the Symbolic Character of Consumer Goods and Activities.* Bloomington: Indiana University Press.

——. 1988b. "Lois Roget: Curatorial Consumer in a Modem Society." In *Culture and Consumption: New Approaches to the Symbolic Character of Consumer Goods and Activities,* 44–53. Bloomington: Indiana University Press.

——. 1988c. "Diderot Unifies and the Diderot Effect." In *Culture and Consumption: New Approaches to the Symbolic Character of Consumer Goods and Activities,* 118–129. Bloomington: Indiana University Press.

——. 1988d. *The Long Interview: A Four-Step Method of Qualitative Inquiry.* Newbury Park, Calif.: Sage Publishers.

——. 1995. "Moses Znaimer and the Future of Television." In *Watching Television: Historic Televisions and Memorabilia from the MZTV Museum,* ed. Liss Jeffries, Sandra Shaul, and Glen Ellis, 42–46. Toronto: Royal Ontario Museum and MZTV Museum.

——. 1997. *Plenitude.* Toronto: Periph: Fluide and www.cultureby.com.

——. 2001. *Transformation.* Toronto: Periph: Fluide and www.cultureby.com.

McCracken, Grant, and Victor J. Roth. 1985. "Does Clothing Have a Code? Empirical Findings and Theoretical Implications in the Study of Clothing as a Means of Communication." *International Journal of Research in Marketing* 6: 13–33.

McCusker, John J. 2001. "Comparing the Purchasing Power of Money in the United States (or Colonies) from 1665 to Any Other Year Including the Present Economic History Services." Available online: http://www.eh.net/hmit/ppowerusd.

McGuire, William I. 1985. "Attitudes and Attitude Change." In *Handbook of Social Psychology,* ed. Gardner Lindzey and Elliott Aronson, vol. 2, 233–346. New York: Random House.

McKendrick, Neil, John Brewer, and J. H. Plumb. 1982. *The Birth of a Consumer Society: The Commercialization of Eighteenth-Century England.* Bloomington: Indiana University Press.

McKenna, Regis. 1991. "Marketing Is Everything." *Harvard Business Review* 69, no. 1 (January–February): 65–79.

McLuhan, Marshall. 1951. *The Mechanical Bride: Folklore of Industrial Man.* New York: Vanguard Press.

McQuarrie, E. F., and David Glen Mick. 1992. "On Resonance: A Critical Pluralistic
   Inquiry into Advertising Rhetoric." *Journal of Consumer Research* 19, no. 2:
   180–197.
——. 1996. "Figures of Rhetoric in Advertising Language." *Journal of Consumer
   Research* 22, no. 4: 420–434.
Mead, Margaret. 1928. *Coming of Age in Samoa: A Psychological Study of Primitive Youth
   for Western Civilisation.* New York: W. Morrow & Company.
Meikle, Jeffrey L. 1979. *Twentieth Century Limited: Industrial Design in America, 1925–
   1939.* Philadelphia: Temple University Press.
——. 1993. "Streamlining 1930–1955." In *Industrial Design: Reflection of a Century,*
   ed. Jocelyn de Noblet, 182–192. Paris: Flammarion/APCI.
Mendes, Sam, dir. 1999. *American Beauty.* Universal City, Calif.: Dream Works.
Merelman, Richard M. 1984. *Making Something of Ourselves: On Culture and Politics in
   the United States.* Berkeley: University of California Press.
Mertz, Elizabeth. 1985. "Beyond Symbolic Anthropology: Introducing Semiotic Media-
   tion." In *Semiotic Mediation: Sociocultural and Psychological Perspectives,* ed.
   Elizabeth Mertz and Richard J. Parmentier, 1–19. Orlando, Fla.: Academic Press.
Mertz, Elizabeth, and Richard J. Parmentier, eds. 1985. *Semiotic Mediation: Sociocultural
   and Psychological Perspectives.* Orlando, Fla.: Academic Press.
Messerschmidt, Donald A., ed. 1981. *Anthropologists at Home in North America.* New
   York: Cambridge University Press.
Mick, David Glen. 1986. "Consumer Research and Semiotics: Exploring the Morphology
   of Signs, Symbols and Significance." *Journal of Consumer Research* 13, no. 2
   (September): 196–213.
——. 1988. "Contributions to the Semiotics of Marketing and Consumer Behavior."
   In *The Semiotic Web: A Yearbook of Semiotics,* ed. Thomas A. Sebeok and Jean
   Umiker-Sebeok, 535–584. Berlin: Mouton.
Mick, David Glen, and Claus Buhl. 1992. "A Meaning-Based Model of Advertising Expe-
   riences." *Journal of Consumer Research* 19, no. 3 (December): 317–338.
Mick, David Glen, James Burroughs, Patrick Hetzel, and Mary Yoko Brannen. 2004.
   "Pursuing the Meaning of Meaning in the Commercial World: An International
   Review of Marketing and Consumer Research Founded on Semiotics." *Semi-
   otica.* Forthcoming.
Miller, Daniel. 2001. "Driven Societies." In *Car Cultures,* ed. Daniel Miller, 1–33. New
   York: Berg.
Miller, Jonathan. 1972. "Plays and Players." In *Nonverbal Communication,* ed. R. A.
   Hinde. Cambridge: Cambridge University Press.
Miller, Michael B. 1981. *The Bon Marche: Bourgeois Culture and the Department Store.*
   Princeton, N.J.: Princeton University Press.
Mills, C. Wright. 1951. *White Collar: The American Middle Classes.* New York: Oxford
   University Press.
Mintz, Sidney. 1985. *Sweetness and Power.* New York: Viking Press.
Montgomery, Charles F. 1982. "The Connoisseurship of Artifacts." In *Material Culture
   Studies in America,* ed. Thomas J. Schlereth, 143–152. Nashville: American Asso-
   ciation for State and Local History.
Morton, Edith F. 1936. *The Attractive Home.* Pennsylvania State College Division of
   Agricultural Extension Circular no. 177.

Motavalli, John. 1988. "Advertising Blunders of the Rich and Famous." *Adweek,* January 11: 18–19.

Mukerji, Chandra. 1983. *From Graven Images: Patterns of Modern Materialism.* New York: Columbia University Press.

Mumford, Lewis. 1934. *Technics and Civilization.* London: Routledge & Kegan Paul.

———. 1961. *The City in History: Its Origins, Its Transformations, and Its Prospects.* New York: Harcourt, Brace & World.

Murphy, Gregory L., and Douglas L. Medin. 1985. "The Role of Theories in Conceptual Coherence." *Psychological Review* 92 (July): 289–316.

Nadel, Alan. 1996. *Containment Culture: American Narratives, Postmodernism, and the Atomic Age.* Durham, N.C.: Duke University Press.

Nader, Ralph. 1972. *Unsafe at Any Speed: The Designed-In Dangers of the American Automobile.* New York: Grossman.

Neich, Roger. 1982. "A Semiological Analysis of Self-Decoration in Mount Hagen, New Guinea." In *The Logic of Culture,* ed. Ino Rossi, 214–231. South Hadley, Mass.: J. F. Bergin.

Nicosia, Francesco M., and Robert N. Mayer. 1976. "Toward a Sociology of Consumption." *Journal of Consumer Research* 3, no. 2 (September): 65–75.

Nisbet, Robert A. 1969. *Social Change and History: Aspects of the Western Theory of Development.* New York: Oxford University Press.

Nissenbaum, Stephen. 1996. *The Battle for Christmas.* New York: Alfred A. Knopf.

Noblet, Jocelyn de. 1993. *Industrial Design Reflection of a Century.* Paris: Flammarion/ APCI.

Nye, David E. 1994. *American Technological Sublime.* Cambridge, Mass.: MIT Press.

Nystrom, Paul H. 1919. *Automobile Selling: A Manual for Dealers.* New York: Motor.

O'Dell, Tom. 2001. "Raggare and the Panic of Mobility." In *Car Cultures,* ed. Daniel Miller, 105–132. New York: Berg.

O'Guinn, Thomas C., Ronald J. Faber, and Marshall Rice. 1985. "Popular Film and Television as Consumer Acculturation Agents: American 1900 to Present." In *Historical Perspective in Consumer Research: National and International Perspectives,* ed. Chin Tiong Tan and Jagdish N. Sheth, 297–301. Singapore: National University of Singapore.

Olson, Clark D. 1985. "Materialism in the Home: The Impact of Artifacts on Dyadic Communication." In *Advances in Consumer Research,* vol. 12, ed. Elizabeth C. Hirschman and Morris B. Holbrook, 388–393. Provo, Utah: Association for Consumer Research.

O'Neill, John. 1978. "The Productive Body: An Essay on the Work of Consumption." *Queen's Quarterly* 85, no. 2 (Summer): 221–230.

Osborne, Peter. 1995. *The Politics of Time: Modernity & Avant-Garde.* New York: Verso.

Packard, Vance Oakley. 1959. *The Status Seekers: An Exploration of Class Behavior in America and the Hidden Barriers That Affect You, Your Community, Your Future.* New York: David McKay Co.

———. 1960. *The Waste Makers.* New York: David McKay Company.

Palladino, Grace. 1996. *Teenagers: An American History.* New York: Basic Books.

Passmore, John Arthur. 1970. *The Perfectibility of Man.* New York: Charles Scribner's Sons.

Paster, James E. 1990. "The Snapshot, the Automobile, and the Americans." In *Roadside*

America: The Automobile in Design and Culture, ed. Jan Jennings, 55–73. Ames, Iowa: Press for the Society for Commercial Archaeology.

Payne, Alexander, dir. 1999. *Election.* New York: MTV Films.

Peirce, Charles S. 1932. *Collected Papers of Charles Sanders Peirce.* Vol. 2. Edited by Charles Hartshorne and Paul Weiss. Cambridge, Mass.: Harvard University Press.

Pells, Richard H. 1985. *The Liberal Mind in a Conservative Age: American Intellectuals in the 1940s and 1950s.* New York: Harper and Row.

Peterman, John. 1999. "The Rise and Fall of the J. Peterman Company." *Harvard Business Review* 77, no. 5: 59–66.

Peterson, Iver. 1999. "Some Perched in Ivory Tower Gain Rosier View of Suburbs." *The New York Times,* December 5: section 1, page 46.

Pine, Joseph, and James H. Gilmore. 1999. *The Experience Economy: Work Is Theatre and Every Business Is a Stage.* Boston: Harvard Business School Press.

Poggioli, Renato. 1968. *The Theory of the Avant-Garde.* Trans. Gerald Fitzgerald. Cambridge, Mass.: Harvard University Press.

Pole, Jack Richon. 1980. *American Individualism and the Promise of Progress.* New York: Oxford University Press.

Pollay, Richard W. 1986. The "Distorted Mirror: Reflections on the Unintended Consequences of Advertising." *Journal of Marketing* 50, no. 2 (April): 18–36.

Pollei, Jennifer. n.d. "Talking about Cars." Available online: http://www.byu.edu/moa/education/cars/quotes.htm.

Pope, Daniel. 1983. *The Making of Modern Advertising.* New York: Basic Books.

Postman, Neil. 1985. *Amusing Ourselves to Death: Public Discourse in the Age of Show Business.* New York: Penguin.

Postrel, Virginia. 1998. *The Future and Its Enemies.* New York: Free Press.

———. 2003. *The Substance of Style: How the Rise of Aesthetic Value Is Remaking Commerce, Culture, and Consciousness.* New York: HarperCollins.

Pratt, Gerry. 1981. "The House as an Expression of Social Worlds." In *Housing and Identity: Cross-Cultural Perspectives,* ed. James S. Duncan, 135–180. London: Croom Helm.

Pray, Doug, dir. 1997. *Hype.* Santa Monica, Calif.: Lions Gate Films.

Price, Martin. 1986. "The Sublime Poem: Pictures and Powers." In *Poets of Sensibility and the Sublime,* ed. Harold Bloom, 31–47. New York: Chelsea House Publishers.

Priestly, J. B. 1964. *Man and Time.* Garden City, N.Y.: Doubleday.

Prown, Jules David. 1980. "Style as Evidence." *Winterthur Portfolio* 15, no. 3 (Autumn): 197–210.

———. 1982. "Mind in Matter: An Introduction to Material Culture Theory and Method." *Winterthur Portfolio* 17, no. 1 (Spring): 1–19.

Prown, Jules David, and Kenneth Haltman. 2000. *American Artifacts: Essays in Material Culture.* East Lansing: Michigan State University Press.

Pulos, Arthur J. 1983. *American Design Ethic: A History of Industrial Design to 1940.* Cambridge, Mass.: MIT Press.

———. 1988. *The American Design Adventure, 1940–1975.* Cambridge, Mass.: MIT Press.

Pursell, Carroll W. 1992. "Telling a Story: The Automobile in American Life." In *Ideas and Images: Developing Interpretive History Exhibits,* ed. Kenneth Ames, Barbara Franco, and Thomas L. Frye, 233–252. Nashville, Tenn.: American Association of State and Local History.

Quimby, Ian, ed. 1978. *Material Culture and the Study of Material Life.* New York: W. W. Norton & Company.

Quinones, Ricardo J. 1972. *The Renaissance Discovery of Time.* Cambridge, Mass.: Harvard University Press.

Rae, John B. 1965. *The American Automobile: A Brief History.* Chicago: University of Chicago Press.

Rainwater, Lee. 1966. "Fear and the House-as-Haven in the Lower Class." *Journal of the American Institute of Planners* 32, no. 1 (February): 23–31.

Rapoport, Amos. 1982. *The Meaning of the Built Environment.* Beverly Hills, Calif.: Sage Publications.

Rassuli, Kathleen H., and Stanley C. Hollander. 1987. "Comparative History as a Research Tool in Consumer Behavior." In *Advances in Consumer Research,* vol. 14, ed. Melanie Wallendorf and Paul Anderson, 442–446. Provo, Utah: Association for Consumer Research.

Rathje, William. 1978. "Archeological Ethnography." In *Explorations in Ethnoarchaeology,* ed. Richard A. Gould, 4–76. Albuquerque: University of New Mexico Press.

Redgap, Curtis. n.d. "An Insider's History of Plymouth: The Brand and the Cars (Part 2)." Available online: http://www.allpar.com/history/inside/plymouth-1.shtml.

Reynolds, Barrie, and Margaret Stott, eds. 1986. *Material Anthropology: Contemporary Approaches in Material Culture.* New York: University Press of America.

Richardson, Miles. 1974. "Images, Objects and the Human Story." In *The Human Mirror: Material and Spatial Images of Man,* ed. Miles Richardson, 3–14. Baton Rouge: Louisiana State University Press.

Richins, Marsha L. 1994a. "Valuing Things: The Public and Private Meanings of Possessions." *Journal of Consumer Research* 21, no. 3 (December): 504–521.

———. 1994b. "Special Possessions and the Expression of Material Values." *Journal of Consumer Research* 21, no. 3 (December): 522–533.

Riesman, David. 1961. *The Lonely Crowd: A Study of the Changing American Character.* New Haven, Conn.: Yale University Press.

———. 1964. "The Suburban Dislocation." In *Abundance for What? And Other Essays,* ed. David Riesman, 226–257. Garden City, N.Y.: Doubleday.

Riesman, David, and Eric Larrabee. 1964. "Autos in America." In *Abundance for What? And Other Essays,* ed. David Riesman, 270–299. Garden City, N.Y.: Doubleday.

Robinson, Charlotte Brenan. 1941. *The Arrangement of Home Furnishings.* Cornell Bulletin for Homemakers Bulletin no. 463.

Rochberg-Halton, Eugene. 1984. "Object Relations, Role Models, and Cultivation of the Self." *Environment and Behavior* 15 (May 3): 347–366.

Rook, Dennis W. 1985. "The Ritual Dimension of Consumer Behavior." *Journal of Consumer Research* 12, no. 3 (December): 251–264.

Rosenberg, Harold. 1962. "Pop Culture, Kitsch Criticism." In *The Tradition of the New,* ed. Harold Rosenberg, 259–268. London: Thames and Hudson.

Rosenblum, Robert. 1975. *Modern Painting and the Northern Romantic Tradition: Friedrich to Rothko.* London: Thames and Hudson.

Ross, Andrew. 1989. *No Respect: Intellectuals & Popular Culture.* New York: Routledge.

Ross, Gary, dir. 1998. *Pleasantville.* Los Angeles: New Line Cinema.

Ross, Kristin. 1995. *Fast Cars, Clean Bodies: Decolonization and the Reordering of French Culture.* Cambridge, Mass.: MIT Press.

Rothschild, Emma. 1973. *Paradise Lost: The Decline of the Auto-Industrial Age.* New York: Random House.

Rudmin, Floyd. 1986. "Psychology of Ownership, Possession and Property: A Selected Bibliography Since 1890." *Psychological Reports* 58: 859–869.

Russell, Rohan. n.d. "Oldsmobile in Australia: The Oldsmobile Starfire." http://home.vicnet.net.au/~oldsclub/starfire.html.

Rydell, Robert W. 1984. *All the World's a Fair: Visions of Empire at American International Expositions, 1876–1916.* Chicago: University of Chicago.

———. 1993. *World of Fairs: The Century-of-Progress Expositions.* Chicago: University of Chicago Press.

Sahlins, Marshall D. 1976. *Culture and Practical Reason.* Chicago: University of Chicago Press.

———. 1981. *Historical Metaphors and Mythical Realities: Structure in the Early History of the Sandwich Islands Kingdom.* Ann Arbor: University of Michigan Press.

———. 1995. *How "Natives" Think: About Captain Cook, for Example.* Chicago: University of Chicago Press.

———. 1996. "The Native Anthropology of Western Cosmology." *Current Anthropology* 37, no. 3 (June): 395–428.

Saile, David G., ed. 1984. *Architecture in Cultural Change: Essays in Built Form and Culture.* Lawrence: University of Kansas, School of Architecture and Urban Design.

Sapir, Edward. 1931. "Communication." In *Encyclopedia of the Social Sciences,* 78–80.

Sapir, J. David, and Jon Christopher Crocker, eds. 1977. *The Social Use of Metaphor: Essays on the Anthropology of Rhetoric.* Philadelphia: University of Pennsylvania Press.

Schatzman, Leonard, and Anselm Strauss. 1955. "Social Class and Modes of Communication." *The American Journal of Sociology* 60, no. 4: 329–338.

Schiesel, Seth. 1997. "New Disney Vision Making the Future a Thing of the Past." *The New York Times,* February 23: section 1, page 24.

Schlereth, Thomas J. 1982. "Material Culture Studies in America, 1876–1976." In *Material Culture Studies in America,* ed. Thomas J. Schlereth, 1–75. Nashville, Tenn.: The American Association for State and Local History.

Schmidt, Leigh Eric. 1995. *Consumer Rites: The Buying and Selling of American Holidays.* Princeton, N.J.: Princeton University Press.

Schneider, David M. 1968. *American Kinship: A Cultural Account.* Englewood Cliffs, N.J.: Prentice Hall.

Schneider, Kenneth R. 1971. *Autokind vs. Mankind: An Analysis of Tyranny, a Proposal for Rebellion, a Plan for Reconstruction.* New York: Norton.

Schudson, Michael. 1984. *Advertising, the Uneasy Persuasion.* New York: Basic Books.

Scott, Linda. 1994. "Images of Advertising: The Need for a Theory of Visual Rhetoric." *Journal of Consumer Research* 21, no. 2 (September): 252–273.

———. 2001. "Advertising, Advertisements." In *International Encyclopedia of the Social and Behavioral Sciences,* vol. 5, ed. Michael Schudson. London: Elsevier.

Seamon, David. 1979. *A Geography of the Lifeworld.* London: Croom Helm.

Sedgwick, Michael. 1983. *Cars of the Fifties and Sixties.* Philadelphia: Temple.

Seeley, John R., R. Alexander Sim, and E. W. Loosley. 1956. *Crestwood Heights: A Study of the Culture of Suburban Life.* Toronto: University of Toronto Press.

Sendak, Maurice. 1963. *Where the Wild Things Are.* New York: Harper and Row.

Sherry, John F. 1984. "Some Implications for Consumer Oral Tradition for Reactive Marketing." In *Advances in Consumer Research*, ed. Thomas C. Kinnear, 741–747. Provo, Utah: Association for Consumer Research.

———. 1987. "Advertising as a Cultural System." In *Marketing and Semiotics: New Directions in the Study of Signs for Sale*, ed. Jean Umiker-Sebeok, 441–461. New York: Mouton de Gruyter.

———. 1991. "Postmodern Alternatives: The Interpretive Turn in Consumer Research." In *Handbook of Consumer Theory and Research*, ed. Harold H. Kassarjian and Thomas Robertson. Englewood Cliffs, N.J.: Prentice Hall.

Shi, David E. 1985. *The Simple Life: Plain Living and High Thinking in American Culture*. New York: Oxford University Press.

Shils, Edward A. 1970. "Deference." In *The Logic of Social Hierarchies*, ed. Edward O. Laumann, Paul M. Siegel, and Robert W. Hodge, 420–448. Chicago: Markham Publishing Company.

Shugan, Steven A. 1982. "Displays and Advertising: A Theory of Seduction." In *Advances in Consumer Research*, ed. Andrew Mitchell, 118–124. Ann Arbor, Mich.: Association for Consumer Research.

Shumsky, Neil L. 1996. *Social Structure and Social Mobility*. New York: Garland Publishing.

Shweder, Richard A. 1984. "Preview: A Colloquy of Culture Theorists." In *Culture Theory: Essays on Mind, Self, and Emotion*, ed. Richard A. Shweder and Robert A. Levine, 1–24. Cambridge: Cambridge University Press.

Shweder, Richard A., and Edmund J. Bourne. 1984. "Does the Concept of the Person Vary Cross-Culturally?" In *Culture Theory: Essays on Mind, Self, and Emotion*, ed. Robert Alan LeVine and Richard A. Shweder, 158–199. New York: Cambridge University Press.

Shweder, Richard A., and Robert A. LeVine, eds. 1984. *Culture Theory: Essays on Mind, Self and Emotion*. Cambridge: Cambridge University Press.

Silk, Gerald. 1984. *Automobile and Culture*. New York: Harry Abrams.

Silverman, Lois H. 1995. "Visitor Meaning-Making in Museums for a New Age." *Curator* 38, no. 3: 161–170.

Silverman, Martin G. 1971. *Disconcerting Issue: Meaning and Struggle in a Resettled Pacific Community*. Chicago: University of Chicago Press.

Silverstein, Michael. 1976. "Shifters, Linguistic Categories, and Cultural Description." In *Meaning in Anthropology*, ed. Keith H. Basso and Henry A. Selby, 11–55. Albuquerque: University of New Mexico Press.

Simmel, Georg. 1971. "Fashion: On Individuality and Social Forms." In *Selected Writings [of] Georg Simmel*, 294–323. Chicago: University of Chicago Press.

Singer, Milton B. 1984. *Man's Glassy Essence: Explorations in Semiotic Anthropology*. Bloomington: Indiana University Press.

Sloan, Alfred P. 1963. *My Years with General Motors*. Garden City, N.Y.: Doubleday.

Smelser, Neil J., and Seymour M. Lipset. 1966. *Social Structure and Mobility in Economic Development*. Chicago: Aldine.

Solomon, Michael R. 1983. "The Role of Products as Social Stimuli: A Symbolic Interactionism Perspective." *Journal of Consumer Research* 10 (December): 319–329.

Solondz, Todd, dir. 1998. *Happiness*. Los Angeles: Focus.

Sorensen, Christian. n.d. "Designing the Automobile." Available online: http://www.byu.edu/moa/education/cars/designing.htm.

Spadafora, David. 1990. *The Idea of Progress in Eighteenth-Century Britain.* New Haven, Conn.: Yale University Press.

Sparke, Penny. 1986. *Design and Culture in the Twentieth Century.* London: Allen and Unwin.

———. 1998. *A Century of Design: Design Pioneers of the 20th Century.* London: Mitchell Beazley.

Spock, Benjamin. 1946. *The Common Sense Book of Baby and Child Care.* New York: Duell, Sloan and Pearce.

Stein, Maurice, and Arthur J. Vidich. 1960. "Identity and History: An Overview." In *Identity and Anxiety: Survival of the Person in Mass Society,* ed. Maurice R. Stein, Arthur J. Vidich, and David Manning White, 17–33. New York: Free Press.

Steinem, Gloria. 1988. *Marilyn: Norma Jean.* New York: Signet.

Stern, Barbara. 1988. "Medieval Allegory: Roots of Advertising Strategy for the Mass Market." *Journal of Marketing* 52 (July): 84–94.

Sternthal, Brian, Ruby Roy Dholakia, and Clark Leavitt. 1978. "The Persuasive Effect of Source Credibility: Tests of Cognitive Response." *Journal of Consumer Research* 4 (March): 252–260.

Stigler, George J. 1974. "The Intellectual and the Market Place." In *Advertising's Role in Society,* ed. John S. Wright and John E. Mertes, 317–325. New York: West Publishing Co.

Strasser, Susan, Charles McGovern, and Matthias Judt, eds. 1998. *Getting and Spending: European and American Consumer Societies in the Twentieth Century.* New York: Cambridge University Press.

Susman, Warren I. 1984a. "Culture and Communications." In *Culture as History: The Transformation of American Society in the Twentieth Century,* ed. Warren I. Susman, 252–270. New York: Pantheon Books.

———. 1984b. "Introduction: Toward a History of the Culture of Abundance—Some Hypotheses." In *Culture as History: The Transformation of American Society in the Twentieth Century,* ed. Warren I. Susman, xix–xxx. New York: Pantheon Books.

Tambiah, Stanley J. 1969. "Animals Are Good to Think and Good to Prohibit." *Ethnology* 8, no. 4 (October): 424–459.

———. 1977. "The Cosmological and Performative Significance of a Thai Cult of Healing through Meditation." *Culture, Medicine, and Psychiatry* 1: 97–132.

Tan, Chin Tiong, and Jagdish N. Sheth, eds. 1985. *Historical Perspective in Consumer Research.* Singapore: School of Management, National University of Singapore.

Teather, J. Lynne. 1990. "The Museum Keepers: The Museums Associations and the Growth of Museum Professionalism." *Museum Management and Curatorship* 9: 25–41.

Thurber, James. 1941. *The Secret Life of Walter Mitty.* New York: Simon and Schuster.

Tognoli, Jerome. 1987. "Residential Environments." In *Handbook of Environmental Psychology,* ed. I. Altman and D. Stokols, 655–690. New York: J. Wiley and Sons.

Tuan, Yi-Fu. 1982. *Segmented Worlds and Self.* Minneapolis: University of Minnesota Press.

Traube, Elizabeth G. 1996. "'The Popular' in American Culture." *Annual Review of Anthropology* 25: 127–151.

Trilling, Lionel. 1971. *Sincerity and Authenticity.* Cambridge, Mass.: Harvard University Press.

Trow, George W. S. 1997. *Within the Context of No Context.* New York: Atlantic Monthly Press.

Turkle, Sherry. 1995. *Life on the Screen: Identity in the Age of the Internet.* New York: Simon and Schuster.

Twitchell, James B. 1983. *Romantic Horizons: Aspects of the Sublime in English Poetry and Painting, 1770–1850.* Columbia: University of Missouri Press.

Umiker-Sebeok, Jean, ed. 1988. *Marketing and Semiotics.* Bloomington: Indiana University Press.

Vance, Bill. n.d. 1953–54 Buick Skylark. Available online: http://www.canadiandriver.com/articles/bv/skylark.htm.

Varenne, Herve. 1977. *Americans Together.* New York: Teachers College Press.

———. 1986. "Doing the Anthropology of America." In *Symbolizing America,* ed. Herve Varenne, 34–45. Lincoln: University of Nebraska Press.

Veblen, Thorstein. 1953/1912. *Theory of the Leisure Class.* New York: Mentor Books.

Vogt, Evon Zartman. 1955. *Modern Homesteaders: The Life of a Twentieth-Century Frontier Community.* Cambridge, Mass.: Belknap Press of Harvard University Press.

von Trier, Lars, dir. 2003. *Dogville.* New York: Lions Gate Entertainment.

Wallendorf, Melanie. 1987. "On the Road Again: The Nature of Qualitative Research on the Consumer Behavior Odyssey." In *Advances in Consumer Research,* vol. 14, ed. Melanie Wallendorf and Paul Anderson, 374–375. Provo, Utah: Association for Consumer Research.

Wallendorf, Melanie, and Eric J. Arnould. 1988. "'My Favorite Things': A Cross-Cultural Inquiry into Object Attachment, Possessiveness, and Social Linkage." *Journal of Consumer Research* 14 (March 4): 531–547.

———. 1991. "'We Gather Together': Consumption Rituals of Thanksgiving Day." *Journal of Consumer Research* 18, no. 1 (June): 13–31.

Warner, W. Lloyd, and James C. Abegglen. 1955. *Occupational Mobility in American Business and Industry, 1928–1952.* Minneapolis: University of Minnesota Press.

Warner, W. Lloyd, J. O. Low, P. S. Lunt, and Leo Srole. 1963. *Yankee City.* New Haven, Conn.: Yale University Press.

Watson, Steven. 1995. *The Birth of the Beat Generation: Visionaries, Rebels, and Hipsters, 1944–1960.* New York: Pantheon Books.

Weil, Stephen E. 1995. "Exclusion Principle." In *A Cabinet of Curiosities: Inquiries into Museums and Their Prospects,* ed. Stephen E. Weil, 75–79. Washington, D.C.: Smithsonian Institution Press.

Weir, Peter, dir. 1998. *The Truman Show.* Los Angeles: Paramount Pictures.

Weiss, Joel, Judith Weinstein, and Eileen Dykes. 1988. *More Than Just a Pretty Face: The Meanings behind the Bat Cave Gallery.* Toronto: Ontario Institute for Studies in Education Working Paper.

Wells, Linda. 1989. "Face Value." *New York Times Magazine,* February 26, part 2: 46, 56, and 72.

Wernick, Andrew. 1994. "Vehicles for Myth: The Shifting Image of the Modern Car." In *Signs of Life in the U.S.A.: Readings on Popular Culture for Writers,* ed. Sonia Maasik and Jack Solomon, 78–94. Boston: Bedford Books.

White, Irving S. 1959. "The Functions of Advertising in Our Culture." *Journal of Marketing* (July): 8–14.

White, Lawrence J. 1971. *The Automobile Industry Since 1945.* Cambridge, Mass.: Harvard University Press.

Whyte, William H., Jr. 1956. *The Organization Man.* New York: Simon and Schuster.

Wicklund, R. A., and P. M. Gollwitzer. 1982. *Symbolic Self-Completion.* Hillsdale: Lawrence Erlbaum.

Williams, Bill. 1977. "GM's '36 Parade of Progress." Available online: http://www.futurliner.com/account.htm.

Williams, Robin. 1966. *American Society.* New York: Knopf.

Williams, Rosalind H. 1982. *Dream Worlds: Mass Consumption in Late Nineteenth-Century France.* Berkeley: University of California Press.

Williamson, Judith. 1978. *Decoding Advertising.* New York: Marion Boyars.

Witenko, Mrs. George J. n.d. Letter to General Motors. From the files of the GM Futurliner Restoration Project. Available online: http://www.futurliner.com/apprec.htm.

Wolf, Arthur P. 1970. "Chinese Kinship and Mourning Dress." In *Family and Kinship in Chinese Society,* ed. Maurice Freedman, 189–207. Palo Alto, Calif.: Stanford University Press.

Wolf, Eric R. 1969. "American Anthropologists and American Society." In *Reinventing Anthropology,* ed. Dell Hymes, 251–263. New York: Pantheon Books.

Wolfe, Alan. 1998. *One Nation, After All.* New York: Viking.

Wolfe, Tom. 1979. *The Right Stuff.* New York: Farrar, Straus, Giroux.

Wright, Gwendolyn. 1980. *Moralism and the Model Home: Domestic Architecture and Cultural Conflict in Chicago, 1873–1913.* Chicago: University of Chicago Press.

———. 1981. *Building the Dream: A Social History of Housing in America.* New York: Pantheon.

Wright, Richard A. 1998. "West of Laramie: A Brief History of the Auto Industry." Available online: http://www.aaca/org/autohistory.

Zagorin, Perez. 1971. *The Court and the Country: The Beginning of the English Revolution.* New York: Atheneum.

Zolotow, Maurice. 1960. *Marilyn Monroe.* New York: Harcourt, Brace and Jovanovich.

Index

Page numbers in italics indicate illustrations.

GRANT McCRACKEN was born and raised in Vancouver, B.C. He holds a Ph.D. from the University of Chicago in cultural anthropology. He has been the director of the Institute of Contemporary Culture and a senior lecturer at the Harvard Business School and is now a visiting scholar at McGill University. He has authored several books including *Culture and Consumption* (Indiana University Press), *Big Hair,* and *Transformation.* He has consulted widely in the corporate world, with organizations including the Coca-Cola Company, IKEA, Chrysler, Kraft, and Kimberly Clark.